★ ★ ★ KEEP ★ ★ ★ SWINGING

A Memoir of Politics and Justice

SEN. JOSEPH L. BRUNO

A POST HILL PRESS BOOK

Keep Swinging:
A Memoir of Politics and Justice
© 2016 by Joseph L. Bruno
All Rights Reserved

ISBN: 978-1-68261-302-3
ISBN (eBook): 978-1-68261-303-0

Cover Design by Quincy Alivio
Cover Photograph courtesy of Tanya Bissaillon
Interior Design and Composition by Greg Johnson/Textbook Perfect

Post Hill Press
posthillpress.com

Published in the United States of America
2 3 4 5 6 7 8 9 10

CONTENTS

FOREWORD

When I first met Joe Bruno, he was ramrod straight and as handsome as a movie star. He was also eighty years old and about to be tried a second time for the same crime, notwithstanding an express prohibition on such double jeopardy in the United States Constitution itself.

We met to discuss the constitutional implications of what the federal government was doing to him. He would eventually be acquitted, not on a technicality, but by a jury on the merits.

My own years as a trial judge in the Superior Court of New Jersey have helped me to bore into character and intellect fairly quickly. In our first meeting, Joe impressed me as a man possessed of intellectual honesty, saint-like patience, and profound love of country, notwithstanding the misguided decisions of those who have run its government.

My initial impression was correct.

We had numerous meetings to address and analyze the judicial mindset and the manner in which it can subtly be moved in one direction or another, depending on the facts in a case and the manner of their presentation.

What to do when the judge in your case sounds more like one of the prosecutors than the neutral arbiter that the Constitution guarantees? What to do when those guarantees are dishonored in a public courtroom of the United States of America by the very people we have hired to uphold them?

Joe is a quick study, and regurgitates clearly what he sees and knows, as the reader will quickly grasp in the pages that follow.

In these pages, the reader will see a small town American success story; an Italian-American Jimmy Stewart, straight out of *It's A Wonderful Life*. He would be embarrassed at the Stewart comparison, but he'd be the first to acknowledge that his life has been wonderful.

He has been a successful businessman, a clean politician in a world of payback and revenge, and a leader willing to buck the tide. He has forged coalitions, achieved compromises, and brought together feuding legislative factions for the common good. All the while he stayed faithful to his basic beliefs that our liberties come for our humanity—not from the government—and the government's first duty is to protect those liberties.

But Joe's political life is more about the fascinating vagaries of human nature than the theories of good government. In these pages, you will meet some household names and characters, like Russell Simmons, George Pataki, Al D'Amato, Rudy Giuliani, Eliot Spitzer—and you will see them, warts and all, interact with Joe in ways my colleagues in the press never seem to convey.

Filled with unvarnished memories, both high and low, using boxing metaphors and elegant moving poetry, Joe gives you here a sprint through the life of a great and decent man. Savor it and learn from it.

In the end you will think of Senator Joseph Bruno as I have. We are all better for him and his public service. The handsome movie star is joyful.

Andrew P. Napolitano
Senior Judicial Analyst, Fox News
Distinguished Visiting Professor of Law, Brooklyn Law School
New York City
July 19, 2016

PREFACE

AND AWAY WE GO!

Here it is, a life story. Honestly, at times, it felt as if it took longer to put on the page than to live it, but now, at last, it's done.

"So what?" one might ask.

A reasonable question. I've asked it myself. And here is my answer. I hope that my experience can help people.

I served in the New York Senate from 1977 to 2008, and for fourteen of those years I was the majority leader, the first full-time businessman ever to hold that post. As a fiscally conservative upstate Republican in a landscape dominated by free-spending downstate Democrats, I was outnumbered. But as one of the so-called "three men in a room," along with the speaker of the Assembly and the governor, I had the constitutional power to shape the budget and a large say in the laws that the Legislature did or didn't pass.

I suppose this would be worth some words, especially since the state was in terrible financial shape when I became leader, with the worst tax burden in the United States. Soon enough we would suffer the worst attack on American soil. Along the way to trying to solve these problems I wound up dealing with people whose names regularly appeared in headlines and gossip columns—Hillary Clinton, Donald Trump, Michael Bloomberg, and Eliot Spitzer, to name a few.

And while these pages contain some of my encounters with the famous and infamous, I never thought that alone would justify the effort for me to tell my story.

Instead, I was thinking about my work, many years ago, with the Jaycees. Assisting community organizations was enormously satisfying, and I have tried to live my life by the line of the Jaycee Creed: "Service to humanity is the best work of life." Back then, I had no conscious interest in elected office. I was, by no means, an "academic," and as a son of a coal miner who spent his early days delivering ice, a life as a politician wasn't in the forefront of my mind as a direct path. But I remember seeing Ronald Reagan, when he was traveling the country for General Electric, speak at the Queensbury Hotel in my hometown of Glens Falls, New York. I sat in front, studying him, his nervousness before he began, his easy style as he launched into his speech, and his ability to entertain and inform an audience, and I recall thinking that when I spoke in public I would try to emulate him. He was a people person, and I was inspired by his ability to communicate. When I watched him, it made me want to become a better communicator. I felt that if I could learn to listen and communicate well, that I could make a difference.

The Jaycee creed, and my glimpse of Reagan, would shape my political career, and it is in the spirit of assisting others that I put together my story, hoping that in some small way reading about my successes and failures might help the reader. This isn't because I was a longtime senator. My role did give me a unique viewpoint, but I never kidded myself that voters thought much of politicians, and the truth is that on occasion I agreed with them. There is no second place when you run for office, you win or lose unlike horse races or golf tournaments. But once the race is over, I learned that you have to shake hands with your opponents and govern. That's what is sometimes missing today, politicians who understand that they are elected not to be self-served, but to provide a better quality of life for the people who elected them and that sometimes takes the willingness to listen and compromise.

More valuable, I think, is that I've lived long enough to see a vanishing America. In that place, once upon a time, we celebrated the ideals of hard work, self-reliance, honesty, essential decency, an attempt by journalists to get their facts straight and to leave the opinions to editorial writers, a justice system committed to the notion of fairness, where public grandstanding by prosecutors and judges was considered indecent, and a political system based on opponents seeking common ground and compromising in order to solve problems.

Not that in the past we always lived up to these ideals, not by a long shot, but even when we failed, we knew what was expected of us. That people no longer seem to care about the erosion of these values troubles me.

On a personal note, I grew up in circumstances that today would be seen as unimaginable poverty. When I was born no social safety net existed, and my father, an Italian immigrant who served in the First World War, was offended by charity of any kind, including government handouts. I was a skinny kid who became a champion light heavyweight boxer, a poor student who managed to graduate from college, a boy from the wrong side of the tracks who married a doctor's daughter, and, after a stint in Korea during the waning days of that war, a businessman who had more ups and downs than a cross-country race course.

In 1976, after I got going as a businessman, I turned to politics, chiefly because I was tired of having the daylights taxed out of me; from the stories I read in the papers about the people doing the taxing, I wouldn't have hired most of them to mow my lawn. Even more infuriating than the tax burden was that the Legislature didn't accomplish much with our money. The year before, New York City nearly went bankrupt; the state was judged to be about the worst spot in the country to locate a business—only Louisiana was worse—and the infrastructure of the Capital Region, where I lived, would've embarrassed a third-world dictator.

Once I won a seat in the state Senate, I made an unhappy discovery. My title came with little clout; I realized that while I could get some things done as Senator, it would be a lot easier and direct if I were leader. To enact the changes I dreamed of, I'd have to be one of those three men in the room, at the table, making decisions about the budget. So, in November 1994, after Republican George Pataki narrowly defeated incumbent Democratic governor Mario Cuomo, I launched a coup to unseat the Republican Senate majority leader, Ralph Marino. Ralph was a nice, soft-spoken guy from

Long Island, with few leadership qualities, and as big a tax-and-spender as Cuomo and Sheldon Silver, a Manhattan Democrat who had recently been elected speaker of the Assembly. No one had ever beaten a sitting majority leader in the history of the state, and neither Pataki nor U.S. Senator Alphonse D'Amato, the de facto Republican boss of New York, wanted me in the position. Had I failed it would've been the end of my career, but I was so disgusted with the state's spending and its tax policies driving out business, I didn't care.

After a nerve-wracking Thanksgiving weekend of phoning other senators and lining up support with a mixture of persuasion and promises of committee chairmanships, I nailed down the votes to become the majority leader, and Ralph was out. He forgave me, and I was later asked by his wife to deliver the eulogy at his funeral along with Mario Cuomo.

Over the next dozen years, sometimes working with and sometimes against Governor Pataki and Speaker Silver, I saw the business climate of New York improve, particularly upstate. One of my biggest supporters was Donald Trump, who raised money for Republicans. Donald was a character—more about him later—but he had demonstrated in the mid-1980s, when he took over the disastrously overdue, over-budget renovation of Wollman Rink in Central Park and completed it in a few months for a couple of million dollars, what I'd been saying ever since arriving in the Senate—that a businesslike approach was better for taxpayers than the slow-moving, expensive grind of government.

In 2006, as George Pataki completed his third four-year term and prepared to enter private life, I was tempted to follow him. Much of what I had set out to do had been done—a revitalized airport, technology parks, improved high-tech education, and bringing nanotechnology to the University at Albany. Still, there was one more project I wanted to see completed: bringing a computer-chip fabrication plant to the Capital Region, a big piece of my dream to see upstate New York compete with Silicon Valley. So I stayed, which was how I came to lock horns with the newly elected Democratic governor, Eliot Spitzer. In later chapters I've documented Spitzer's fifteen months in the Governor's Mansion—the strangest period of my years in politics. All I'll say here is that while I never claimed to own a crystal ball, I had to be among the first to recognize that Spitzer was unbalanced, an opinion I see no reason to change now, eight years after he departed Albany in disgrace.

The chip plant would be built, but I'd come to regret my decision to remain in the Senate, because I wound up in the ugliest fight of my life, being prosecuted for something that the United States Supreme Court ruled wasn't a crime at all—the supposed theft of honest services.

Which brings me to the last reason I'm telling my story. The federal government spent three years investigating me, and I fought the government in court for another five, all of which gave me a close look at a legal system overwhelmed by uncontrolled prosecutorial discretion and a judge who many thought enabled the prosecutors. I was lucky in that I had the persistence and the ability to raise the money to fight. I was even luckier to have the support of my entire family and so many great friends who stepped up and publicly supported me, despite great personal jeopardy at times. My son, daughter, and Kay were by my side in court every single day, and that meant everything to me. Most people don't have my resources to fight back against the unfairness of this system, and the horrid impact these trials had on me, my family, and friends, continues to rankle me.

Yes, the tales of corruption are legendary. After my two trials were done, Assembly Speaker Silver was convicted of selling his office, and Dean Skelos, the senator who replaced me as majority leader, was convicted of extortion. Both were prosecuted by the U. S. Attorney's office, which had won prosecutions against other legislators and Wall Streeters. Yet, reported with less fanfare, probably because it isn't as entertaining as the public scourging of an elected official or a hedge-fund manager, is that a number of these convictions have been thrown out by the courts. In the end, if we don't change this behavior, everyone is at risk.

One final observation, if I may, and I kept it in mind while I dove back into my past. Someone once told me that you can gauge a life by what was accomplished, how long the odds were against succeeding, and the price you paid for your success.

I believe I accomplished things worth reading about—things that no one in his right mind would have predicted for me when I was a boy. As for the price—it was high, higher than I ever anticipated, and, as you'll see, I'm still paying it.

Was it all worth it? This book is also my attempt to answer that question.

1

COURTROOM 6

The United States of America versus Joseph L. Bruno...

I couldn't believe it. Not those words. I felt like I was standing outside myself. Trapped in a crazy nightmare. I blinked. On the wall behind the judge's bench, I saw the Great Seal of the United States, the eagle grasping an olive branch in one talon and thirteen arrows in the other.

Really? My country was prosecuting me? I was the enemy? An eighty-year-old enemy, no less. A veteran of Korea who had served in the New York State Senate for thirty-two years.

Yes, they were. On this cold gray Monday morning, November 2, 2009, I'd come through security at the James T. Foley United States Courthouse in Albany, walked down the hallway, and entered the courtroom, with its dark mahogany furniture and pastel, blue and gray carpet, then sat in a chair at the defendant's table and glanced at the rows of potential jurors seated behind me.

And what was my crime? Not tax evasion, that's for sure. The feds had gone through fourteen years of my returns and hadn't found a penny out of place. The government had bigger things in mind for me. Assistant U.S. Attorneys Elizabeth C. Coombe and William C. Pericak had conjured up a headline-grabbing, eight-count, thirty-five-page indictment that basically claimed I'd deprived the citizens of my state of honest services.

I wasn't doing my job, was that it? Me, who went sixteen hours a day, whose family and staff accused of being a workaholic?

1

The honest-services statue was ludicrous—"a weapon of mass discretion," according to one legal scholar.[1] So what was I being tried for? *The New York Times*, no friend of mine, speculated that it wasn't necessarily a matter of "what's illegal in Albany but what's legal."[2]

Ah, I get it. I was being prosecuted for following rules I'd tried to change as the majority leader of the Senate, only to have my ideas shot down by Governor Eliot Spitzer. Now all the government had to do was put retired Senator Joe Bruno in jail, and presto—they'll clean up Albany.

If that doesn't make sense to you, you're not alone, but you'll never go broke betting against overreaching government prosecutors, and for these folks the honest-services law was awfully handy. Justice Antonin Scalia would quip that you could use it to indict "a mayor for using the prestige of his office to get a table at a restaurant without a reservation."[3]

Maybe Coombe and Pericak wanted to nail me for that. For using my name when I made a reservation at Jack's Oyster House.

Now was no time for jokes. Still, I kept thinking that if the eagle on the Great Seal knew what was going on below him, he'd fall off the wall, dead.

My mind wandered. I was standing outside myself again, but I no longer wondered how I'd wound up in Courtroom 6.

I began wondering how all of this had started, if there was one identifiable moment when, long ago, I had become who I was going to be.

Yes, I decided, there was a moment…

2

HOMETOWN, U.S.A.

A single moment that had shaped my future, a moment in September. My whole life altered by that excruciating, indelible moment.

And it only took me a lifetime to figure it out.

I couldn't have known it back then. Not while it was happening. Not in 1946, when I was a fast-talking seventeen-year-old senior at Saint Mary's Academy, a middleweight who loved to box and ignored his homework to take any job I could find, from delivering newspapers to matching quarters with my schoolmates so I could buy a class ring. Not as I sweated through my shirt in the blistering sun of that September afternoon and stood on the parched grass outside 25 Walnut Street in Glens Falls, a rundown duplex, with my maternal grandmother's family, the Ricciardellis, on one side, and all ten of the Brunos on the other, crammed into the three bedrooms upstairs with just a commode, no sink, no hot water, and three rooms downstairs, where we bathed once a week in a tub in the kitchen—the two girls on Friday night, the six boys on Saturday, with water heated in iron pots. To make space for their children, our parents slept on a pullout couch in the living room, and there was a wood stove in the kitchen that went out at night, so in the winter I froze my ass off even though we slept two in a bed and bundled up in sweaters and coats to sleep.

Welcome to Hometown, U.S.A., the name bestowed on Glens Falls, New York, by *Look* in April 1944, when the magazine began publishing, with glorious color photographs, its series on the city flourishing in the

3

foothills of the Adirondacks, a six-part, patriotic love letter to its nine-teen thousand residents, all of whom, if you believed the articles, appeared to live in a Norman Rockwell painting with views of the Hudson River. For some reason, *Look* failed to mention the east end, where the Brunos resided, perhaps because the hardscrabble lives of the east-enders were not as effective an advertisement for the American dream as pictures of young-sters riding bicycles past the grand homes on Glen Street or a businessmen's luncheon in the opulent dining room of the Queensbury Hotel.

Any of the shoppers strolling under the stately elms downtown or enjoying a malted at the soda fountain in Kresge's could tell you that the east end was where the dagos and micks clustered, scrambling to get by in the shadows of the D & H Railroad depot, where boys had hugged their parents and sweethearts before going off to war, and where the sooty rectan-gle of Singleton's coal yard doubled as a playground for the neighborhood kids, who often hopped a boxcar there and rode it to Hanks Candy Co. to feast on packages of discarded chocolates. There were red-brick factories almost everywhere you looked that smudged the sky with smoke and sup-plied the customers who anesthetized their assorted sorrows in the taverns, pungent with sweat and tobacco, and owned by ex-bootleggers. The one redeemable feature of the east end, or so some of the illustrious citizens said, were the mom-and-pop bakeries and grocery stores along the narrow streets, excellent places to buy homemade wine or bread but otherwise, if you had half a brain, you'd keep out. Those east-enders, particularly the kids, were tough.

Neither I, nor my seven brothers and sisters, ranging in age from twenty-one to seven, were feeling especially tough on that blazing after-noon as a listless breeze blew dust in our faces, and we watched our father, Vialiano, as dark and handsome as a matinee idol, storm past us to the street. In 1910, when Vito was fourteen, he had emigrated from Bologna, Italy, and by now his muscles had muscles—his stomach was so hard he let his sons punch it for fun—the result of working every minute of overtime he could get shoveling coal into a furnace at a plant that produced tissue paper, trudging back and forth over the South Glens Falls Bridge because the bus cost a dime each way. By nature, Vito was reticent, a patient father

4

and listener, but he was a ferocious protector of the people he loved, and at the moment his anger was visible in the corded veins in his neck as he gave the ambulance driver holy hell in his fractured English, yelling at him to turn on the air conditioning because our mother—forty-three years old and wasted away to skeletal proportions—was strapped on a stretcher in back and almost suffocating in the September heat that was indistinguishable from the worst dog days of summer.

My mother, Rachel Catherine and always called "Katie," was in that ambulance because she had just returned from the Lahey Clinic in Boston. For a long time she had suffered from the aftereffects of a botched gall bladder operation. Before her surgery, she was a robust woman with an alabaster complexion and twinkling brown eyes who possessed boundless energy for tending to her husband and children, cooking, cleaning, and marching us over to Warren Street on Sundays for nine o'clock Mass at Saint Mary's, her daughters in home-sewn dresses and her sons in their one decent set of clothes, purchased at the Economy Department Store. A Glens Falls native, my mother could read and write English and Italian. Thus, when many of our neighbors received a letter from Italy or wanted to write one, they came to see Katie, who also served as the local psychotherapist, listening to their problems and offering advice and whatever assistance she could.

I was a small boy the day Ma came home from her first surgery, and so relieved to see her I probably followed her from room to room as Pa and the neighbors streaming in to visit celebrated with pasta in rich tomato sauce and newly pressed wine. Six months later, Ma had stomach pains, and her skin and the whites of her eyes were yellow with jaundice. A doctor discovered that during her gallbladder operation, the surgeon had cut into a bile duct so that bile was leaking into her abdomen, which had become infected. An operation was scheduled to insert a tube to bypass the injured duct, which her body continuously rejected, and this was the start of a torturous odyssey of seven surgeries and months away from us recuperating. Ma grew sicker; I can still see her stretched out on the couch, shivering with chills while Pa heated bricks on the stove then wrapped them in a blanket and used it as a heating pad for his wife. Ma never complained, though, and made the most of it when she was home. My oldest sister Rose had assumed the household chores, and Ma sat in her rocking chair, instructing her on how to prepare meals, and fighting off her pain to help Rose bathe the youngest children, and even working at the polls on Election Day, from six in the morning till nine-thirty at night, because it paid $15.

I remember how concerned the adults around me were when Ma became pregnant with Art and then Bob. From what I could make out, everyone worried whether Ma, with her trouble keeping down food and little strength, would survive the deliveries. I dearly love my youngest brothers, but it was during these years that I began to resent the Catholic Church for its condemning birth control as sinful. Most of the Italian—and Irish—grownups in the east end were staunch Catholics, and there they were, in the midst of the Depression, barely able to put food on their tables, and still having more kids. Why? Because the Church told them they'd fry if they didn't. Yet what assistance did the Church offer the devout Brunos? When Ma was too sick to attend Mass, Father O'Connor made house calls to give her Communion. And Saint Mary's sent a fruit basket after she died.

I didn't realize it on that September afternoon, but Ma's going to the Lahey Clinic had been her last hope. As it worked out, the doctors at Lahey, among the finest in the country, had been unable to help her, and now she was supposed to be taken to the Koch Nursing Home on Glen Street for palliative care. My father's medical insurance had covered the hospitalization, not the ambulance ride from Boston to the nursing home. Originally, Pa had been told the cost would be $75. He had saved up those funds, only to be informed by the ambulance driver, who had stopped at our house to collect payment, that the cost was $125. After Pa got done shouting, the driver had agreed to start up the engine and turn on the air conditioning, but he refused to deliver Ma to Koch or to unload her from the ambulance until he got paid.

Pa was fifty bucks short. And he was flat broke.

To understand what happened next, to appreciate the desperation my father must have felt, and his humiliation, you have to understand his enormous pride and his belief, as strong as his faith in God, that to have integrity you had to make your own way, and you weren't entitled, regardless of how difficult your circumstances, to break the law or to take anything you didn't earn. During Prohibition, my father's brother, Dominick, who lived on the street behind us, was a successful bootlegger, and he offered Pa a chance to join him. My parents had three children and needed the money, but my father rejected his brother's offer. Then the Depression hit, and although Pa struggled to feed his family, raising rabbits and chickens in a coop he built from a shipping crate and planting a garden, he refused to accept the same government assistance that our neighbors accepted. Nor would he permit the firemen, who ran a charity drive at Christmastime, to give us the same presents that they gave the other poor kids.

Now, however, his wife was a prisoner and his children expected him to rescue her.

I can scarcely imagine how difficult it was for my father to swallow his pride for the following five or six hours, and, along with two friends, Dominick Russo and Giuseppe Didio, go from house to house for help. The people they asked were generally no better off than the Brunos, though none of them had a loved one stuck in an ambulance. Henry Lamberti and Pietro Villa ponied up fifty cents; John Popi, Carmela DiPaldo, and Aurora Pagano each kicked in a quarter. I know the names and amounts because someone made a list. My father couldn't write, and in all likelihood he insisted that either Dominick or Giuseppe keep track of the contributions, because he intended to repay everybody. The list read like an Italian phone book, and there were one hundred and fourteen names on it. I know all of this because thirty-five years later, when my father passed away, the list was in the Coleman toolbox that he used to store his personal papers.

I'm not sure whether Pa repaid those people, but I wouldn't bet against it.

My mother was taken to Koch Nursing Home, where she remained until spring. One Saturday in April, Pa walked us over there to see her. Mom was lying in bed with tubes running into one of her thin pale arms. Her children crowded around her. She patted my youngest brothers on their heads. I don't recall what anyone said, though somebody must have said something, but I had the impression that my mother, despite her fight to live for her husband and children, understood that she would soon be leaving us.

In the morning, there was a loud knock on the kitchen door. My father, still in his underwear, opened the door, and our neighbor, who had gotten the phone call from the nursing home, told him that Mom had passed away. It was Easter Sunday, 1947. She was forty-four years old. It was the first time I ever saw my father cry.

As broken up as I was about her death, with the passing of time what has never left me was the memory of my father being unable to pay her ambulance while she lay helpless on that stretcher.

Ask me why I stayed in the New York State Senate for thirty-two years. Ask me why I dedicated much of my adult life learning how to operate the levers of power, to shift funds to save a school, for instance, or to reinvigorate a financially bereft community. Ask me. I'll give you chapter and verse on the wages of powerlessness, its horror, its degradation, and the wounds that never heal.

Ask me, and I'll tell you about a hot September afternoon, seventy years ago.

3

WHATEVER YOU WANT

Throughout my mother's illness and after her death, my father held the family together. He did this with a combination of working long hours and handing out advice, and among his favorite sayings was "Whatever you want, you have to work hard to get it."

I listened and, as a boy, grabbed any opportunity that came my way. At the age of nine, I began waking up before six, walking over to Voher and Donahue's Bakery, and carrying metal trays of doughnuts and cinnamon buns to McMullen and Levin, a shirt-and-dress manufacturer. I could see the factory from the back of our house, and the whole undertaking took about an hour, the worst part of it being in the winter, when I woke up in the dark and had to walk through the bitter cold and kept slipping on the ice and snow, trying to balance the trays. I was paid in day-old baked goods, and during that year my family ate lemon pies and éclairs for breakfast. By the following year, I graduated to a paper route with a hundred and twenty-four customers who paid three cents for the paper, and I kept a penny.

After school and in the summers, I pulled weeds, cut grass, unloaded watermelons from box cars, carried bags at the railroad station for tips, put out the produce at Central Market, collected coal that fell outside the fence at Singleton's, put it in a burlap bag, and brought it home to burn in the stove. My scariest job was answering a phone for a taxi company seven days a week from three in the afternoon until two in the morning, many of the customers belligerent drunks who relished screaming at the kid in

9

the office. I was paid fifty cents a shift, an arrangement that would land an employer in jail if he tried it today. When my stint at the taxi company ended, I got hired to set up the bowling pins at the Knights of Columbus on weekday evenings, usually keeping at it until midnight.

My chief recollection of these years is of being tired and miserable, and feeling as though I was inferior to other children. My clothes smelled of coal smoke, and because we couldn't afford a dentist, I used to stick pieces of white paper in my mouth to hide the decay staining my teeth. The single image that has never left me—an image that contains all of the pain and frustration of my childhood—is of kids squealing with delight and riding ponies down Walnut Street while I had to watch because my parents didn't have the nickels for their children to take a turn.

As for my future, all I knew was that I didn't want to be poor, so I worked as hard as I could while it gradually occurred to me that, contrary to Pa's advice, hard work wasn't a guaranteed ticket out of poverty—you had to get a job that paid well. My ticket out could've been an education. The Bruno children attended Saint Mary's Academy, an imposing stone edifice on the outskirts of the downtown. Because my parents couldn't afford the tuition, I assume the church let us attend for free, but even there I felt as if I were a six-headed duck, beginning with the fact that I didn't have a uniform like the other students—again because my family didn't have the money. With the hours I was working I frequently fell asleep in class, and the nuns considered me a lost cause. I did my best to avoid the sister the students referred to as "King Kong," who once smacked my brother, Pete, in the head so violently that it took him a day to regain his hearing. I managed to escape his fate, but I was a regular at detention, where I discovered a copy of Dale Carnegie's *How to Win Friends and Influence People*.

The nun snatched the book from me, held it up and mocked me by saying, "Look what he's reading." Then she smacked me on the back of the head and ordered me to do my homework.

Probably because I wanted to prove that I could do something worthwhile, I got it in my head that I wanted to be an altar boy. This news was greeted with healthy skepticism by my homeroom teacher, Sister Marsha. She spoke to Sister Rose Madeleine, who the students referred to as "King

Kong," and Sister Rose told my teacher that I was too dumb to learn Latin. Sister Marsha offered to teach me after school, and I accepted and studied myself silly and became an altar boy, winning an award that was presented to me one Sunday when the church was full. The faithful applauded my efforts. I liked the award and the applause, tangible proof that I'd accomplished a goal. The same was true with the Boy Scouts and its merit badges, and I flourished as a Scout. However, the skill I picked up during those years that gave me my strongest sense of self-reliance was learning how to box.

The Sagamore Street Playground was a quarter-mile from my house, and when I first started hanging around there I was the proverbial ninety-pound weakling, which I guess was an invitation for the bigger kids to pick on me. I got beat up on more than one unceremonious occasion. Still, I figured it was my playground too, and I was stubborn enough not to let them chase me away from the swings and the slide and the baseball or football game. In the 1930s, anti-bullying campaigns were limited to your ability to defend yourself, and I was blessed that on a summer afternoon a guy in his twenties came over to say hello. His name was Bob Coons; he was a middleweight boxer from New York City; and he promised that he could show me how to handle bullies.

For weeks, Bob practiced with me, getting down on his knees and rotating around—and wearing out his pants—while I circled him, leading with my left and punching straight ahead with my right just as he taught me. I fell in love with the rhythm and physicality of boxing, the combina-

translating it into a dance along with jabs and hooks.

The next time a kid came after me, it was a two-punch affair, and I wasn't the one with the bloody nose, and after that I knew all I'd ever need to know about bullies. From then on, I took care of myself and looked after some of the smaller kids in the playground.

It was excellent training for a future politician.

★ ★ ★

One of the most pernicious aspects of poverty is that it is hard to imagine a better life beyond the riches one might see in the media—in my day, the magazine photos of Hollywood stars and European royalty—not necessarily the most helpful guide for plotting a realistic escape plan. For me, there was the example of my Uncle Dominick, my father's brother, who owned a tavern, The Blue Room, with a hotel upstairs and a grocery store next to the bar, with his family living upstairs. I don't know if anything indecent went on in the hotel rooms, but Ma told me to keep away from there, as if my morals would be compromised by the proximity to alleged sin. The word in my family, though, was that Uncle Dominick had been a bootlegger and, given my upbringing, I didn't consider a life of crime an option.

Fortunately, the Rotary Club of Glens Falls appreciated this challenge and had a program designed to pair needy kids with some of the city's more successful citizens. It was known as the Buddy Club. Every Saturday, for a nickel, we could go to the YMCA on Glen Street to play in the gym and swim in the pool, and each of us who participated had a sponsor from the Rotary. My sponsor was Dr. Mitchell, a tall, bespectacled man whose serious demeanor was both intimidating and encouraging. Every week I used to meet with him and we'd talk for five or ten minutes, and he would sign a slip of paper that I'd visited. Dr. Mitchell became, I now realize, someone I wanted to emulate, and he and his family resided in the Broadacres section of Glens Falls—a bucolic slice of heaven dotted with magnificent homes. I had Christmas dinner with them, and it was in that house that I got my first glimpse of the world beyond the six crowded rooms on Walnut Street.

Now, at least, I had something to shoot for.

And going to the YMCA altered my life in a way I had never anticipated, for it was there, standing across from me at a Ping-Pong table, that I met Barbara Frasier, called Bobbie. I was fourteen, and Bobbie was a year younger. We would later confess to each other that it was love at first sight, though being so young neither of us knew squat about the subject. But the Y was a wonderful place to find a partner, because they held weekly dances, and it was swaying to big-band music that we became boyfriend and girlfriend.

Bobbie was a demure, strawberry blond who, even then, had a poise and grace that was totally foreign to me. I'd soon discover that she came by those qualities honestly enough, growing up less than a mile—and a world away—from the east end. Her house was one of the big, comfortable Victorians on Glen Street, directly across from Glens Falls High School and half a block from First Presbyterian, where her family prayed on Sundays.

Her father, Dr. Nelson Frasier, was an austere man, a graduate of New York University Medical School who completed his surgical training at Bellevue Hospital in Manhattan and entered the U.S. Army Medical Corps as a first lieutenant during World War I, serving at the base hospital in Langres, France. Following the Armistice, he married Jesse McNeal, an Albany native three years his senior, opened an office in their home, established a busy practice as a surgeon and ultimately became chief of staff at the hospital. Jesse was a beautiful, high-spirited woman a few inches under five feet, who loved to cook and bake, and no one I've ever known was kinder to me. The Fraziers had two other daughters, Margaret and Jean, and initially they were less kind to me than their mother, acting as though a loutish Italian-Catholic alien had arrived from a wretched galaxy to disrupt their happy clan by stealing their sister.

Dr. Frazier wasn't directly rude to me—he was too well-bred for that—but he told Bobbie in no uncertain terms that she should not go out with me. Looking back, I can understand the reaction of her father and sisters, because to this day, I'm not exactly sure what Bobbie saw in me. She was a good student, an excellent dancer, softball player, and skier and, unlike me, deeply involved in the whirl of activities at her school— the French club and the prom committee, to name a couple of them. The one thing I had going for me was that I was the opposite of shy. I'd say whatever was on my mind, and I wasn't afraid to ask for something if I wanted it—a talent I perfected out of necessity as I was always in the position of needing a job. Bobbie, on the other hand, was quiet and shy. I suppose we thought our lives would be easier if we could fix our imperfections with the qualities of the other.

I got the best of that deal. I never made Bobbie less shy, but whatever gentlemanly skills I developed, I owe to her. After we started to date, I realized that my grammar and my language, which seemed normal at home, was a disaster. Gently, and insistently, Bobbie corrected my English, striking "ain't" and "youse" from my vocabulary, handing out a few pointers about agreements between subject and verb, and suggesting that as a rule profanity wasn't the most succinct way to express yourself. I could've been insulted, but Bobbie was such a generous soul; she offered her suggestions as though she were sharing these wonderful secrets; and so it was impossible for me to be hurt. Then, too, I knew that her seeing me came at some cost to her, because she respected her father, and his disapproval of me wounded her, as did the snide comments from her sisters, one of them being that if Bobbie married me, she'd have dark, wiry-haired Italian babies.

Her mother was her ally, and she didn't report to Dr. Frazier that their daughter had set up a signal with me, leaving the light on in her room so I'd know her father wasn't home, and it was safe to call her on the phone. In order to go to the movies or dances with me, she told her father that she was meeting her girlfriends, and when I brought her home we had to say goodnight while standing behind the thick trunk of an oak tree. We were young, and our rebellion held as much allure as our romance. Yet I was uncertain about my future, and the idea that I would marry Bobbie seemed unrealistic. Despite my brashness, even I didn't think I could punch that high above my weight.

I was about to graduate from Saint Mary's, a miracle rivaled by the fishes and loaves. My best grade in four years of high school was a 92 in Civics, with the others being just barely adequate for me to get my diploma. Now I needed a job, and Fred Hovey, the most prominent ice dealer in town, a shrewd, hard-working man who plowed his profits into buying land, hired me to help deliver ice from one of his trucks. I worked six and a half days a week for $14, a sum that I doubted would impress Bobbie's father.

"Why don't you go to college?" Bobbie asked me one night. Bobbie, upon graduating from Glens Falls High School, would become a student at the Edgewood Park School in Briarcliff Manor, a two-year program that prepared young women for semiprofessional careers but didn't stint on the high-toned cultural stuff that Bobbie liked.

"With my grades? Are you kidding?"

"No," she replied quietly. "I'm not."

I knew Bobbie was right. If my life was going to catch up with my ambition, I'd need a college degree, so I got permission from Mr. Hovey to borrow his truck and drove down to Loudonville, a suburb of Albany, where in the 1930s Franciscan friars had established Saint Bernardine of Siena College. When I arrived on campus, the place was so jammed with returning veterans paying their way with the G.I. Bill that classes were held in Quonset huts.

I met with a dean, a friar who was as sympathetic and forgiving as the founder of his order, Saint Francis of Assisi. Upon inspecting my transcript, the dean said that he wasn't sure my grades warranted an acceptance and noted that I hadn't taken any admission exams.

"I'll take the tests," I said. "And do the work. I promise."

He must've heard the desperation in my voice, because when I climbed behind the wheel of the truck, I was no longer just another Italian Glens Falls east-ender. I was a real American college boy.

Electric refrigerators weren't mass produced until after the Second World War, and it was a while before they were a familiar presence in American kitchens. Before then, food was stored in an icebox, and in every town you'd see ice trucks driving up and down the streets. Our days began before dawn when I had to walk three miles to Glenwood Avenue, where Fred Hovey had his home and his company's ice houses. We worked into the evening, and I had to make up the hours I spent at Siena. First, we cut up the ice in the storage sheds with chainsaws, and I saw more than one careless guy slice into his own leg and splatter the white-blue blocks with blood. Using tongs, we loaded up the truck, and then we were off on our daily rounds. Delivering ice in the summer and fall was back-breaking, and you got soaked hauling it into houses and sliding it into the boxes. Yet all of this was a day at the beach compared to what we had to do in January and February, cutting blocks of ice from a pond and transferring them to ice houses.

With our breath smoking in the frigid gusts that shook the bare branches of the trees, we began by scraping the snow off the pond with plows attached to horses that, on occasion, protested their working conditions by refusing to move or trying to kick you. Then, using a motorized saw, we attacked the ice, cutting blocks that were thirty inches thick, fifteen feet wide, and weighed a minimum of three hundred pounds. Once we squared off the ice, we used crowbars to free it from the surrounding ice until it resembled a raft and began floating it to shore.

By now, our hands and feet were numb, and we had to load the ice onto an elevator that lifted the ice over the traffic on Glenwood Avenue. The worst job was the final step: as the elevator lowered the ice onto mini-tracks that led into the storage sheds, the switchers had to guide the blocks by grabbing them and stopping their movement with a pike. If the switcher forgot to plant his feet, he'd wind up getting clocked by the ice and knocked off his feet, which always made everyone laugh and infuriated the poor fellow on the ground, who sometimes stood up and punched one of his giddy co-workers in the face.

Between working for Hovey Ice and driving fifty miles in wet clothes three days a week to Siena, I felt as though I were trapped in a frozen Hell.

Then I got smart—and lucky.

Smart because I transferred to Skidmore, a women's college in Saratoga Springs that had recently opened a co-ed extension in Glens Falls to accommodate the World War II veterans. Professors were brought from Saratoga; tuition was cheap; and because so many of the veterans were employed, the extension had a generous selection of evening classes.

My luck was that the Irving brothers, who had the ice route in Hudson Falls, decided to retire. That meant Fred Hovey needed a new guy for his truck, and I asked him for the job. In 1948, I figured it was a brave thing to do. Today, however, I can see that his answer was a foregone conclusion, and this taught me an aspect of deal making that I didn't fully appreciate until years later: know who you are asking and how your request will be considered. In Fred's case, I knew that he liked me. More important, I knew that he had made his own way in the world and revered hard work; and I sensed that he was itching to give a kid a chance.

Fred looked me up and down. "How the hell you gonna do it? One guy on a truck?"

"Don't worry. I'll do it."

He thought for a moment, rubbing his chin. "I'll tell you what. I'll let you have the truck and ice for a week—no charge. Let's see how you do."

I made a small fortune, or at least that was how it felt to me as I emptied my pockets at night and piled the crumpled, wet bills on my dresser. The route became mine. I paid Fred seventy cents for a three-hundred-pound cake of ice, and sold it for $3. I never sold less than a hundred cakes a week, and most weeks I sold more.

Finally, I could afford an engagement ring, and I asked Bobbie to marry me.

And she said yes.

4

YOU'RE IN THE ARMY NOW

Barbara and I were married on March 25, 1950, in the rectory of Saint Mary's, not in the church, because it was Lent and no big to-dos were allowed. I wasn't sure God had the time to worry about where we took our vows, but the priest said He did. Dr. Frazier made up for the modest ceremony by paying for a reception at the Queensbury Hotel. During my spring break, Bobbie and I honeymooned in New York City. For eleven bucks a night, we stayed at the Hotel Commodore, with its opulent lobby that included a waterfall, and when we returned to Glens Falls, I moved into the Frazier's house—at her father's insistence. It was his way of helping us, and I suspect that he thought Bobbie and I were children ourselves and still needed a parental hand. He was right: I was twenty; my new bride was nineteen.

Dr. Frazier and I were on much better terms. Once I slipped the engagement ring on Bobbie's finger (and had a well-paid job and a full schedule of college courses), he accepted that his daughter wanted to marry me regardless of whether he approved, and his own problems must have outweighed any disappointment he might have felt about Bobbie's selection of a son-in-law. Due to the onset of Huntington's disease, the doctor had to close his practice. He had made some solid investments and bought enough insurance that he and his family were on a sound financial footing, but he was unable to tend to his house and grounds, so I handled those chores for him.

Jessie, my mother-in-law, who had long been in my corner, was thrilled to have me around. She loved to cook and bake. Her husband had little appetite, and her daughters were watching their figures. However, I came in from work and school starving, and I ate from one end of the house to the other. Not a pie or cake or cookie that Jessie took out of the oven was safe from me, and she used to stand over me smiling as I polished off everything she prepared.

Bobbie, intimately acquainted with the details of my childhood, also seemed to be on a mission to make certain that I never went hungry again, and frequently when I came back to Glens Falls to go to class she'd bring me something to eat, claiming that she could track me down by looking for the puddles my ice truck left in the street.

As I settled into married life, I began to see the fuzzy shapes of a better future, but seven thousand miles away events developed that would sidetrack me and give me a glimpse of horrors that I'd never forget.

In June 1950, aided by the Soviet Union, Communist North Korea invaded U.S.-backed South Korea. The United Nations condemned the attack, and President Harry Truman ordered American troops to assist the South Koreans. The fight was referred to as a "police action," and history would dub it the "Forgotten War," because it was dwarfed by our efforts in World War II and it didn't divide the country in the same manner as Vietnam.

I could've found some way to avoid serving, but I believed our country had a responsibility to help free nations and that it was my patriotic duty to do my share. My father and father-in-law had served in World War I; two of my brothers planned to join the Navy; and my brother, Vito, was in ROTC at Siena and would become a career Army officer. So, believing that I'd get drafted after finishing at Skidmore, I chose to enlist in the Naval Reserve and was accepted into the officer-training program. I had to attend meetings each month, which I didn't mind at all, and then one summer I was sent on a two-week cruise, where I became so seasick I was tempted to jump overboard.

You didn't have to be a military genius to conclude that I'd be more effective on land, and in the winter of 1952, I spoke to someone at my local draft board.

With visions of myself dying with my head stuck in a metal toilet bowl, I said, "Please, you gotta draft me. If you don't, I'll end up in the Navy, and I can't do any more time at sea."

That last year of college I got my first taste of politics, winning an election to become the president of the Skidmore annex. The dean was less than thrilled with the results—I wasn't the best student he'd ever met—and he ordered a rerun of the election. I won again, and the dean gave up. The fighting in Korea seemed to be raging on a distant planet in May when I graduated with a degree in business administration, but it got a lot closer by August when the Army drafted me. I reported to Fort Devens in Massachusetts for processing, and while I was there a letter was forwarded to me from the Navy with instructions to report to Newport, Rhode Island, for my officer training. Never has writing a response given me such pleasure: On the bottom of the Navy's letter, I wrote: "I'm sorry, but I'm in the Army now."

I completed basic training at Camp Breckenridge, Kentucky. After five years of hauling ice, I was in better shape than a lot of the draftees and, thanks to my experience in the Boy Scouts, I actually enjoyed the training—pushing myself to the point of exhaustion during calisthenics, on marches and the obstacle course, and learning how to clean, fieldstrip, and fire an M-1 Garand. I was selected as an acting sergeant and discovered that many of the men who arrived with me took exception to my promotion. Their view was: "Who the hell died and made you king?"

A number of the soldiers began to question my authority, and in my first encounter with New York City swagger, one big mouth busted my chops for a month when I led the platoon during training sessions. One morning, we were marching, and I ordered everyone to pick up the pace, and he refused. I told him to knock it off, which he interpreted as an invitation to tell me to go fuck myself in front of the other men and to explain, at length, the variety of methods he would employ to kick my ass.

I invited him to meet me behind the barracks, where I learned that his mouth was faster than his fists. I hit him some nice combos, and then landed a right that knocked him against the barracks and through the window.

The next morning, the company commander sent for the big mouth and asked him how he got hurt. He replied that he'd fallen down the stairs. Of course, the commander knew he was lying and summoned me.

"What happened?" he asked me.

"What did he tell you?" I replied.

He told me, and I said, "I guess that's what happened."

I could've wound up in the stockade, but the commander clearly didn't want that to occur. He ordered us back to the barracks. I thanked the guy I'd hit for not squealing, and we shook hands. Later, he became one of my closer friends, and a much better soldier.

By the time basic training ended, I'd taken a test to be an officer and did well enough to get my name on the list. While I waited, I was in a maintenance platoon, and after a couple of months, I went into the company commander's office and asked if he'd heard anything about my starting at officer's candidate school.

He said, "There's no telling. But you're better off here than in Korea."

"Frankly, sir, I'd rather be in Korea."

Within days, I received my orders, and I was glad to be on my way. Then I realized we'd be traveling by ship. That tempered my excitement.

We flew to California, boarded the troop transports, and set sail, passing through one of the worst hurricanes ever recorded. This is pure speculation, but it is possible that I might belong in the *Guinness Book of Records* for consecutive hours spent on my knees throwing up. I had no shortage of company in the head, which was backed up and overflowed with waste that formed a foul-smelling lake around us. Except for the nausea, the retching, and the pain in my empty stomach, my recall of the crossing is as hazy as a fever dream. We docked in Yokohama, Japan, and after the weather cleared, we continued on to Korea.

My first memory, as the ship entered the harbor at Pusan, was an odor of raw sewage so strong I began breathing through my mouth. We were herded onto a train, and by nightfall we were stuck in a tunnel. It was pitch black and we were nervous, listening to the boom of artillery. We didn't know why we had stopped. Were we being attacked? Smoke filled the tunnel and came through the open windows. It was a while before we figured out that it was coal smoke from the train. Then we were moving again, out through the night, with flashes of artillery, like heat lightning, in the distance. We got off the train, coated from head to toe with coal dust, and jumped onto trucks that ferried us to Camp Casey.

The camp, which sprawled across thousands of acres, was less than a dozen miles from the Demilitarized Zone, that lethal, desolate strip of no-man's land that separated North and South Korea. The war had ground down to a stalemate and was about to conclude, though the North Koreans were still patrolling nearby. I was assigned to F Company, 2nd Battalion, 35th Infantry Regiment, 25th Division. The highlight of each day was mail call when I could stretch out on my bunk and read Bobbie's letter. My unit's primary job was pulling up barbed wire and searching foxholes and bunkers where soldiers, ours and theirs, had died. It was horrible work unearthing the decomposed bodies, and the stink of death was overwhelming. We were also tasked with locating unexploded bombs and bringing in the experts to set them off. That was frightening enough, but the area was seeded with mines, and a couple of guys died stepping on them, and a truck and a bulldozer hit some mines and rolled over, killing the drivers.

I heard that a single-elimination boxing tournament was being put together. The first bouts would be at the company level. The winner would go on to battalion, then regiment, and finally fight for the division championship. The tournament was a big deal among the soldiers because we were in the 25th Division, which had been partially formed from the division in the huge bestseller *From Here to Eternity*, and one of the novel's main characters, Private Robert E. Lee Prewitt, was a boxer. And I thought: This is a good opportunity to get a break from digging up the dead.

I made it through the company and battalion matches with ease. Even though we wore headgear and fought with fourteen-ounce gloves, some of the fighters got hurt; one guy I remember, a pal of mine, got his brains scrambled and never did return to the company. My opponents were genuine tough guys who liked to fight, but fought as if they were unfamiliar with the more technical demands of boxing, and I had the feeling, in some of the clinches, that they were disappointed because they couldn't knee me in the nuts. Once I moved up to regiment, I was assigned to Special Services so I could join the regimental boxing team. Now, my days were spent training, which was wonderful until I had to walk back to my unit in the dark with the occasional South Korean and North Korean patrols firing at each other.

There was a lot of betting on the semifinal matches of the regimental tournament, and at one point, when the crowd disagreed with the decision, a riot erupted. The military police had to be called, and the MPs used nightsticks to restore order. President Truman had ordered the integration of the forces in Korea, but there was still a fair amount of racial hostility on both sides. I hadn't seen a lot of it out in the field, but during the tournament was another matter. As I walked out for my fight, my opponent, a black fellow about my weight—a hundred and seventy-five pounds but a couple of inches shorter than my five-foot ten and built like a tank—fell in beside me. He was fierce-looking with a shaved head and Fu Manchu moustache, and as we reached the ring, he turned toward me, spit in my face, and said, "You're dead, motherfucker."

I thought he was being overly optimistic, but the company cook, who was my corner man and water boy, said to me, "If I were you, I'd faint or act sick or something and hightail it out of here."

"Thanks for the encouragement."

Then my trainer said, "Stay away from this guy. If he hits you, he's going to hurt you. Just box him. Be smart. You're faster than he is."

My knees were knocking when I got out to the center of the ring. My opponent didn't even want to touch gloves and glared at me as the referee issued his instructions. We went to our corners until the bell rang. The guy came charging at me, swinging wildly and knocking me against the ropes. While I was prepping for my fights, a trainer had mentioned that I was a counterpuncher and didn't start fighting until I'd been hit hard, and someday, he'd warned, I'd get hurt. As I came off the ropes, I figured maybe this was the day, because I stood in the middle of the ring, toe-to-toe with the man who'd predicted that he'd kill me, and exchanged punches with him.

The troops, believing we were going to knock each other out, loved it. I heard them screaming for blood. Yet as I'd discover repeatedly throughout my life, appearances can be deceiving. My opponent was punching like crazy, but I knew how to protect myself and had my head hunched down between my shoulders. He was round-housing, so most of his punches were striking my upper arms and hitting me with less force. I was punching straight ahead as Bob Coons had taught me in the playground—left, right, left, right, each one hitting the guy square in the puss. This went on for maybe ninety seconds—an eternity in the ring. Sweat stung my eyes. I could barely see the face I was hitting, but I heard the thwack-thwack-thwack of the punches landing. Just as I was about to run out of gas and started thinking that I couldn't keep firing rights and lefts at him, and when I dropped my hands, he'd kill me, the guy went down like a ton of bricks.

He was saved by the bell and, with help, made it back to his corner. I can't recall whether the ref stopped the fight or we went a couple of more rounds, but I do remember someone holding up my arm and declaring me the winner.

The championship fight was the next evening. My former opponent attended the match. His eyes were swollen shut, and his nose looked like it was on the side of the face. I hardly had a mark on me and felt bad seeing him. My sympathy, however, didn't last long, because I was fighting his buddy, another black guy who was bigger and stronger than his friend, and he told me: "You see his face? That's gonna look handsome when I get done with you."

He came right for me when the bell sounded. He was so strong that he knocked me against the ropes with one punch to the shoulder. I had my hands up to protect myself, but he was pummeling the hell out of me. I tried to swing, but I couldn't get any momentum against him. The round ended, and my corner man informed me that I hadn't thrown one damn punch, and I was getting beat three ways to Sunday.

"No shit," I replied.

"Move more. Circle him."

"There's a plan," I said, thinking that it was far easier said than done. The guy was the strongest man I'd ever met, and I had the distinct impression that he didn't like white people in general and me in particular.

Round two was a repeat of round one. My opponent charged and shoved me against the ropes while swinging away at my head. I bunched up, and he was hitting my hands, my arms, and my shoulders. I was getting pissed off being his punching bag, and I remember leaning back into the ropes, and suddenly springing toward the guy, throwing a flurry of left and right jabs that nailed him square in the face. I backed him up into the center of the ring, keeping after him with the jabs, and I was flabbergasted when he went over backward and stayed on the canvas. The ref either had a bet on the fight or was a real bloodthirsty son of a bitch: he didn't even start counting to ten, and at least fifteen or twenty seconds passed before the bell rang, and I had to go to my corner.

The ref should've stopped the fight because in round three my opponent could hardly get his hands up to defend himself. I was exhausted, but I knew if I kept on punching I'd win. That was what happened, and so I became the division champion.

It was the proudest moment of my life.

5

CHASING THE
AMERICAN DREAM

While I was boxing, I was promoted from private to private first class to corporal to staff sergeant. After I won the championship, my company commander offered to promote me to first sergeant for the company. His reasoning was that I was now an official ass-kicker and, with the shortage of troops, the Army was drafting ex-jailbirds and releasing soldiers from stockades to fill quotas, which led to more than a few behavior problems.

I was also offered a chance to go to Japan to continue boxing, and I talked it over with my trainer.

He asked, "You wanna be a pro boxer?"

"Hell no. I'm just trying to kill time here."

He said, "Well, once you get to Japan, you're gonna meet guys who might want to turn pro, and who knows how you'll wind up. Cauliflower ears. Blind. Punch drunk."

He had a point, so I became the company first sergeant. I did give a loud mouth a stupendous beating, and that was the end of the problems. I spent thirteen or fourteen months in Korea, and though I got seasick on the ship home, I managed, in between visits to the head, to win $3,400 playing poker. We docked in New York City, and I was mustered out at Fort Dix, New Jersey. Bobbie had taken a train down from Glens Falls, and we spent a night in New York City before I moved back into her parents' house.

During my first few weeks at home, I considered applying to law school. Bobbie supported the idea, but her sister, Peggy, said to me, "Don't you think it's about time you get a job?" Add her comment to the fact that the memory of my childhood poverty was never far away, I decided to consult the classifieds. I'd read that you could earn more money in sales than in any entry-level job in business, so I answered an ad for a position as a salesman with Nash-Ringel, Inc. The company, owned by Morty Nash and Stan Ringel, was selling the Amana Food Plan throughout the Capital Region.

Amana manufactured freezers to replace the ice boxes in homes. By the mid-1950s, Americans were averaging almost four children per family, and that was a lot of mouths to feed. The parents of the baby boomers had grown up during the Depression, so they were inclined to stretch a dollar, and the Amana Plan was designed to appeal to them. Families would get the freezer at a discounted price, and they'd buy a three-month supply of food, also at a discount, which would be delivered to the house. Part of what I explained to potential buyers during my two-hour pitch was that you could pay for the freezer with the savings in your food budget, and the food itself was healthier because it was frozen as soon as it was picked or harvested.

I used to drive down to Albany at seven in the morning and, after a sales meeting, we'd go out to book pitches. You knocked on the door. Usually a housewife answered and glared at you as if you were a bill collector. Sometimes they shouted out a window to get off their steps. You had to have stamina and a can-do attitude, and I lived by the advice my sales manager had given me: "When somebody slams a door in your face, you don't walk to the next house—you run."

Nothing I ever did was better training for politics—trying to get people to sit down long enough to hear what I had to say; meeting and talking to them in their living rooms; answering their questions; figuring out how you could help them; and at the end closing the deal. Generally, during the day, I spoke to housewives, and I had to return when the husbands were there; both signatures were required for the sale; and while wives were eager for help with the grocery shopping, the husbands tended to focus on the cost.

Seven days a week, I worked the morning, grabbed lunch, then kept at it through dinner and didn't get home until eleven at night. And here was what I learned: I could sell. I enjoyed listening to people, could explain things clearly, and never quit regardless of how often I got turned down. I became a star and was promoted to sales manager. Morty and Stan cut a deal with the owners of Fowler's, a fancy department store in Glens Falls. They agreed to sell the Amana Plan, and I worked out of a cubicle in the store. I put together a sales organization and had women prospecting for appointments over the phone, and if their leads paid off, they received a percentage of the sale. I was making ten grand a year, enormous money in those days. Bobbie and I were now living in a rented place on Fred Hovey's property. We had been trying to start a family without any success, but we were optimistic and, using my poker winnings for a down payment, bought a four-bedroom bungalow at 14 Haviland Avenue in South Glens Falls.

I'll never forget the sadness on Bobbie's face when she gave me the news. The doctor had told her that it would be hard for her to conceive. Bobbie responded by saying that we should start taking in foster children. We took in several and became quite close to a brother and sister, Michele and Mike. They were five and three, and it was clear, from their rotted teeth and bony frames, that they had been neglected. It was wonderful providing them with care, and we tried to adopt the children, but their mother wouldn't give them up.

We searched for a child to adopt. The Catholic organizations wouldn't help because Bobbi was Presbyterian. At last, we found a place in Burlington, Vermont, where pregnant teenagers who wouldn't be able to keep their babies went to give birth. We made arrangements to adopt a boy who was nine days old. We were already calling him "Joey" when the social worker handed him to us and said: "Maybe you'd better go to the Howard Johnson's down the road, get a cup of coffee, and see if you really want to take this step."

Bobbie and I went to HoJo's and looked at each other across the table. "What're we doing here?" she asked.

"Let's go get our son."

We brought Joey home, and a few years later we returned to Vermont to adopt a girl, our daughter, Susan. She was nine or ten days old and cute as heck. Joey was with us when we went to court to talk with the judge, who apparently had known the grandparents of Susan's biological mother and seemed reluctant to place Susan with us. I guessed that he was either upset that the mother hadn't kept the child or that he, too, was opposed to mixed marriages. The social worker made an impassioned plea on our behalf. The judge basically ignored her and spoke to Joey, who was dressed up in a coat and tie. Joey answered the judge politely, and the judge said, "I can see you did a pretty good job with this young man—so far."

A year later, when it came time to formalize the adoption, the judge initially indicated that he might want us to bring Susan back. That was one of the most traumatic moments in our lives, though he changed his mind, and Susan was ours.

★ ★ ★

I was growing weary of selling the Amana Plan, repeating the canned pitch and pressing people for the hundred-dollar, ten-percent deposit. One in five couples wouldn't pass the credit check, and you'd lose the sale and the hours you spent talking to them. This problem was somewhat alleviated by selling out of Fowler's, where people already had established credit, but at bottom I think I wanted to sell a product grander—and more complex—than freezers. I got my chance when Morty Nash and Stan Ringel came to a parting of the ways, and I decided to go with Stan, who had arranged to sell mutual funds from the brokerage and investment house First Albany Corporation, which had recently been founded by a well-known lawyer, Daniel V. McNamee Jr.

The world of finance was new to me and fascinating. We spent maybe nine months at First Albany and did nicely enough that Stan had a brainstorm. He decided that we should go out on our own and found two companies that sold a pair of related products—Balanced Investors would sell mutual funds and Balanced Planning would sell insurance. The pitch was a beaut—a plan for living or dying. You'd use the mutual funds to invest for your children's education and your retirement, and you'd buy life insurance to cover these costs if you died before you'd finished saving.

Stan, whose mind moved a mile a minute, was always the idea guy, and I was the hard-working street guy. My contribution was as necessary as Stan's, so I said that I'd go with him if I were a full partner. He thought it over for a second and agreed.

I believed in what we were selling. I'd seen how my father-in-law's shrewd planning had saved his family when Huntington's had forced him to retire, and how my mother's illness had devastated my family. I began to spread the word in Glens Falls by becoming active in the community. I joined the Chamber of Commerce and became chairman of the membership committee. I was president of the Optimist Club and the Saint Mary's Alumni Association (which, given my grades, must have made some nuns giggle and others faint). I was the regional president of the Jaycees, and later I was elected state vice president. The groups provided a host of services to the community—much as the Rotary had done when I was a kid—and I was meeting the kind of people who were interested in what Stan and I were selling.

One thing you learn in the boxing ring is that just when things are breaking your way, you can get knocked on your ass, and this lesson was about to become invaluable to me.

As our business was finding its legs, a national company providing services identical to ours contacted Stan and offered to buy us. We did a stock swap with them in lieu of payment. We started out doing fairly well with offices in Albany, Rochester, and Syracuse. Within a couple years, their stock became one of the fastest selling on the New York Stock Exchange.

Then one evening I'm at a formal dinner with a group of high rollers, and I overheard the fellow next to me say to his friend, "Did you hear what's going on with _____ and their financial planning?"

Another fellow added: "Yeah, I read about it in the *Wall Street Journal*. It's horrible."

"What?" I said, panic spreading through me. "What's horrible?"

It turned out that a VP of the corporation was running a scam. He would locate a dead person, get his Social Security number, create the phony sale of a life insurance policy—let's say for $5 million—and lay off most of the policy on the secondary market. After a while, the death would be reported, and the insurance proceeds would wind up in the company coffers as income and helped goose up the stock price.

The government got wise, and bankruptcy followed, with a scammer or two getting sent to prison.

I'd thought I was going to get rich. Now Stan and I were broke. And Christ, I had a family, and over the next few months I often didn't know where I was going to get my next two dollars. I did some part-time work and put on a good act, but the most helpful thing I did was repeat to myself a poem I remembered:

I am sore wounded but not slain.
I will lay me down and bleed a while,
And then rise up to fight again.

I had no idea where I'd read it. I just repeated it to myself with the blind faith the nuns had expected of us when we recited the Rosary.

Next thing I know, Stan got us into the encyclopedia business, working for Harry Bobley in Cincinnati, Ohio. Harry was no bigger than five-four, but he was the most dapper little guy you ever saw, and when he got up to talk he was spellbinding. He had a sales director who was equally effective—Noah Bower, a big guy with a nose the size of a snowplow. He was the most effective salesman I ever met, and I learned a lot from him about how to motivate a crowd. Stan and I alternated weeks in Cincinnati. I'd take a sleeper car out there on Sundays. We sold the encyclopedias much as I'd sold the Amana Plan. We had an operation in a prestigious department store, and a sales force that went door to door. Again, the baby boom helped us out. There were lots of young children, and parents, hoping their kids would go to college, wanted books for them.

Things were going gangbusters. Then—boom! Harry had been selling vitamins through the mail, and the FDA went after him, claiming that he was practicing medicine without a license. I thought it was bullshit, but the manager of the department store called me in and said:

"You gotta go."

Talk about humiliation. We didn't do anything wrong, and I remember sitting in the manager's office for an hour waiting to talk to him while he was on the phone flirting with some girl. When he got off, I told him that I'd just hired a sales manager, and he replied: "I don't give a shit who you hired. Get your stuff and your people and get out of here."

And so I went, reciting to myself, *I am sore wounded but not slain....*

Undaunted, Stan dug up another opportunity, peddling a sophisticated alarm system manufactured by Westinghouse. Stan and I visited the company for a demonstration. They had the system on a wall, and they blew smoke at it, and the alarm went off, and we were told that it would automatically place a call to the fire department and police station. Today, these systems are commonplace, but back then it was a revelation. They gave us a detailed pitch, and when they were done, I said, "It works fine on the wall, but you don't have it wired into a house. How do you know it's going to work in a house?"

Rolling his eyes to indicate that I was as technologically savvy as a caveman, the presenter answered, "You know what we're making on the floor right below us here?"

"Not a clue."

"You can't go there because they're making the reactors for atomic subs. That's what we're making. Now, if they can make a reactor for an atomic submarine, don't you think we can build an alarm system?"

His logic was irrefutable, but I would've been more comfortable if I'd seen the alarm under battle conditions.

Stan and I signed on to represent the Northeast. We had to raise twenty or thirty grand, and I went to my brothers and a handful of other investors. Our marketing plan was solid. First, we would sell the mayor of a town, then the fire and police chiefs, and let the word spread. The mayor of Glens Falls was a close friend; I sold him one. I sold a system to a fire captain, and to the family of a reporter at the local *Post-Star*, and I put in a system at my house.

And guess what?

The alarms started going off in the middle of the night for no reason. There was a siren on the roof, and I'll be damned if it didn't sound like the Soviets were coming to bomb us.

The fire chief paid me a visit. "Joe, you've got to knock this off. We've got trucks responding. The cops got patrol cars going to the scene."

Westinghouse tried to fix the problem; no dice. Understandably, it was difficult to sell these systems when your whole city was vibrating with false alarms every day. Stan and I were beside ourselves and shut down our business and sued Westinghouse, eventually settling for enough that we could repay our investors.

There we were, Stan and me, knocked on our collective ass again.

6

IF AT FIRST
YOU DON'T SUCCEED

If you want to accomplish something meaningful and to earn a living for your family in the process, brains can come in handy. Luck might be even better. Best of all, though, is hard work.

Think about it. You're born with your smarts; schooling helps but chiefly expands and refines your natural ability. Luck, most of us learn early, is a finicky pal. First off, it runs in two directions, and good luck is generally nothing more than a prelude to a meeting with its less cheerful sibling. Furthermore, luck depends on events you didn't create—on moves someone else is making, frequently someone you don't know or never heard of.

Ah, but hard work—that's elementary arithmetic. There are twenty-four hours in a day. That never changes, whether your highborn or lowborn, gifted or not. Thus, the more you work, the better your odds. Most appealing to me, it is the one area of your life that you can control.

This belief accounted for another of my favorite sayings, which I quoted for decades without knowing the author (who turns out to be Basil King, a Canadian clergyman and author).

Be bold and mighty forces will come to your aid.

Boiled down to its essence: If you stand in the middle of the highway long enough and don't flinch at the traffic zooming by, you improve your chances of luck hitting you head-on.

That's what Stan and I did. We dusted ourselves off from the West-inghouse disaster and got back in the game. Stan had been reading about intercoms manufactured by the Swedish communications giant Ericsson, a cutting-edge gadget that businesses could hook up to their existing phone systems to communicate inside their office. Stan and I got ourselves a fran-chise, and I started selling the Ericssons. This was back in the day when the American Telephone and Telegraph Company—Ma Bell—had a monopoly, controlling not only access to the lines but to the equipment. I told poten-tial customers that the Ericsson intercom, which was connected internally and separate from the AT&T system, was more sophisticated than what they could rent from Ma Bell: It had a privacy button so you could continue listen-ing to a conversation and speak with someone in your office, and an executive override that allowed you to break into a conversation. Yet even though the savings on their AT&T rental fees would pay for the new intercoms, it was a tough sell. Ma Bell had been around since 1879 and was American business royalty. I kept setting up appointments, but it was a hard slog.

Well, I figured at least Stan and I were up and running again.

★ ★ ★

In an effort to meet people who might become customers, I got involved with the New York State Association of Young Republicans. One day, I got a call from a guy I met in that group, Joe Boyd. It was 1966, and Governor Nelson A. Rockefeller was running for reelection, and Joe asked me to join

the campaign staff. At the time, the Republican Party was already begin-ning to fragment into moderate and far-right wings, a split that would continue to widen for the next half-century. Rockefeller was a moderate, which was fine with me, but I wasn't a fan of his tax-and-spend ways. Still, I was curious to see what a campaign looked like from the inside, especially one that was shaping up into a real battle. Four years earlier, Rockefeller had defeated the Democrat, Robert M. Morgenthau, a former U.S. Attor-ney for the Southern District of New York, with 53 percent of the vote. However, in 1966, there was going to be five other candidates crowding the ballot, and three of them had a serious following. Frank D. O'Connor, the president of the New York City Council, was nominated by the Democrats;

Professor Paul L. Adams, a dean at Roberts Wesleyan College outside Rochester, was put up by the Conservatives; and Franklin D. Roosevelt Jr. had the Liberal line.

I signed on as an advance man, and my responsibility, along with seven or eight other guys, was to make certain that everything was in order when Rocky arrived at an event. I enjoyed watching him go through the crowd with that big smile, pumping hands and saying, "Hiya fellah, hiya fellah," and because he was so rich and famous everyone wanted to touch him. Serving on an advance team was an excellent education for an aspiring politician, though frankly I didn't see that in my future. Still, I learned the things a candidate had to know: First and foremost, money makes your life easier. I remember a lunch for twenty-five hundred at the New York Hilton where I signed a check for a hundred grand, and requisitioning a helicopter for the campaign by simply telling the company to send the bill to Rockefeller.

More important for my later career, I discovered the basic questions you had to answer if you were going to be an effective campaigner. When you arrived, what door do you use? Where are you going to speak? How do you turn on the lights? Is there a lectern? Who is going to be up there with you? Do you have a list of the people you have to mention? And last but not least—where is the men's room?

Once, we were in a bus on the campus of Colgate College. It was raining cats and dogs, and we were running late. We go into a building, and the governor had to take a leak, so there we are darting up and down hallways searching for a toilet. We find one; Rockefeller relieves himself, and then we go looking for the auditorium and think we've found it. In we go through a door and wind up on the stage in our dripping raincoats with the standing room-only crowd staring at us as if we've just arrived from another galaxy.

The governor won reelection with just 44 percent of the vote. I went home thinking that I'd had some fun, but now I had to get back to business.

I picked up where I'd left off, mostly getting rejected and making the occasional sale, and working as the deputy director of Urban Renewal in Glens

Falls. Bobbie and I had moved from our bungalow to a small three-bedroom on Owen Avenue in Queensbury. Contrary to the doctor's prediction that Bobbie would never be able to get pregnant, she did—twice. We had our son Ken and then our daughter Catherine, so we were now blessed to be a family of six, and while we were enjoying our good fortune, fate was about to deal me a straight flush and demonstrate, once again, that although you can't control circumstances, you can be bold enough to go all in when you're dealt a winning hand.

During the 1950s, Thomas F. Carter was the owner of a two-way radio business in Dallas, Texas. He was also a tinkerer and invented a gizmo that could hook up one of his two-ways to a regular phone. It was a revolutionary step forward in communications, allowing someone who—let's say—was out in the middle of nowhere and needed to contact a customer, to call his office on the radio, where a secretary could patch him into their phone system. The gizmo was christened the "Carterfone," and it changed the industry in a way that I suspect Thomas Carter never imagined.

Understandably, AT&T was less than ecstatic about the invention. The company had claimed that third-party add-ons wouldn't meet their high technical standards and threatened the integrity of their system, a position that the law had supported in the past. Of course, monopolies are afraid of creative small fries whose innovations threaten their market, and the behemoth's response was heavy-handed. Ma Bell let it be known that that it would cut off service to any of its customers who dared use a Carterfone. I suppose at AT&T corporate headquarters, they figured that should settle the matter: I mean, how the heck can you do business without a phone?

The big brains at AT&T who made the decision didn't factor in one crucial variable: Thomas Carter had a king-sized set of brass balls. He filed an antitrust suit against Ma Bell, and it turned out that the members of the Federal Communications Commission were as brave as Carter. In 1968, the FCC declared that while AT&T was legally permitted to set technical requirements for add-ons, they couldn't stop people from using equipment that met its standards.

Bam-bam-bam! Lady Luck was pounding on the door. Stan and I heard about the ruling, and we became the first company in New York State to compete with Ma Bell. It was a no-brainer. We already had a stable of technical people who installed and maintained our intercoms, and it was easy to contract with companies in Canada and Korea to buy phones. I revised my intercom talk to customers, asking them to take out a pencil and a piece of paper, calculate the cost of our equipment versus their leasing expense from AT&T, and tell me which was more reasonable. I already knew the answer. With Ma Bell's overhead, their charges couldn't possibly be lower than ours.

Still, I was having trouble getting a foothold. Cutting edge technology sounds great to the average person, but those running a business hear nothing but trouble. Usually the rejections were polite, but occasionally I'd hear: "What, a new phone system? And not from AT&T? Are you kidding? Those phones are the lifeblood of my company. Who's gonna service it? Your guys? Who the hell are your guys? I like you, Bruno, OK? But I think you need a psychiatrist."

One thing about luck—sometimes it takes a while for your ship to come in. I worked around the clock, driving down to our office in Albany and taking trains and planes around the state. Our equipment was more sophisticated than what was available from AT&T. Our people installed the systems, running the wires to an interconnect box on the outside wall, which attached our phones to Ma Bell's wires on the other side, and that was that.

Stan and I had been operating under our old corporate banner, Balanced Planning Service, but now we took on the more august sounding United Telecommunications Corporation.

In 1968, I was elected president of the New York State Young Republicans. I can't say that it did anything for my business, but I figured it couldn't hurt getting to know people around the state. Remember, this was an era when there were just three ways to communicate: in person, through the mail, or on the phone. So organizations played an important role in passing along information that today is disseminated via e-mail, websites, and Skype.

The Young Republicans were quite active, and in 1968 I threw myself into helping candidates in a handful of key Assembly races. Lo and behold, the Assembly went from Democratic to Republican, and Perry B. Duryea Jr., a tall, silver-haired lobsterman from Montauk, Long Island, who had been in the Assembly since 1961, was chosen as speaker by his caucus. I was given more credit than I deserved for my efforts in the election, and the next thing I know I get a phone call from Speaker Duryea's office asking if I'd like a position on his staff.

Even though I could have used the money, I said no thank you: my plate was full. I believed in those new intercoms and phone systems, and damn it, sooner or later I was going to make other people believe in them too. The following year, the speaker's office contacted me again, suggesting that I take a part-time position as a special assistant to the speaker, something flexible that would fit into my schedule, for which I'd earn twenty grand.

I asked what they wanted me to do, because while I couldn't really afford to turn down the offer, I wasn't interested in a kiss-on-the-cheek for helping in the election. I met with Speaker Duryea and his executive assistant, Henry Mund. They needed someone to organize their employment practices. The speaker's responsibility wasn't to be a manger, and Perry was being overwhelmed with new hires. Typically what happens in the wake of a power shift in a legislature is that anyone who can hands out jobs to their spouses, cousins, friends, girlfriends, former college roommates, and maybe even the kid who cuts their grass.

I relished a challenge, believed I could be useful, and became a special assistant to the speaker. How to fix the problem was easy; doing it was not. Dorothy Glough was in charge of the fiscal office. She was a no-nonsense lady, and when we spoke, I tried to be as charming as I could, because I was concerned about making her feel as if I were stepping on her toes. I explained what was going on and told her no one could go on the payroll without the signature of the speaker or my signature on his behalf. Then I contacted the county chairmen and said that they would have to recommend the job candidates, adding that it would be nice, you know, if they actually had some qualifications.

Dorothy was a true professional about that rule, but people would come into her office expecting to be put on the payroll, be informed that they needed me to sign off, and go nuts. Dorothy was a willing partner of mine because she knew that the hiring practices were a mess, and she handled the situation with both steel and grace. Then Perry started to take a lot of flak from disappointed applicants and from senior members who wanted to give out jobs, which is one of the great advantages of incumbency, because people you hire will work like crazy for you come the next election. Perry appreciated what I was doing, but for peace to reign in his caucus, he had to make a number of exceptions to my system.

Yet I was pleased with what I had done, aligning my business instincts with a moribund political practice. I asked myself: What was the result the speaker was seeking? And I pursued that goal, and though it was far from perfect, it was better than how I had found it.

Bobbie and I began thinking about moving again, and with my salary from the Assembly and selling our place in Queensbury, I thought I could manage it. By 1972, our four children were sharing bedrooms, and I, who grew up sharing a bed with my siblings, wanted each of my own kids to have their own room. And I needed to be closer to Albany, no more than a half-hour away, because commuting from Glens Falls was cutting into the time I could spend with my family. Bobbie and I had always dreamed of having a house with some land in the country. We both wanted horses. When I was courting Bobbie, she used to ride with me, holding on for dear life, but she loved the idea of taking care of animals in a barn she owned. I was excited about riding horses ever since I was a child and other children rode ponies while I watched from the sideline because my family didn't have the nickel it cost for a ride.

In Brunswick, a town in Rensselaer County, we located a house with fourteen acres on Bulson Road, a rolling lane that wound through green countryside. It was perfect. We bought it, and I began my life as a gentleman farmer.

7

WELCOME TO THE ARENA

Once we were settled in Brunswick, I kept my part-time job with Speaker Duryea because I needed the money. As I remember it, our gross sales at Coradian were less than $1 million a year, and our budget was so tight that Stan and I stopped drawing paychecks. On the positive side, my commute to Latham and downtown Albany was shorter, and my flirtation with politics was over, another reason I'd wanted to leave Queensbury.

I'd been active in the community, and naturally drawn into political circles, serving as a Warren County Republican committeeman and the president of the Warren County Young Republican Club. I had considered a run for the Assembly, but the county GOP leaders weren't with me because I had to run in a primary against an incumbent. My view was that the incumbent, relying on the Warren County machine to reelect him, wasn't doing much. The view of the machine was predictable: why risk potential trouble in the general election by letting a newcomer primary a guy who already held the seat? Who needs it? Go away, Bruno. Leave us alone.

Being hard-headed, I continued to explore the possibility until it became clear to me, from counting votes, that I'd get beat two to one, and I wound up supporting the incumbent. Even so, my daring to suggest he wasn't qualified and acting as though I might do something about that made me more than a few enemies, and I was glad to be done with the infighting.

41

Truthfully, I wondered why I ever wanted to get involved in politics in the first place. It was a butt-ugly business. They don't hand out trophies for second place so anything goes in pursuit of a win. It was worse than boxing, where at least if a guy hits you below the belt, the ref can penalize him and he could lose the fight on points. Politics—no refs, no points, only votes, and you had to keep your eyes on the ballot box.

Not long before moving to Brunswick, I got a look at how nasty a campaign could be in the one election that I'd ever lose—a race to become the statewide president of the Jaycees, not exactly the grand prize of political horse racing, right? Yet you would've thought we were running to see who was going to rule the Roman Empire.

I'd been the regional president and state vice president, and before leaving for the state convention in Jamestown, I lined up all my delegates, talking to them on the phone, finding out their concerns, recruiting people to join my slate. My opponent's name was Curt Bauer, and as I drove to Jamestown, I was confident that I had the votes to beat him.

When I checked into the hotel, the desk clerk was so nasty to me I had the impression that he thought I'd just busted out of prison. I was given a suite on the top floor. That sounded good until the desk clerk informed me that the elevator was out of order. I walked up seven flights of stairs and sat on the bed to make some calls. Guess what? The phone didn't work. I hoofed it back down to the lobby and made my calls from a pay phone, inviting my delegates to meet. They came, complaining about the walk upstairs, and one by one they began to peel off, saying they wanted to wait on their decision. The people on my slate did the same thing. It took me about a minute to figure out what was happening. My opponent was from Jamestown.

A third of the way through the roll-call vote on the convention floor not one person had voted for me, and I conceded the election.

Lesson learned, and a bitter, humiliating one at that. I told myself that I was done, and I was for a few years—until a winter day in Brunswick, when Frank Bentley, a shrewd, old-time Republican pol, showed up, and everything changed.

★ ★ ★

On our property, a chicken coop had been converted into a ski shack, and on weekends when I was working in the barn or chopping wood, I used to take a break and go in and warm up by the fireplace. I was sitting there when a guy knocked on the door, and I told him to come in. It was Frank. He had to be in his eighties, but he was spry and feisty, and his hearing was fine except for his trouble hearing the word "no." He introduced himself, and we talked about our state electoral district. The 41st included Rensselaer County, parts of Columbia and Saratoga counties, and the city of Cohoes, which was in the Democratic stronghold of Albany County.

Frank said, "You'd make a good chairman for the Rensselaer County Republicans."

"I'm done with politics."

"I'm glad you'll think it over."

"That's not what I said."

"Wise decision."

Frank came back on Saturdays five or six weeks in a row. During our chats, I learned that the state senator from the 41st, Douglas Hudson, a farmer who lived in Castleton, had started out in 1952 as chairman of the Rensselaer County GOP, so the job had the prospect of upward mobility. Frank was pressing me so hard because Doug was giving up the chairmanship, and the competition for the post between the Brunswick town chairman and a bunch of other hopefuls—all of them overeager and underqualified—had become poisonous.

"Joe, you could win," Frank said. "But you got to do it before anyone gets to know you."

"You trying to flatter me?"

Frank laughed. "What I mean is, because you're new here no one dislikes you yet. Stick around, that'll change."

I talked it over with Bobbie. She disliked the pettiness of politics—an opinion, I shared—but she said if that was what I wanted, then I should pursue it. I phoned the town chairmen around Rensselaer County, and their reaction was positive. I spoke to Stan. He said that it couldn't hurt

Coradian, which was what I had concluded, and in late November 1974, at a meeting in the Uncle Sam Room of the Holiday Inn in Troy, I was elected chairman.

I spent the next year building relationships. Hugh Carey, a former Democratic congressman from Brooklyn, had been elected governor. A downstate Democrat in the Executive Mansion is rarely good news for upstaters. I repeatedly made this point around Rensselaer County as I tried to draw more people to the committee. I became close to two powerful GOP chairmen, John Sharp in Columbia County and Jim Foley in Saratoga County. Both thought that Doug Hudson, who was nearing seventy, ought to retire from the Senate, and they asked me if I'd be interested in being the candidate, saying that the district needed a business-minded go-getter.

I had four reasons for agreeing:

The first was that I believed in the exalted place of public service in American life, and yet I wouldn't have hired half of the elected officials I'd met to be clerks. They lacked the capacity for pragmatic thinking and hard work, and I seldom met one who had the guts to start a business. Yet these were the folks who passed the laws I had to live by—who determined my taxes and what should be done with the money. It made my blood boil.

Second, I had become disgusted with tax-and-spend government. Why couldn't the governor and Legislature limit their expenditures to the revenue they took in? And why did they have to take in such big chunks of my money? This was plain-vanilla conservatism, and I'd learn that there were answers to my questions, although just then I was unaware of them.

My one specific goal was to get the funding to upgrade the Albany County Airport. I suppose there were officials who thought all you'd ever need in the Capital Region were government jobs, but those people couldn't do arithmetic. You needed profits and salaries to tax to pay for those jobs. And how could you attract major corporations to the region with that run-down airport? Executives would land here, take a look around, figure what they were seeing was a reflection of the area and its workforce, and get back on the plane.

Finally, and perhaps most important, I just felt that the timing was right. It's been said that a good politician is someone who is at the right place at the right time, and knows it. Well, a long-serving senator was retiring; the Republicans had no idea who would replace him; and people weren't getting along—a perfect opportunity for a newcomer.

At the urging of Frank Bentley, John Sharp, and Jim Foley, who wanted peace to reign among Republicans in the 41st, I asked Doug Hudson to be my campaign chairman. Doug almost choked when he agreed, but he signed on. Nor was the county executive, Bill Murphy, pleased when I stopped by his house to tell him. I had helped Bill become the county executive, but he went berserk when I gave him the news, saying that he had always intended to run for the seat. I could've used Bill's help, but calculated that I could make it without him, so off I went, blissfully unaware that around the district some voters saw me as a carpetbagger who was shoving aside the man who truly deserved Doug's seat, Thomas G. Cholakis.

The Cholakis family had been a fixture in Troy for a couple of generations and owned the popular Mayflower restaurant. Tom Cholakis and his older brother, Constantine, had been active in politics and the Greek community. In 1968, Con had been elected district attorney of the county. He was enormously popular with the electorate; he'd been an excellent DA; and he was now a judge in county court. Tom, a resident of North Greenbush, had a lower profile than Con, but he had been elected to the county legislature, which put him a step ahead of yours truly. Nonetheless, he was unhappy when word got out that I was vying for the nomination. Tom was a friend of John Sharp and pressured him not to support me. John refused.

To run, I had to step down as chairman of the Rensselaer committee, and Dorothy Birkmayer Fonks took my place. Still, I had plenty of friends across all the Republican committees in the district, and I received the GOP endorsement, beating Tom by a vote of 38,353 to 6,836. While this wasn't the same as winning the Senate seat, it was close, because for the last decade the district had sent a Republican senator to Albany. The Conservatives had endorsed Tom, so he decided to go against the committee and try to take the GOP line from me in a primary.

I always thought that my secret weapon was that I could outwork anyone, and that was what I did—in the process losing twenty pounds I didn't have to lose. I started at seven in the morning, shaking hands with people on their way to work and finishing up at night in bowling alleys, where I tried to avoid the guys who had been knocking back beers and who, upon seeing me, shouted that all politicians should go shoot themselves. Usually, I ignored the drunks, but once one of them got up in my face, berating me, and I replied, "Why don't you go fuck yourself?" Not the most politic response, but I doubted that he was going to vote for me.

The crux of my campaign was a theme that I'd be sounding for the remainder of my political career: I pressed the governor to deal with the shrinking industrial base upstate and the dreadful business climate, the inevitable result of high taxes. I pointed out that the governor had helped New York City: now it was time to help the people north of Westchester. Given the experiences of my childhood, one particular concern was that as the fiscal situation became dire in many rural communities, there was a terrible shortage of doctors, and I wanted the Health Department to make sure residents in these areas had access to care.

Initially, I wasn't doing as well as I'd expected. Lynn Mueller, the director of community affairs at Garden Way Manufacturing in Troy, was a clever, energetic operative who was part of an advertising agency, First Tuesday, in Buffalo, and Lynn did a lot of work for GOP candidates, including me. Lynn thought that there could be some confusion among voters between Tom and Con Cholakis, and because Con was so popular, the electorate might be under the impression that I was running against Con. Lynn and a couple other guys came up with a radio ad that I believe helped to turn that around. Here's my imperfect memory of it:

Two fellows are talking, and one says to the other: "Hey, that's a hot race in the forty-first. Who you voting for?"

"For Cholakis."

"Why?"

"Because Cholakis is a great judge."

"But it's his brother, Tom, not Con, who's running against Joe Bruno."

"Tom? Not Con? Then I'm voting for Joe Bruno."

That ad brought a silly attack from the Cholakis team, who accused me of prejudice, because I had referred to Con as a "Greek" judge. They were told that Con had been described as a "great judge," but I suspect they already knew.

The ridiculous charges persisted. Tom accused me of violating election law by displaying my brochures and bumper stickers at the Rensselaer County Republican booth at the Schaghticoke Fair. I hadn't used a nickel of committee funds to pay for my literature, and I showed the canceled checks to the board of elections, who saw nothing wrong.

This was run-of-the-mill pettiness, but what happened next was beyond cruel. A woman called my house and asked for my wife. When Bobbie came to the phone, the woman said: "You think your husband is out campaigning? He isn't. He's with another woman."

She called again on other evenings, telling Bobbie the same lies. After that, Bobbie hung up whenever she heard the woman's voice. It was one thing for me to be attacked in public, but another for someone to try and hurt my wife. I was furious—the boxer in me was never far below the surface—and it would've been satisfying to deck someone. But anger in a campaign is best used to push yourself to do more campaigning even though you feel as though you are about to pass out from exhaustion.

The primary was held on September 14, 1976, and in the unofficial count I beat Tom Cholakis 8,933 to 6,568. There was a celebration at the Holiday Inn. It was after three when I finally climbed into bed, and I got up the next day to see the kids off to school and to phone supporters to thank them. According to the *Troy Record*, Tom claimed that the low turnout was responsible for my victory, but the fact is I outworked him, the proof being that I won the city of Troy, where Tom and his family had a huge advantage in connections and name recognition, by a two-to-one margin.

My Democratic opponent in the election would be Daniel Ashley, a Rensselaer County legislator, and because the 41st was heavily Republican, I was less worried about Dan than I had been about Tom. However, Tom still had the Conservative line on the ballot, which would sap votes from me in November, so I met with him twice in late September to discuss unifying our party. Tom told me—and reporters—that he was dropping out of the race and would not actively campaign. He refused to endorse me, a refusal I took to be sour grapes. Losing is tough, and I figured Tom would eventually get over his bruised feelings, and I didn't give it a second thought.

That was a mistake.

In early October, my campaign did a poll. I'm not a big believer in polling. Occasionally, the numbers can tell you where you are off track or where you need to focus your efforts, but the results are usually a momentary snapshot that can lead a candidate toward overconfidence and laziness or paranoia and revamping your positions until you sound drug-addled when you explain yourself to audiences. The poll said that if the election were held just then, I'd win, Tom would finish second, and Dan third. It wasn't surprising that a Democrat in the 41st would trail two Republicans, and one of them endorsed by the Conservative Party.

A weasel employed by my campaign saw the poll and decided that it was real news. From what I understand, the weasel persuaded Tom that my poll indicated he'd be a significant factor in the election. Next thing I know, I hear from a supporter who spotted Tom eating lunch with Edward McDonough, the Democratic county chairman, at Hess's Tavern in Watervliet. Tom and Ed, I was told, spoke for an hour and a half and made over a dozen calls.[1] The next day, Tom announced that he was back in the race.

This was revenge with some wishful thinking sprinkled on top. Tom knew he couldn't win, but if he received a substantial percentage of the vote—say, 30 percent—he'd hand the election to the Democrats, and who knew if he cooked up some deal with Ed McDonough. Or maybe Tom thought that if he stopped me from taking the Senate seat now, he could beat Ashley in the next election.

My Democratic opponent, Dan Ashley, was no less petty than Tom. Dan told reporters that one of my advisers had been indicted. He was referring to Lynn Mueller, and ironically, this was an omen of things to come for me. Yes, in 1973, Lynn had been indicted for a vote-siphoning scheme, a charge so ridiculous that a judge threw out the indictment, declaring that the law used to charge him was unconstitutional. I thought it was bullshit when Lynn was charged, and my opinion hasn't changed since then.

Aiming to knock Dan off his high horse, I told the media that because Dan was an employee of Hudson Valley Community College and a member of the Rensselaer County Legislature, he was voting on pay raises that benefited him and his colleagues.

I have no idea whether any of this nonsense works, but there was no shortage of it during the campaign. On Election Day, the early returns showed that I was down by 5,000 votes, in all likelihood because of Tom holding the Conservative line. In the end, I won, receiving 65,183 votes to Dan's 57,936, and Tom's 13,908.[2] I was still angry about the double-dealing—remember, this was my first big election, and I hadn't yet learned that one of the main tasks of politics is mending fences. I told Bill Fagan of the *Troy Record* that I didn't think Tom had handled himself "as a gentleman or a man of integrity," and added that it was his kind of behavior that turned people off to government.[3]

Then I went home, happy about the win and that the campaign was over.

8

SELLING CORADIAN AND A SHORT HISTORY OF EIGHTEEN YEARS IN THE POLITICAL VINEYARD

On Election Day, in a burst of optimism, I went to Kelly Clothes and bought a new suit. I had to leave the jacket and pants to be altered, and when the salesman told me I could pick up the suit on Thursday, I replied: "By then, I'll either be a has-been or a senator-elect."

The salesman didn't appear to know what I was talking about.

"I'm running for the seat in the forty-first district."

He chuckled. "Oh, good luck."

On Thursday, I floated into Kelly Clothes on a cloud of post-election euphoria. My picture had been in the papers, with the story of my win, and the salespeople descended on me, offering their congratulations, standing close by while I waited for my suit to be brought out. This seemed to happen everywhere I went. Politics, I knew, was the national pastime of the Capital Region, but I wasn't prepared to be treated as if I'd just homered in the ninth to win the seventh game of the World Series. I could hardly believe that I'd been elected and began to appreciate the cliché of pinching yourself to make sure you weren't dreaming. I felt sandwiched between my disbelief and my joy at winning, but even remembering the stress of the campaign, the fundraising, the early mornings and late nights, didn't make it thoroughly real.

The round of parties and my swearing-in, hiring staff, and moving into the Legislative Office Building (LOB) in Albany helped to dispel the dreamlike quality, but it was my father who underscored for me the reality of what had happened. Pa had attended the events after the election, saying little, and then one day, long after the hoopla was done, he asked me in his broken English: "How it possible you get where you are? Where it come from? How you do it?"

His question almost brought me to tears. He couldn't fathom how I had traveled from his ramshackle house to the grandeur of the Senate chambers. I recalled those immigrants in the east end of Glens Falls, and how they'd go to Peter Fiore, the head committeeman, if they needed work or to trim some red tape at city hall—if you asked them, they'd tell you Peter was the president of the United States. Now, looking at Pa, his lined, weathered face, I remembered that while his children were growing up, he worked three jobs—stoking a furnace, cleaning a grocery store in exchange for food, and getting some work from the city, cutting grass in the summer and shoveling snow in the winter, because everyone knew Pa desperately needed the money. His pleasures were limited: an occasional glass of red from a jug of homemade wine while he smoked one of those little Italian stogies that stunk to high heaven.

Trying to help my father understand the role he'd played in my life—and the lives of all his children—I said to him: "You worked hard. You taught us to work hard. You never went on welfare. You taught us to be honest. You never took anything that didn't belong to you. You taught us that if you want something bad, you had to really work for it. You taught me those things. You taught all of us those things, Pop."

My father nodded, as if it were dawning on him that he had helped to guide his children's journeys, and that made me as proud as I'd ever been to become a senator.

As I began to learn the ropes at the Senate, Coradian took off. Rolm Corporation, in Santa Clara, California, had developed a telephone network, relying on computers that could be installed and upgraded and enlarged with new software instead of forcing a company to buy new equipment. Coradian was ultimately named the sole distributor of the product for upstate New York, then New York City and northern New Jersey. Our sales exploded: In 1975, we were approaching $2 million; by 1978, we were doing more than $7 million. Two years later, we went public, and on paper, at least, I was worth $5 million. Rolm also went public, and I paid about fourteen grand for a thousand shares that would later be worth more than half a million bucks. *Inc.* magazine published a list of the fastest growing public companies in the United States, and Coradian was on it in 1980 and 1981.

All those decades of struggle to establish some financial stability for my wife and children, and now that I had it, I discovered that I enjoyed being a senator more than making money. I never wanted to be dependent on my government salary—the system would own you then—so I vowed that I'd always have an outside income. And initially, I was ecstatic about my windfall. I remember getting a check for $450,000 and taking it home and showing Bobbie, and it was such a kick looking at the check that I was reluctant to cash it. Yet I was careless with my new-found cash. I didn't drink or gamble, but it was fun buying stocks—even when the share price plunged. I remember losing thirty grand on a stock in a couple of weeks, and I didn't think twice about it. I could afford it, so why not?

Besides, I had important work to do. From my office at the LOB, I could actually help people.

During the next eighteen years, one lesson that I learned repeatedly was that while New Yorkers complain about their high taxes, their criticism is not quite what it seems. That was because more often than not the spending that citizens oppose was done in someone else's community: when that money was spent in the neighborhood of the folks sounding off, those weren't taxes. No sir. That was a wise investment in the future.

I think of this as the It-Depends-on-Whose-Ox-is-Getting-Gored phenomenon, and it was challenging for fiscally conservative legislators. If you fought for your district's fair share, then your opponent in the next primary or general election could use it against you and charge you with talking a better game than you played.

It was a delicate balancing act, and I did my best to help my constituents while calling on the Legislature to pass a law that would tie spending to tax collections. To compensate for these limits on taxation, I pushed for a more businesslike approach, using tax dollars to encourage the expansion of the state economy. I can't say that this won me a lot of friends among the old-timers in the Senate and Assembly, and it was during these early years that I developed a reputation for being a maverick who wouldn't shut up.

In 1978, I ran against A. Jerome McCormick, a Democrat from the town of Clifton Park, and I coasted, winning with more than 60 percent of the vote. By now, I loved the campaigning, because it was an extension of what I did during my term, meeting people, hearing them out, telling them what I was trying to accomplish. The key to winning over voters was touching them, shaking their hands or taking a picture with them if one of my staff members was around with a Polaroid. So wherever I went—to the hardware store, to the supermarket, to county fairs, or out to eat with Bobbie and the kids—I introduced myself and extended my hand.

I'd learned this in the 1960s. I had a friend, Ben Patrick, a smart, successful businessman. Ben would tell anybody who would listen how he hated politicians, that they were all phonies. I was working for Perry Duryea, but Ben made an exception for me because we were neighbors and our wives were friends. So one day, when Jerry Solomon, later the longtime congressman, was running to become the town supervisor of Queensbury, I asked Ben who he was voting for. Ben replied, "None of those bastards." Shortly after that remark, Ben was out eating dinner with Harriet, his wife, and Jerry entered the restaurant, said hello to everyone and left his palm card. Ben told me that he was pissed Jerry had interrupted his meal, and he'd told the candidate to get lost. Undeterred, Jerry kept working the place. Later, on Election Day, I bumped into Ben, and he said that he and

Harriet had voted for Jerry. I laughed; Jerry won his race and I never forgot the story.

Good thing too, because I'd need every bit of campaign wisdom I could muster in 1980, when I faced a candidate who proved to be my last tough opponent, Edward "Ned" Pattison. The Pattisons had a higher profile in Troy than the Cholakis family. In 1813, Ned's great-great grandfather had founded a law firm in the city that became one of the oldest in the United States, and his grandfather and father, also lawyers, had been active in several charitable organizations. After graduating from Cornell Law School and serving as a lieutenant in the Army, Ned went to work at the family firm. In 1969, he won an election for county treasurer, and in 1974, in the backlash against Republicans that followed the Watergate scandal and the resignation of President Nixon, Ned was elected to Congress, a noteworthy achievement considering that the Troy area hadn't sent a Democrat to the House of Representatives in more than a century.[1]

Ned had an impeccable reputation for honesty. He was an outspoken critic of the Vietnam War, refusing to continue military aid to South Vietnam, and he was the sole congressman to confess to *Playboy* magazine that he'd smoked pot. Ned lasted in Washington until 1978, when my friend from Queensbury, Jerry Solomon, a very conservative Republican, ousted him. Ned had a couple of major problems in that election. He was too liberal for his district, and he was an avid supporter of President Jimmy Carter. With inflation climbing into the double digits, the prime rate at 11 percent, and 30-year mortgages at more than 10 percent, the economy was sluggish, and Ned was hard-pressed to persuade voters to return him to Congress.

Due to his record in Washington and that Jerry had beat him by eight percentage points, I was surprised that Ned ran against me. Scuttlebutt was that he and his campaign people had superimposed the areas he'd won in the congressional race over my district and predicted that his vote total would exceed mine. I doubted that rubbing two maps together had any more to do with electoral outcomes than rubbing a genie's lamp—every contest has its own candidates and issues—but I got nervous when I saw polls that had us neck and neck.

Ned was a reserved, pipe-smoking professorial type, and his campaign tactic was to go to events and talk for hours to demonstrate how conversant he was with the matters at hand. One-on-one, Ned was a pleasant guy, but that fall he lambasted me for not being him: I was a backslapper and glad hander, a shoe-leather politician who went door-to-door and store-to-store and stood in front of factories at seven in the morning and outside of supermarkets. That was an accurate description: I even got chased away from a store in Clifton Park, probably owned by a Democrat, and when I refused to budge the owner called the cops, who tried to make me feel like a second-class citizen because I dared to ask folks for their vote.

And my style wasn't Ned's most cutting criticism of me. Worst of all, he said, I was a *businessman*, a double-dipper who enriched myself while I was supposed to be working for the people. In contrast, Ned claimed, he was a former lawyer and a former professor at Rensselaer Polytechnic Institute, who, unlike Joe Bruno, would focus on being a senator.

He attacked me in ads on television, and maybe the attacks were hurting me in the polls, but I guessed that the Pattison name, combined with the prestige of Ned's four-year walk across the national stage and his constantly trumpeting his rectitude, were appealing to the sample who answered the pollsters' questions on the phone.

An hour-long debate between us was scheduled by a local TV station, WRGB, and Ned and I went to the studio on Balltown Road in Niskayuna. My staff and I had done our homework. In 1977, Congress had almost tripled the payroll tax, and as I recall, Ned had cast a deciding vote to move the bill along. The debate began, and after the standard blah-blah-blah both of us had lifted from our stump speeches, I asked Ned why he had voted for the tax hike. He denied voting for it. I asked him again, and he repeated his denial. I reached for a folder, saying, "Let me refresh your memory," and I read off the record of his vote. Then I said: "You are denying it and lying to the public and you shouldn't do that."

Ned took offense. If you want to infuriate someone enthralled by his own righteousness, there's nothing like catching him in a lie, and before Judy Sanders, WRGB's venerable political reporter, could restore order, I said: "Not only are you lying about this, but"—I held out his campaign brochure—"right here it says you are a former lawyer. Were you disbarred?"

Ned snapped back: "Of course, I wasn't."

"Then you're a lawyer."

"Of course, I am."

"Then why are you saying you're a former lawyer? And you say you'll be a full-time senator. That you don't teach at RPI. But you do teach there. Why are you lying to the public?"

Our debate got heated, and honest to God, I thought Ned was going to have a breakdown. I continued to push him on his tax-hike vote, asking him to clarify his position to the public, until he screamed: "Yes, I voted for it, but—"

"But nothing. You're lying in your brochure. You're lying to the public."

The debate ended, and as I walked out, Ned double-timed it over to me, spitting and sputtering, and I thought he was going to throw a punch. Our aides got between us, and Ned asked, "Why would you do that? Why would you say those things about me?"

"Because they're true and if you can't handle it, then don't run."

After that evening, the polls showed that I started pulling away from Ned, and I beat him with 56 percent of the vote.

So much for using vote maps to predict an election.

As my third term got underway, Rolm told us that by 1983, Coradian would no longer have exclusive distribution rights in New York to its equipment. Rolm had become a giant in the industry, and its telephone system accounted for most of our sales. Coradian, because of the economic slowdown, was already in financial trouble: by the spring of 1981, our stock was trading at under $6 a share while the year before it had been at $18. Rolm had offered to buy us, swapping our shares for theirs, and I'd wanted to sell.

Robert Schwartz, who was the president and chief operating officer of Coradian, convinced Stan Ringel that it was a bad deal. I have to give Bob credit for his honesty, if not his business acumen. He said that he'd only make $800,000, but if he stuck around and grew the company, he'd make a lot more. Stan and I stood to make millions if we sold, and I argued with Stan that we should take our payout and go. Right before the Rolm offer came off the table, I was tempted to call Rolm's president, Ken Oshman, and ask him to help me convince Stan to sell. I never made that call, one of the few times I've ignored my instincts.

In the fall of 1981, I was named the chairman of Coradian's executive committee and the CEO. One of my first official acts was to call Bob and say: "Get your stuff and get out of the office. And don't forget to leave your keys."

Between my duties at Coradian and the Senate, I was going fourteen, fifteen hours a day, seven days a week. I was exhausted, but I wanted to salvage something from the company that I'd helped to found. In a preview of my later legal trouble, I was accused of an ethical conflict because for five years Coradian had a modest state contract. It was a preposterous accusation, and I was cleared by the State Commission on Government Integrity, but the rumors persisted. The struggles at Coradian occupied me until 1990, when I cut a deal to sell it to Mitel, a Canadian company that agreed to pay $10 million and take on $13 million in debt. The deal led to the rumor that I'd pocketed millions—instead of less than $400,000, which is what my stock was worth. Mitel asked me to stay on for twenty-four months at the same compensation I'd received at Coradian, $110,000 a year.

I don't believe Stan ever recovered from rejecting the Rolm offer. Over the years, he used to count how much we would've been worth had we completed the stock swap, and it was well into the millions. As much as I regretted not having the money, my deepest regret was disregarding my impulse to make that phone call. Usually, I went with my gut, and when I didn't, I lived to regret it, particularly years later, when I knew I should retire from the Senate but stayed long enough to be the target of a vendetta that would drag me through the courts.

In November 1994, I won my tenth election. I'd been a member of numerous standing committees: Commerce; Economic Development and Small

Business; Banks; Civil Service and Pensions; Consumer Protection; Finance; Higher Education; and I'd chaired the Legislative Commission on Public and Private Cooperation. I'd played a leading role in passing the second new-car lemon law—and the first used-car lemon law—in the country. I knew that I was there to pass laws. That was the glamor, getting your name on bills. One year I passed more new bills than any other legislator, and people would tell me what a huge accomplishment it was.

In retrospect, it was a lot of puff. I can't even remember what some of those bills were—nor does anyone else. I'm sure they did people some good. Most of them, though, sat on the books and did nothing at all. My greatest satisfaction, in those eighteen years, was helping individuals with problems large and small, and I drove my staff to try and solve any issue from a friend or stranger that wound up on their desks.

Now and then, I got to help folks that I knew well, and it was the best feeling in the world. Take the case of Lester and Helen Cole, the neighbors who had sold me our house on Bulson Road. Lester became one of my closest friends. He had operated a business on Hoosick Street for forty or fifty years, but was forced, via eminent domain, to sell his building when the road was widened.

The guy from the Department of Transportation low-balled him on the price. When Lester went to complain, the son of a bitch climbed all over him and threatened that the DOT would do this, that, and the other thing if Lester didn't fall in line.

Distraught, Lester explained the situation to me. This was the heavy hand of government at its absolute worst, and I phoned the DOT commissioner and raised holy hell. The commissioner contacted the SOB, who then proceeded to tell Lester: "Since you talked to Bruno, I'm really gonna give you a hosing. You won't get one more cent. If you don't like it, go to court. If you win, I'll appeal. I promise you'll be waiting a long time for your money."

When Lester told me that story, I went berserk and called the commissioner again and was less friendly than I'd been during the first call. The guy was sent to another office to make someone else unhappy, and Lester ended up getting a fair price for his property.

The main reason that legislating was so unsatisfying was that as one senator in a crowd of other senators, your power to change just about anything was limited, because it was the governor, the majority leader of the Senate and the speaker of the Assembly who determined the allocation of funding, and you couldn't do anything without money.

For example, I'd come into office wanting to improve the Albany airport. I put together a group of movers and shakers from the chamber of commerce and got us an appointment to present our ideas to Governor Mario Cuomo. Personally, I liked Mario, even though he never tired of teasing me about my looks and my hair, which was a lot thicker than his. I recall asking him a pointed question in front of journalists, and when one of the reporters asked him why he didn't answer me, Cuomo declared: "Because he's the best-looking guy in the Senate." His non sequitur broke up the room, and defused the tension, but Mario wasn't always so amusing, and behind closed doors he could be impatient and dismissive. The afternoon I walked into his office with the businesspeople, he was polite enough, shaking hands, making small talk. Then one fellow in our group told him what we were after, and the governor replied, "Are you nuts? Get out of here. That's a county airport. Use county money."

End of meeting.

Seeing a gaggle of movers and shakers, who were accustomed to being treated like royalty, getting booted out the door had some entertainment value, but it doesn't get an airport the facelift it needs.

Yet the governor was also capable of showing some real class. I was an unrelenting critic of his budget increases, and in 1990, he sent out a letter attacking me in my district. However, prior to the mailing, he had Gerald Crotty, his counsel and secretary, send me a copy of it and inform me when it was being sent. The governor could've blindsided me, a common bit of political pettiness, but he chose the high road.

A year later, Mario went back to his combative self, when we were locked in a battle over a nearly $5 billion gap in the budget. Just then, pundits and politicos were predicting that Cuomo was gearing up for a run against President George H. W. Bush, and suddenly, on a Saturday, Cuomo had a tantrum and decided that he had to discuss the budget impasse immediately. Ralph Marino, the Senate majority leader, was at home in Long Island and couldn't get to the meeting. Ralph phoned me and asked me to go. I was in the barn in my jeans, and ran into the house, jumped in the shower and dressed, and went to the governor's office.

I'd seen Mario Cuomo be upset and unpleasant, but I'd never, ever seen in him in this kind of full-blown outrage. He had some choice words for the Republicans and said that we were refusing to do a budget to keep him from running for president and had destroyed his career.

I sat there, trying to explain our problems with the budget, but the governor was too busy calling us every name in the book to let me interrupt him.

Whether Mario Cuomo believed that the Republican majority in the New York State Senate was the real reason he didn't seek the presidency remains a question in search of an answer, though a week before Christmas that was what he told reporters when he announced that he wasn't going to run.

Following this confrontation, and my experience chasing funding for the airport, I recognized that the only way I'd have enough power to stand up to a governor and make the changes I'd been mulling over since my election in 1976 was to become the majority leader of the Senate.

Any senator who tells you that he or she hasn't daydreamed about being elected to that post is kidding themselves. But having the opportunity, and seeing that you had it, was another matter.

In the fall of 1994, I saw my chance.

9

FINALLY, A CHANCE

Anger is a good motivator. Outrage is even better.

Let's start with my anger. After eighteen years in the Senate, my most frustrating experience was interacting with Senate Majority Leader Ralph Marino, a Republican from Oyster Bay, Long Island. In 1988, I'd helped Ralph become the leader by rounding up support for him among the upstaters in the Senate, who worried that a leader from Long Island wouldn't go to bat for their constituents. Here is as good a spot as any to mention that the infighting among legislators has less to do with Democrat versus Republican than with the downstate-upstate divide. Dealing with downstate legislators, I frequently had the impression that they would've been content if the land north of Westchester had remained pastures and woodlands, perfect for fishing cabins, summer camps, and grand estates with milkmaids and stable boys.

Ralph's predecessor, Warren Andersen, a low-key lawyer, had been from Binghamton. He was a prime mover behind the magnificent Tuition Assistance Program and wasn't shy about spending money on upstate infrastructure, his most famous project being an extension of Interstate 88 that linked Albany to Binghamton and was referred to as "Warren Anderson's Driveway."[1] He also did his share for downstate, helping to drag New York City back from the edge of bankruptcy in 1975 and pumping money into the Metropolitan Transportation Authority to improve the subway system.[2]

Yet Warren also advocated for some tax cuts, an issue dear to almost every Republican in the Senate—but not Ralph Marino.

Ralph rarely encountered a tax dollar he didn't want to spend, particularly in his district, which spanned Nassau and Suffolk counties. Ralph was so cozy with the free-spending Mario Cuomo that it was as if Ralph worked for the governor, and through their efforts the budget grew by more than forty percent in a half-dozen years.

Reporters often described Ralph as "courtly." In political-speak that translated into "wishy-washy," and in my opinion Ralph was the opposite of a leader. His nickname was "Mumbles," a comment on his performance at news conferences, which was an embarrassment to Senate Republicans, especially because we were confronting the smooth-talking Cuomo.

Ralph would stand up before the media and start by saying, "Uhh... Well, I'm glad you're all here. Uhh..."

A reporter would call out: "Can you speak up, Ralph?"

"Uhh, yeah. Can you hear me now? Umm, we have some things to talk about."

"C'mon, Ralph," another reporter would say as the media surged forward, struggling to hear him. "Speak up!"

Ralph was no more understandable at our Senate conferences. He would sit at the head of the table in a room on the third floor of the Capitol and mumble generalities about the budget, and when I'd request specifics, in the hope of controlling the increase, one of his staffers would reply that they really couldn't give us the details on spending.

This would send my blood pressure soaring, while the other senators hurled questions at Ralph and received the same evasive answers from his minions.

Mentioning Ralph's staffers leads me to my outrage—one staffer, actually, his counsel, Angelo Mangia. Angelo was a ruthless, miserable, baby-faced prick in his thirties. I could imagine him as a kid being bullied at school and, upon becoming the right-hand man of the Senate majority leader, getting his revenge by kicking anybody within range. If you wanted to see Ralph, first you had to see Angelo. His office was next door to the leader's, and when you'd pass by there would be nine or ten people waiting to see him. Three hours later, you'd go by again, and most of the same people were still waiting. Nor did things improve after Angelo let you in—unless you happened to enjoy explaining what you needed to an arrogant little bastard who could've cared less about you and your constituents.

I went to speak to Ralph about Angelo and brought a few members with me, members who were allies of the leader. We told him about our problems, and Ralph said, "Yeah, but Angelo's OK."

"OK?" I replied. "He's got zero people skills, and it's a reflection on you."

Ralph didn't appear to care. I went to Plan B and invited Angelo to lunch.

"Communication is important," I told him. "Listening to people and giving them a decent response. I'm a team player, and I want to be helpful to Ralph. Can't you find a way to work with me and the other members?"

Angelo was all sweetness and light as we ate, but by close of business that day he was as difficult as he'd ever been.

The final straw came at the conclusion of the legislative session. I had a bill up: I can't recall what it was, but I remember that there wasn't a lot of funding involved, and it was important to people in my district. I know that I'd talked it through with Ralph, and I had his backing.

As the session concludes, the Senate votes on something like four hundred bills in a few hours so they won't die of debate. I checked the list of bills scheduled for a vote and saw that my bill wasn't on it. Frantically, because time was short, I started tracking down what had happened and found out that Angelo had scratched my bill off the list.

I dashed over to talk to him. His door was shut, and I couldn't get in, so I barged into Ralph's office. He appeared stunned at my breach of protocol—my daring to go around Angelo. Before Ralph could get a word out, I said, "Angelo had my bill set aside. I need to know why. You'd approved it, and I've promised people that it would pass."

"What do you want me to do, Joe?"

"Get Angelo in here."

Ralph called Angelo, and when he came in, not even bothering to glance at me, Ralph asked: "What happened to Joe's bill?"

"We had too many bills so I had it taken off the list."

I said, "Angelo, I made a commitment about this bill after getting the approval of the committee chairman and the leader."

Ralph said, "Oh, put it on, Angelo. What's the big deal?"

"I'm not going to do that," Angelo said.

Ralph shrugged. "What can I do?"

I felt as if the top of my head was about to pop off. "What can you do? You're the leader! You tell him what the hell to do or to get the hell out of here!"

Angelo didn't appreciate my suggestion. He stormed out. I wouldn't have believed what happened next if I hadn't seen it. Ralph left me standing there and ran after Angelo, pleading with him not to leave.

"Fuck him!" I shouted to Ralph. "Let him go!"

After five of the longest minutes of my life, Ralph returned and sat at his desk with his head in his hands.

"I don't know where he went," Ralph said. "We can't find him."

I said, "You're the leader. If you let that pipsqueak get away with this, you ought to be ashamed of yourself."

"I need Angelo to finish the session."

"You gotta get on the phone and push that bill to the floor."

I stood over Ralph until he made the calls that got my bill passed. Unfortunately for Ralph, Angelo had picked the wrong time to jerk me around. I decided on the spot that I wanted to be the majority leader if for no other reason than to throw out Angelo. And my timing was fortuitous. I had a relatively new friend in the Senate, George Pataki, and George was hoping to become governor.

George Pataki, who received his undergraduate degree from Yale before going on to Columbia Law School, was tall and lanky with a boyish open face and a somewhat nonchalant attitude toward his clothing. At first glance, you could mistake him for a privileged Ivy Leaguer, but George had grown up on a farm in Peekskill in the Hudson Valley, graduating from the local public schools, and had gone off to the Ivy League by working and receiving academic scholarships—the first generation of his family to attend college. After serving as the mayor of his hometown, George spent eight years in the Assembly, and as his fourth term was ending in 1992, he announced that he was going to take on the incumbent Republican, Senator Mary Goodhue, in a primary.

Let's pick up the story there, in the late summer of 1992.

Ralph Marino was furious at George for challenging Mary. She was a classy, solid senator and the lone woman Republican in the Senate. More than ever, women were taking their place in state and national politics, and 1992 was shaping up into what would become known as "the Year of the Woman," with four women being elected to the United States Senate.[3] I'd known Mary for all of her fourteen years in Albany. We sat next to each other and had a warm camaraderie even though we disagreed about taxes. Mary was seventy-one and her husband had passed away at the start of her last term, and she was spending a lot of time away from the Senate. As I remember it, she didn't come back for the budget vote, and she had told me that she planned to retire. She had been a mentor to George when he served as a lawyer on her staff, and she wasn't angry that George wanted her seat, but Ralph wouldn't hear of it and bombarded Mary with requests to stay put. For Ralph, it wasn't just that he'd be losing the one woman in his conference, it was also that he knew Pataki, a vocal opponent of runaway spending, would press him and Mario Cuomo about their tax increases.

Mary explained her situation to me, and I said: "Forget what Ralph wants. What do you want?"

"I don't know what to do. Ralph is pressuring me. He says I don't have to do anything, and after the election, I can come and go as I please."

Mary was a good soldier, and perhaps she wasn't ready to relinquish her seat, and announced that she was running. It was one of those primaries that made you heartsick. Pataki criticized Mary as a disinterested tax-and-spender, and his campaign intimated that she was getting up in years and perhaps too scattered to be an effective senator. George won the primary and the election, but by unseating a woman who was so popular with her colleagues, he arrived in the Senate a persona non grata. Ralph and the New York City members treated him like a leper, and his fiscal position alienated a fair number of upstate Republican senators when he proved to be the pain in the ass on taxes that Ralph had feared and voted against the budget in 1993 and 1994, which made the rest of us look as if we approved the jump in spending.

Still, I liked George and befriended him. With his earnestness, he reminded me of Jimmy Stewart in *Mr. Smith Goes to Washington*. He was impressive, very intelligent, and it was obvious that he had the guts to challenge Cuomo, a plan that U.S. Senator Alphonse D'Amato, a product of the powerful Nassau County Republican machine, encouraged. Al was popular with his constituents because he helped everyone he could, and for his troubles the media called him "Senator Pothole." He didn't give a damn and focused on assisting Republicans all over New York State, making him a de facto political boss, a status that did not sit well with Ralph Marino. Al had his people do a survey to find out which qualities a candidate needed to defeat the governor, and going over the checklist they saw that Pataki had nine out of nine. I thought his main assets as a statewide candidate were that he was pro-choice and opposed wild government spending. I also felt that Cuomo was underestimating the anger in the suburbs about property taxes. The governor may have preferred to consider those taxes a local matter, but he wasn't fooling suburbanites. They knew that the lion's share of those funds went to the schools, and they wanted the state to do more to offset these costs instead of handing over their tax dollars to special interests that did almost nothing for them and everything for the incumbents who doled out the money.

I introduced George to my old friend, Bill Powers, a hard-nosed, get-it-done ex-Marine who was now the chairman of the New York State Republican Committee. Bill was a neighbor of mine, and years before I'd pushed for him to become head of the Rensselaer County GOP. He'd done a bang-up job and was producing similar results as state chairman, wiping out the party's debt, eventually helping to build Republican majorities in two-thirds of the counties, and getting behind a batch of winning mayoral candidates, Rudolph Giuliani among them.[4]

Once Bill got on board with the idea of a Pataki candidacy, I phoned Lewis Golub, who, with his cousin Neil, operated the family's Price Chopper supermarket chain. The Golubs had been among my strongest and most generous supporters.

"Lew," I said. "I'm bringing George Pataki over to meet you."

"What's a Pataki? What does it mean?"

"It's the name of the next governor. That's what it means."

"You kidding me?"

"No." I thought that George had a shot at winning—a long shot—for the simple reason that, after a dozen years, New Yorkers were suffering from Cuomo exhaustion and tired of the never-ending rise in taxes.

Lew agreed to sit with Pataki and listen to him, and he wound up being a finance chair for his campaign and raised a sizable amount of money. Long story short, I did that with a lot of people, and I began to offer George some unsolicited advice. He used to walk around with a stack of manila folders under his arm, and one afternoon I saw him bending down in the hallway picking them up.

I asked to speak with him in his office, and once we were inside, I closed the door and said, "I know you're a guy who cares more about the work than the look, but—you're going to the convention in May, and you'll probably be nominated for governor. I'm hoping you're gonna get elected, but you gotta start looking gubernatorial. Christ, you gotta start looking the part."

"What's wrong with—"

"What's wrong? Go look in a mirror. Look at your shirt—it's wrinkled. Your tie is two inches off center. Your suit is baggy. And your shoes look as if you just came out of the pasture."

George gaped at me, not hurt, though partially stunned.

I continued: "Go buy a dozen shirts, some new suits and shoes. Start looking gubernatorial. You're in politics and, like it or not, perception is everything."

George was good-natured about my advice, and I gave him some dynamite motivational tapes from Earl Nightingale that I liked. I don't know if he listened to the tapes, but I noticed that he began to dress more like a governor. I'd bet Ralph Marino noticed it too, and when I and a group of Republican senators went to see Ralph and asked him who he was supporting, Ralph said that he was for Herb London—one of the state's great political hybrids, a Jewish, pro-life New York University professor who had run on the Conservative Party line against Cuomo in 1990. A Senate majority leader refusing to support one of his own against an incumbent governor was pathetic, yet Ralph hadn't forgiven George for taking out Mary Goodhue and for accepting support from Change-NY, an organization of rabid anti-taxers that had fought Ralph's reelection in 1992.

"I'll back anyone except Pataki," he said.

Before the convention, I spoke privately with Ralph. "I'm going to be on the floor working the delegates for Pataki. If you go there to get London nominated, you and I are done. I'll no longer be supporting you. I want you to know that upfront. All bets will be off."

Ralph looked over at me as if I were sharing nothing more important to him than the weather report. "Do whatever you want," he replied, most likely thinking that I was bluffing.

I wasn't.

The convention was held at the Sheraton New York Hotel and Towers and, after checking in, I went to watch George, surrounded by campaign staff, practice his convention speech. I didn't expect him to be in Mario's league as an orator—few are—but George's speech was lacking. I listened for twenty minutes. Then I interrupted him and said, "George, tear up what you're reading and tell me why you want to be governor. What makes you think you're qualified? What's your vision for New York State? Why should the delegates be proud to have you as their candidate? You know why; nobody has to prompt you; you don't have to write it out. Try telling me."

George began talking, and after a while, he was giving a good speech, though he was still making notes when I left to go downstairs to the ballroom.

Sure enough, Ralph Marino was out in the sea of delegates, trying to line up support for Herb London. Ralph had no chance of keeping George off the Republican primary ballot in September. All George needed was 50 percent of the delegates, and he was far above that number. Ralph was trying to get London 25 percent of the delegates so he would also be on the primary ballot.[5] Not that London could beat George, but he would make him spend time and money on a primary, and the candidate who benefitted from that tussle was Mario Cuomo. It was a shameful way for a Republican leader to behave, and I'll be damned if, during the three hours of voting, Ralph didn't almost pull it off.

I think Herb London was somewhere close to 23 percent when Senator Roy Goodman, a wealthy, liberal Republican from the Upper East Side of Manhattan, headed for the microphone. Later, I was told that Roy was poised to announce that his delegation might switch its votes from Bill Green, a former congressman from Roy's district, to Herb, which would've given him the 25 percent for the primary ballot. I don't know if this is true, because Roy didn't get a chance to speak. As state chairman, Bill Powers was presiding over the convention, and before Roy reached the mic, someone—a Pataki supporter, no doubt—yelled, "Move to adjourn!" and it was seconded, and Bill slammed down the gavel and called out: "This meeting is adjourned!"[6]

All hell broke loose. Herb told the media that he might go to court to challenge the adjournment, and his supporters were talking about getting him on the primary ballot by collecting signatures on petitions.[7] The cure for such talk was some old-fashioned, political horse trading: Herb was promised that he could run for comptroller on the Republican line.

★ ★ ★

George chose Betsy McCaughey, a historian and conservative thinker, as his running mate, and the silly season was underway. Ralph formally endorsed George in September and stated at a news conference that George had promised him his support as leader if he won. George was noncommittal when asked, though both he and Al D'Amato had assured me that I'd be leader if George made it. Just then, I didn't take their talk seriously, knowing that if I wanted the job I'd have to get it on my own. George and Al were politicians, and I'd been around too long not to know that politicians tend to promise the sun and moon when it was expedient and to develop amnesia later on when it was in their interest to forget their promises.

Pataki jumped out ahead of Cuomo in the polls, but it was going to be tough for him to win, and not merely due to George challenging a sitting governor. I was concerned about a minor-party candidate, Tom Golisano, a mega-wealthy businessman from outside Rochester and founder of the Independence Party. He had buckets of cash to spend, and if Tom wasn't on the ballot, I thought the majority of his votes would've gone to George.

The race was a bitter one, charges and countercharges flying like shrapnel, and it turned out to be, up until then, the most expensive gubernatorial election in the state's history. I raised money, called in in every favor I was owed, and attended rally after rally. In a perfect demonstration of how the downstate-upstate split functions in New York politics, Mayor Giuliani called a press conference at City Hall, and though Rudy was the first Republican mayor of the city since John Lindsay departed in 1973, he endorsed Cuomo for governor, blasting George as vague, unsympathetic to the needs of the city, and a protégé of Al D'Amato.[8]

By the end of October, George's lead over Mario had evaporated: a *New York Times*/WCBS-TV News Poll showed that he was trailing the governor by double the margin of error. In addition, the poll confirmed my earlier fears about Tom Golisano. Upstate, George was losing seventeen percent of his vote to Tom, a margin that could cost him the governorship.[9]

To his credit, George didn't slow down, and on the Saturday before the election, I attended a rally with him and his wife, Libby. We were outside the Executive Mansion, and two or three hundred Democrats showed up, and it got rough. People were shoving and throwing punches and calling each other names. George got Libby into a car, but the governor and I stood there on Eagle Street, in the middle of it, and I remember being on the sidewalk across from the mansion, and we were trying to get George up on some stairs so his supporters could see him. An Albany policeman ordered me off the curb and into the street. I didn't budge, and he shoved me, saying, "I told you to move."

I started to shove him back, not the smartest choice I ever made, but somewhere the theme song from *Rocky* was playing, and maybe the boxer in me was inspired. The policeman threatened to arrest me. Somebody who was watching told him: "I don't think you wanna go there," but I was pissed off and decided to explain the right of assembly to the cop. He wasn't overly impressed by my civics lesson and, if memory serves, Albany Mayor Jerry Jennings had to straighten out the mess.

Meanwhile, Ralph didn't lift a finger to help the Pataki campaign, and the morning before Election Day, his picture appeared on the front page of a New York City tabloid alongside a shot of Mario Cuomo. Ralph wasn't endorsing the governor, but he had attended an event on Long Island with him, and the imagery annoyed Republican politicos, and I knew that I was one step closer to becoming the majority leader of the Senate.

The night of the election, I was at the Hilton Hotel in New York City with George and Libby, Al D'Amato, and a band of Pataki supporters. By seven o'clock, as we sat down for dinner, George believed that he might lose, and he was understandably anxious about it. We made it through the meal, and George asked me to come up to his suite. We sat on the bed, watching the coverage on TV. The polls were about to close when Guy Velella, a Republican senator from the Bronx, joined us. The returns showed Pataki leading. The State Police entered and tried to shoo us out, because it seemed as though George was going to be governor.

More visitors arrived, and the troopers ordered them to go.

"You two stay," George said to Guy and me.

Every five minutes the room would start to fill, and every six minutes the troopers would chase out the newcomers. It was like a Marx Brothers' movie, and it went on until Cuomo conceded the election (which George won with just under 49 percent of the vote.) The troopers hustled George down the back stairs to the room where he could speak to his supporters. I was behind him onstage. George was at the podium, acknowledging people, which in the first excited flush of an election victory I felt was a mistake, because you are bound to forget someone. In George's case, he forgot to mention me. I wasn't put out. I had an agenda of my own. The next morning, I grabbed a cup of coffee with Al D'Amato, and he went into overdrive, saying, "Yep, you're the man. You're going to be the leader. George and I got to make that happen."

I returned to Albany thinking that, at best, my chances were fifty-fifty.

10

MR. LEADER

Initially, the pledges of support from Pataki and D'Amato seemed to be nothing but lip service. For the moment, Ralph Marino had saved his job by flying to Florida after the election and meeting with Al. From what I heard, Ralph said that he was searching for a position in the private sector and, if Al would help him, he promised to retire within a couple of years. Ralph added that he wouldn't give the newly elected governor any trouble, though he got stubborn when Al insisted that he dump Angelo. Evidently, Ralph's counsel treated New York State and United States senators with the same contempt.

George and Al decided that they ought to let things lie and go with Marino—that he'd gotten religion and would be cooperative. I was disappointed, but I wanted to be a team player, and I told reporters, who were speculating that I was up for majority leader, that I wasn't seeking the post, and I intended to keep my word.

Then Ralph made a mistake.

There was a bill that George didn't want passed while he was governor-elect, one that raised pension benefits for public employees. George asked Ralph to hold off on the vote, and he agreed. Two days later, Ralph changed his mind and said that he wanted to think some more about the bill.

George went berserk. I called him and Al to inform them that I was going to run for leader. Neither one approved or disapproved.

I got out a legal pad and proceeded to do some arithmetic. There were thirty-six Republican senators, and I needed nineteen of them to win. Ralph wouldn't vote for me, but I would, so bottom line I had to convince eighteen out of thirty-five. I never thought about losing and told myself that I could do it—no sweat, Joe, right?—but my confidence was tempered by the realization that I could fail and failing to take out a leader wasn't free. I'd lose any meaningful assignments and my member-item funding, so my district would get almost nothing in state assistance. If I didn't resign, Ralph would find a candidate to primary me, a candidate who would be fat and happy with campaign cash.

I met with Bill Powers. With his knack for raising money and his success at electing Republicans, Bill was respected by the senators I had to persuade, and I wanted to make certain that he was in my corner.

"I'm going to run for leader," I said. "I'm going to start making phone calls, OK?"

Bill wasn't one to waste words. "Go for it."

On November 20, the Sunday evening before Thanksgiving, I sat in my bedroom and reached for the phone. I knew that I had to penetrate Long Island, Ralph's turf, to prove to my colleagues that I was for real. My ace in the hole with these guys was that in August, following the convention, I'd spoken to Joe Mondello, the longtime GOP boss of Nassau County. Joe had the power to give a thumbs-up or down to any moves Republican state legislators from Nassau might make. I'd bumped into Joe at Saratoga Racetrack. I didn't know him well, but I said hello, and we talked. I'd heard that Joe disliked Ralph, who, at the urging of Angelo, had tried, behind the scenes, to weaken the county leader. They failed to hurt Joe, but I guessed that it left him with a hankering for some payback, and I was glad to give Joe the opportunity.

I said, "If you hear anything about my wanting to replace Ralph, all I'm going to ask you to do is nothing. Don't tell them yes about supporting Bruno and don't tell them no. Just say that they're on their own."

Joe held out his hand, and we shook. "Don't worry about it," he said.

My first call that Sunday was to Dean Skelos. If possible, Dean disliked Angelo Mangia more than I—"Senator Mangia," we called him—and

Dean resented Ralph for letting him run roughshod over the conference. I filled in Dean, and he climbed aboard.

My next call was to Guy Velella in the Bronx. That was a formality: On election night, I'd spoken with Guy in Pataki's hotel suite, and he was behind me.

"Go get 'em, Joe," he said.

I tried a few more senators, but they weren't home. That night, I fell asleep knowing that I had three votes and wondering where I'd find the other sixteen.

On Monday morning, I phoned Owen Johnson, a conservative from Suffolk County who had been in the Senate for more than twenty years. Even though I was close to Owen, I had to be careful. I'd shed my own blood if I didn't get rid of Ralph—that was a given—but so would any senators who the leader discovered were behind me. Thus, my pitch was critical to rounding up the votes, and it was informed by my experience in sales, where I'd learned that I had to emphasize why whatever you were selling benefitted the listener, not the talker.

Here, as best as I can remember, is what I said to Owen and the other senators I contacted:

"I'm running for leader. Ralph and his staff demean us every chance they get, and we're not in control of our destiny. Powers, D'Amato, and Pataki are behind me. I've already got Dean and Guy voting for me, and I hope I can count on you. I need nineteen votes. Once I get there, I'm going to announce that I've got a majority of the conference, and I need you standing with me at the press conference. If I don't get to nineteen, then we never talked. You were never with me."

Owen signed on, and I moved down my list: Kemp Hannon in Garden City, Long Island; John DeFrancisco in Syracuse; Jim Seward in Oneonta; and Bill Larkin in Orange County. As eager as I was to reach my goal, I listened carefully to everyone's answers. Counting votes is an art form. The counter must control his optimism, never an easy task for politicians, because falling in love with your own wishes—and believing that others are on your side—is one of the chief hazards of the game.

On Monday, I went from eight in the morning until ten at night. By November 22, a Tuesday, I checked and rechecked my pad over breakfast and saw that I had fourteen votes. I phoned John Daly, a friend of Pataki and of mine. John represented Niagara County, but he was in his Albany office. I pitched him and received a lukewarm response of support. I didn't add his vote to the total, and before I could place another call, the phone rang. It was Johnny DeFrancisco.

"Hey," he said, "Daly called me and said if you're going to run, he's going to run. He wants my vote for leader."

Oh, Jesus. I'd worried that once I'd showed the balls to challenge Marino, others might follow suit. After logging fourteen yes votes, I'd figured that it wouldn't come up, and now it was clear that I'd been too optimistic, a trap that I'd sworn to avoid.

"What did you tell Daly?" I asked.

"I told him that if he'd been in touch earlier, I'd have voted for him. But now I can't. I'm committed to Bruno."

"Thank you very much for that."

I hung up and called Daly.

I said, "What're you doing?"

"I'm going to run—that's what I'm doing."

"Let me share something with you. I've been making calls. I've got votes lined up. And you haven't done a single thing."

I thought that would scare him off. He didn't say anything.

"Let's have lunch," I said. "Today."

We had a quick lunch downtown. I convinced Daly that I had such a head start, he couldn't catch me. I added that if he tried, the result would be that Marino would survive as the leader, and Angelo would be around to make him miserable. However, if I won, I could appoint Daly to a deputy-leader spot.

Before I picked up the check, my vote total had increased to fifteen.

★ ★ ★

One of the stunning aspects of my try for leader was that Ralph Martino never appeared to get wind of it. Part of that was the media didn't completely grasp what was going on until I had enough support, but mainly I suspect that Ralph and Angelo doubted that anyone would have the nerve to pursue the post: overthrowing a majority leader is a political no-no and had never been successfully done. In fact, while I'd been having lunch with John Daly, Ralph was up the block at the Fort Orange Club, attending a luncheon with his key staffers. He asked if anything important was going on, and he was told no, it was business as usual. Ralph drove to Rochester to spend Thanksgiving with his mother.

His spokesman, John McCardle, informed the media that Ralph had scheduled a conference for December 1 to vote for the next majority leader, a vote that Ralph expected to win. James Dao, a reporter for *The New York Times*, sniffed out some behind-the-scenes activity by me, but Dao quoted Charlie Cook, a senator from Sullivan County. I hadn't spoken to Charlie, and he told *The Times* that he doubted any challenge would succeed.[1]

All of this was a lucky break for me. Had Ralph become aware of my plan, he would've been able to stop it by rewarding his allies and punishing the insurgents.

Late that afternoon, as I was chasing my last four votes, the phone rang. It was Al D'Amato. "Joe, what the fuck are you doing?"

"Running for leader."

"You're telling people that I'm supporting you, and that Pataki's supporting you."

"That's exactly what I'm saying."

His voice rising to a higher octave than usual, he said, "Stop saying that—immediately."

"Why? Aren't you supporting me?"

"I've talked to some people, and they say you can't make it."

I smelled politics and did my damndest not to gag on the stink. "Really? Why can't I make it?"

"You're too confrontational. You're too much of a maverick. And you'll be trouble."

This was beginning to make sense. Pataki was going to be one of the three men in a room negotiating the budget with the speaker of the Assembly and the Senate majority leader. By law, the governor had no more power than these two legislators—unless neither the speaker nor the leader understood their roles or were unwilling to play them. Sheldon Silver, a big-spending Democrat from Manhattan's Lower East Side, who had become speaker in February after Saul Weprin died, was well aware of his power in relation to the governor. Furthermore, Shelly had a reputation for tying his adversaries in knots by leaving the table and refusing, until the last second, to discuss any compromise. I wasn't a tax-and-spender, and my style was more operatic than Shelly's, but like him I understood the leader's position in relation to the governor. Pataki and D'Amato had seen me in action, and they must have determined things would go smoother with a more malleable leader.

I asked Al, "Who should get the job?"

"Ron Stafford. I need you to support Ron and you can take over the Finance Committee."

That confirmed my suspicion. Ron was from Plattsburgh and among my dearest friends in the Senate. He was a sweetheart of a guy, but an effective majority leader, one who was willing to shoulder his legal responsibilities, couldn't be a sweetheart. Ron was chairman of finance, and he loved that position: more pay and more power, but not enough of either to give you insomnia or migraines.

Al said, "Ron's got a lot of votes."

Only through a substantial exertion of self-discipline did I refrain from suggesting to Al that he go take a flying leap. I'd spoken to Ron, and he was voting for me. Pataki and D'Amato must've called and, after telling Ron that I couldn't win, said that they needed him. Ron was a good man: he'd do anything to help and become majority leader if it were a done deal, but he wasn't aggressive and wouldn't jeopardize his chairmanship.

"Al, Ron doesn't have one vote, because he knows that once he makes a phone call, he's done being finance chair. If either Ralph or I win, he's gone."

That sounded harsh, except those were rules for this variety of raw, down-and-dirty politics. Its tools were trading, cajoling, and threatening, and you had to be prepared to tell a friend that if you're not with me, you're nowhere. I won't do anything to hurt you, but you'll be at the back of the line when you want something or need my help.

"Ron has votes," Al said. "He does."

"Let's get him on the phone."

I remember that Al had to get off then, and later that day there was a conference call with Al, Ron, and Ron's best friend, Doug Barclay, a former senator from Oswego County who was now a partner in a law firm.

For openers, I said, "Ron, tell me how many calls you've made to ask for support."

"I've got a list right here of people who will support me."

"I'm sure you got names on a piece of paper, but how many calls have you made asking people to support you for leader?"

He hemmed and hawed.

I said, "Let me tell you how many. None. OK? I've got fifteen votes, and I would've heard about it if you'd been in touch with any of them."

"Joe," Ron said, "if I'm leader, you'll be finance chair."

Al and Doug tried to persuade me that I should take it. I cut them off, saying: "Nohow, no way. And Ron—you haven't spoken to anybody about being leader, and if you don't call back tomorrow and say you're supporting me, I'm going to commit the finance chair to someone already onboard. Trust me. I'll give it away."

Early Wednesday, I heard from D'Amato again. He asked me to stop making calls.

"I hate saying no to you, Al, but—"

"No?"

"That's right. No."

Ron checked in; he was with me. Jim Wright from Watertown, Nick Spano from Yonkers, and Tom Libous from Binghamton signed on. By Thanksgiving Day, I had twenty-one votes. About four o'clock, just before sitting down with my family for dinner, I was getting dressed in the bedroom when the phone rang. I picked up, and it was Ralph Marino.

"I guess you got the votes," he said.

"I do."

"Yeah, I heard."

"Anything I can do to be helpful to you, Ralph, I will."

"I appreciate that."

Ralph hung up, and I actually fell to my knees to thank God. Not that I was going to be the majority leader of the Senate—you don't bother God with the small stuff—but that the battle was over.

My prayers had been premature. We were still at the table and tucking into slices of pumpkin pie when Ralph called back.

"I'm not giving up," he said.

"Look, I know you're listening to Angelo, and frankly he's the reason a bunch of guys backed me. Make the transition hard on everyone, and I won't help you."

That threat didn't persuade him.

We had a news conference scheduled for eleven on Friday to announce that I would be the new leader, but we had to keep putting it off, because I couldn't get in touch with Ralph. We rescheduled for noon, then one. Finally, I got Ralph on the line.

"Tell me where you are," I said.

"I'm done."

"Thank you, Ralph."

We made a date to have lunch, and I promised that he could stick around without a problem from me or choose a painless exit.

Ralph said he was grateful and chose to go in February.

11

PREFACE:
FUTURE IMAGINED

Before I negotiated my first budget, I got in my car and toured the
Capital Region to remind myself of my goals. I passed the empty
office buildings, dark storefronts, and barren lots—one of which held
my attention, an overgrown field along Washington Avenue Extension in
Albany. I drove through my Senate district, into Luther Forest, and down
Columbia Turnpike to the East Greenbush site of the Sterling-Winthrop
Research Institute.

The pharmaceutical company had left the area in 1991, and I parked
and walked the grounds, gazing up at the abandoned, cream-and-brown
brick buildings. It was a cold, gray afternoon, and the wind was blowing,
and I can still remember the sadness I felt thinking that more than a thousand people used to work at the institute, and now the pigeons were using
it as a hotel. I listened to them cooing up on the window ledges and hoped
the birds were having a ball because now that I was in charge of the Senate,
I was confident that they wouldn't be hanging around there forever.

I headed over to the train station in Rensselaer. It was a rundown shell
that would've been more appalling if my next stop hadn't been the Albany
County airport, which resembled a bus station in a town that time forgot.
That evening, when I walked into my house, I knew that as leader I'd be
buried in mundane tasks that could distract me from fixing this crumbling

infrastructure and the lethargic economy that went with it. But as I sat down to dinner with my wife and children, I promised myself that I'd keep my eye on the ball, and I wouldn't leave the Senate until I'd made good on this pledge.

12

ROUND 1:
THREE MEN IN A RING

During his campaign, Governor Pataki had pledged to reduce the tax burden. For his first three years in office he did everything he could to make good on that promise, and I worked to help him. In a February 1995 address, the governor said that he wanted a reduction of $6.8 billion over four years. That was his opening gambit, and I doubted that he'd get it. Yet he gave state workers the jitters, which got worse when the governor proposed cutting five percent of the workforce, more than 11,000 jobs, but added that he'd only lay off a thousand people, and the remainder would be accomplished by retirement and attrition.

I defended his proposal in the media and told the *Times Union*: "We're not talking about an ax. We're not even talking a pen knife."[1]

By then, the governor was laying off some five hundred state workers Mario Cuomo had hired right after he lost the election, even though Pataki had asked Mario to hold off on the hiring. Pataki followed those layoffs by getting rid of close to four hundred nonunion appointees, saving almost $50 million but increasing the anxiety around the Capital Region, including my own district, which was loaded with thousands of unionized state employees. It appeared to some as if the governor was unaware of how crucial these jobs were to the economic stability of the area, to say nothing of the sense of well-being among so many people. That became even clearer when the governor set off a storm by suggesting that 6,000 state data-center employees be relocated to former IBM buildings in Kingston, Poughkeepsie, and Endicott—his plan to persuade the company to remain in New York and to cut hundreds of more jobs.[2]

In that overheated atmosphere, I knew the chances of miscommunication were high between the governor and me—in business I'd seen a host of problems created by the simplest of misunderstandings—so I had a hotline installed that allowed the governor and me to call each other directly without going through assistants. I called him frequently, because Pataki and I were not on the same page when it came to moving jobs. I was hearing about the move—and the cuts—from my constituents, and so was Mike Hoblock, a Republican senator from Albany County, and we went to speak with Pataki, explaining that we had to be careful because the fallout would create political trouble for us later on. Pataki understood, but he didn't revise his game plan, not right away, and it cost Mike his seat, which went to the Democrat Neil Breslin in 1996.

I felt part of Pataki's problem was that he was advised by his staff, most of whom were from downstate. Furthermore, and this wouldn't become clear until the following year, both the staff and Pataki himself sometimes had an idealistic view of what they could accomplish and not enough appreciation for the power granted by the State constitution to the Senate leader and Assembly speaker. Pataki learned the hard way, and so did I, and eventually we both discovered when to push and when to back off.

Unfortunately, Zenia Mucha, the governor's director of communications, never learned.

Zenia, who come to Pataki from Senator D'Amato, was the governor's fiercest advocate and protector and, for all intents and purposes, ran the office. Zenia was smart, extremely strong-willed, and seemed to strike fear into the hearts of her co-workers. I rarely heard her complete a sentence without salting it up with a *fuck* or a *prick*, and frequently while I was meeting with the governor she'd barge in and enter the conversation unannounced, and I'd say, "Hey, Zenia, this is my time, why don't you set your own time?"

Usually, before disappearing, she'd eye me as though she wished that she could order the palace guard to drag me off to the dungeon. On one afternoon, however, after the governor and I had talked through some of the moves and tax cuts and reached a compromise, and I assured him that I was going to help make another of his big campaign promises come true, passing a death-penalty bill, I mentioned that it would help if he announced that we were together on the jobs issue. At that moment, Zenia walked in, and the governor told her what we wanted to do.

Zenia said, "What? You agreed to what?"

Pataki told her again, and she snapped, "No, we're not going to do that."

"Why the hell not?" I asked.

"Because we're not."

"Look, Zenia, the governor and I have agreed that this is mutually beneficial and it's better for the people of this state if we move forward and stop arguing about it in public."

"No," she said to me.

Pataki broke in. "Joe, maybe we should talk further about this."

It sounded as though he was backing down, but most of us had aides we respected enough that they could change our minds or, at the very least, give us pause before finalizing a decision. Zenia was a handful, but that didn't mean she wasn't astute, and I didn't blame the governor for hesitating.

Yet, in this situation, a little theater was in order to demonstrate, as much to Zenia as the governor, that I was impatient with sudden reversals.

Before leaving I said, "Are you kidding me? We spent a half hour talking about it, and come to a decision and Zenia comes in and tells us what we can and can't do? Who the fuck is running this state?"

I recount the story to demonstrate how convoluted getting anything done becomes. It's not just the governor, senators, and members of the Assembly all of us have to worry about, but the advice of people who surround them.

Not long afterward, I drew a line in the sand, basically telling Pataki, "Those jobs are going downstate over my dead body. Go find another place or get new businesses to come in or do whatever else you want to do. But they're not moving."

It was a promise that I'd fight him tooth and nail in public, and it was a harsh way to do business, but once in a while that was the only option you had to get yourself heard over the strident interference of advisers.

The earliest hit I took from the media as leader was when I recommended one of my brothers to be a special assistant to the State Office of Alcoholism and Substance Abuse Services, a position for which he was more than qualified, having worked in the field for fifteen years. When one of my sons was hired by the Office General Services, this proved to be too much for *The New York Times*, which accused me of running my own jobs program.[3]

Because Pataki was reducing state employment and I'd spoken out against handouts for people who don't work and been accused of being a racist, I should've seen it coming. Yet as I told *The Times*, I didn't think my family should suffer because I was in the Senate. The newspaper claimed that I had it backward: why should my family be advantaged by my position?

I didn't reply to that question, though the newspaper had certainly hired a family member or two over the years, and I doubted that I should take the hit for creating the spoils system, since it dated back to the nineteenth century.[4]

That was just the warm-up for the criticism I received when the first budget I negotiated as leader was late.

From the outset I knew that Assembly Speaker Silver, a Democrat, would fight the tax cuts, because he needed the money for programs his downstate constituents wanted. Normally, the speaker counterattacked by doing nothing, and he did plenty of that during 1995, along with getting on the radio and accusing Pataki of helping the rich at the expense of the middle class. My response was to wait Shelly out, let the budget impasse drag on, and amuse the journalists who covered state politics. I'd always begin these news conferences by saying, "Maybe I've said this before," and since I always said the same thing, the reporters were already laughing when I came out with my explanation: "We can't get a budget because Shelly is doing what he does best—nothing."

Shelly had his own bagful of stock replies. He'd say that all Bruno cared about was getting something done—he doesn't care what. All he cares about is being on time. He doesn't know how to run a government or be realistic or reasonable.

It was a game Shelly and I played—blame the other person and try to make it stick. Or take credit for any programs or decisions that work out well—even if you didn't originally support them.

The media was an appreciative audience. Reporters relish pointing out how stupid and inept people in government are, and though I'd also apply those adjectives to some elected officials, the measure of their worth isn't when the budget gets wrapped up. The budget had been late every year since 1983, and I didn't think it was a tragedy, because I never accepted that an on-time budget was better than a late budget if it included high taxes, huge spending, and projects that don't do the taxpayers any good. I mean, think about it. You pay a contractor to build your dream house; you're supposed to move in April 1; and you push and push the contractor and, against his better judgment, he finishes on time. You move in. The next day, the roof collapses. Not good. Another couple builds their dream house. They harass the contractor to finish by April 1. He tells them to relax, he'll get it done—correctly. They move in on June 1. Nothing goes boom.

Where would you rather live?

Pressure for an on-time budget came from the media, good-government organizations, some of the voters, and entities anxious to pocket their funding, yet I wouldn't swear that any of those raising a racket were familiar with the details contained in the 2,000 pages. Democrats or Republicans, depending on which of us were getting—or not getting—the appropriations we wanted, also hollered about a late budget. That was political jousting for advantage, not a sign of fiscal responsibility, and the outrage you often heard was the battle over whose ox was getting gored.

The truth is that most proposals that come before the Legislature have merit and deserve funding. The state can't afford it, so a lot of excellent programs go without. What determines who walks away with a prize is the result of political headbutting. There are winners and losers, but I assure you that many times winning and losing doesn't have a thing to do with merit.

For me, the most effective method of dealing with the racket was also the easiest: I ignored it, because I didn't care about the noise. I cared about economic development and job creation, which would improve the quality of life in the state. Everything else was a distraction.

Governor Pataki, Shelly Silver, and I—the three men in the room—were getting gutted in the papers, on TV, and the radio for our alleged inability to close a deal, and here is as good a spot as any to talk about a term of art in New York State politics that has been transformed into an epithet—*Three Men in a Room*. The phrase refers to the way the final budget is negotiated among the governor, the speaker of the Assembly, and the Senate majority leader. A former Democratic state senator, Seymour Lachman, wrote a screed about the three men, and his subtitle said it all: *The Inside Story of Power and Betrayal in an American Statehouse*.

Give me a break.

In the spring of 1995, I attempted to make the process more transparent and bipartisan at the request of my Democratic colleague, Senator Nancy Larraine Hoffmann. I had the Senate Finance Committee go over the differences in the Senate and Assembly operations budget in public, but no one seemed to care, and it didn't pass the budget any faster.

Sometimes I thought what the media, the citizens groups, and some of the electorate wanted was for us to rent an auditorium, stick the governor onstage, and seat 211 people—the combined total of the Assembly and the Senate back then—in the audience and have them scream at each other. That wouldn't get us anywhere, and while three men in a room wasn't the most open way to nail down a budget, the approach is a form of representative democracy. Here's how it works. The speaker and the majority leader are responsible to their conferences and their districts. This meant that Shelly had to keep his Democratic conference happy or they wouldn't reelect him speaker, and he had to deliver for the people in his election district or they wouldn't return him to Albany. I had to tend to my Republican conference or I was gone just like I'd replaced Ralph Marino, and I had to win the Senate race in my district.

And the governor had to fall somewhere between the two of us or the people of New York would retire him.

I viewed this arrangement as fair. Yes, the Republicans in the Senate got more funding than the Democrats, another frequent criticism, but the reverse was true in the Assembly.

The funniest line of attack was when the three men were drawn and quartered for the alleged crime of doling out funds to help them and their allies get reelected, as if politicians should be above self-interest—say, like journalists.

Let's see: A Pulitzer Prize-winning reporter gets a call from a source who has a bang-up story for him, and the reporter says, "No thanks. I already have my Pulitzer. Call my pal, Bill."

Or the director of a nonprofit government watchdog entity receives the news that a donor has bequeathed $1 million to his organization, and the director says, "Oh, we've got enough. Give it to another group."

Are there things that could be handled better by elected officials? Absolutely. But I was always a fan of the Winston Churchill dictum: "Democracy is the worst form of government, except for all those other forms that have been tried from time to time."

Besides, it gave the chronically dissatisfied something to yell about, as if every problem could be traced to the fact that three men had the final say on spending, and no amount of transparency was going to quiet this disgruntled choir.

Anyway, in the spring of 1995, the budget fight got especially heated because the governor refused to approve any emergency funding to pay legislators, their aides, and himself. People were suffering, and their stories appeared in the papers, and a federal judge got into the act, ordering the governor to restart the paychecks. Shelly was in fine form, accusing the governor of extortion and asking Albany District Attorney Sol Greenburg to investigate. Greenburg politely declined the invitation. I was taking a fair amount of flak from my constituents, and I felt as though I were starring in a Vaudevillian melodrama.

The governor also had another budget challenge. Pataki had promised the voters that he wouldn't OK a budget that included member items. This was impossible, and Pataki, Silver, and I knew it. So the governor began referring to the member items as "member initiatives," which was nice way of saying the same thing. Talking to reporters, who asked the governor about the $150 million in these initiatives included in the budget, Pataki relied on his *Mr. Smith Goes to Washington* approach, saying that he felt bad about carving up the pork, but gee, what else could he do? Shelly was his usual reticent self: why bother explaining what everyone knew anyway? That wasn't my approach. I gave it to them straight, without the sugar coating, saying that it may not be the best system, but it's the one we have. When a reporter noted that a number of the projects financed were in Rensselaer and Saratoga counties, my response was to reiterate what the reporter already knew. That was my district.

I didn't lose a wink of sleep over helping my constituents. I'd been elected to do that. Also, there had been Senate majority leaders from downstate and from western New York, and I felt that the Capital Region had gotten the short end of the stick, an inescapable conclusion if you bothered to look at its sorry public infrastructure. When journalists and assorted self-proclaimed citizen watchdogs—frequently employees of nonprofit groups who annoyed me more than reporters because they bashed elected officials as a means of raising money to pay themselves—observed that tax dollars tended to flow into the districts of the more powerful legislators, I responded by saying, "Go over to the railroad station. Go over to our airport. It is an embarrassment for the capital of New York State. How do you expect jobs to come here? How do you expect us to grow here? We're the Empire State!"

And while I spoke these words, I thought: I wasn't born with any power. I acquired it through hard work, and anyone else so inclined was welcome to do the same.

That wasn't going to happen, though. Some folks prefer the comfy seats on the sidelines, where they get to sling mud and preserve what they consider their moral superiority.

In addition, I didn't see the appropriations as wanton spending, and when I was criticized I'd say that we were investing in the people and the economy of New York. And think about it. People get jobs—they go to the movies, to drug stores, to restaurants, and to the dry cleaner's. The companies also buy locally, and that's what an economy is all about. And everyone pays taxes, and those taxes build our roads, pay for our schools, and every goodie the government provides.

I didn't want to argue or split phony moral hairs. I wanted to help people. Of course, this didn't get done without the seemingly endless, back-and-forth discussions between my office and the governor, sometimes between our staffs, and other times between us. I remember that we had boiled down our differences on the budget to maybe four issues, and I thought I'd reached a compromise on them with Pataki. I filled in Abe Lackman, a terrific numbers guy who had worked as Giuliani's budget director and who I hired to take over as secretary of the Senate Finance Committee. Abe was about to button up the budget with the Assembly when he got a call from Patricia Woodworth, the governor's budget director. Patti had heard about my talk with Pataki, but she didn't know the details, and Abe told her. They didn't sound right to her, and she asked Abe to hold off until she could double-check with Pataki. Sure enough, Patti called back and said I had it all wrong—the governor hadn't compromised his position.

When Abe informed me, I was so irritated I didn't even have the chance to start cursing before I got on the hotline. Pataki picked up and told me he was in a meeting.

"I don't give a shit. I'm coming down," and when I got there, I learned another lesson about miscommunication.

I let the governor know that I genuinely thought we had a deal, and he replied, "Joe, just because I'm nodding my head doesn't mean I agree. All it means is that I'm listening to you."

Perfect. I now had a running joke that I would use with the governor. Whenever he nodded, I'd say, "Are you being polite? Or does that mean yes?"

In 1995, I saw to it that funds were appropriated to renovate the Saratoga Performing Arts Center; for East Greenbush, I got the money to build a center for children and senior citizens, and to start developing a health research center on the Sterling Winthrop site. There was money for salt storage in Schaghticoke, a community center in Moreau, and I promised the Alliance of State Arts Councils that I would push for money to nourish the arts.

I knew this ran counter to the perception by some that conservative Republicans are dollar-crazed barbarians. However, not only did I believe the arts were important to education, which was why I helped to establish a scholarship program for students at the New York State Summer School of Orchestral Studies, I also felt that if you wanted to attract major-league corporations, the arts had to thrive to give the area the cachet that attracted sophisticated business leaders. Therefore, over the years, I made sure the arts got a steady infusion of funding. Just looking over a partial list published in the *Albany Business Review* I see that the Junior Museum in Troy was awarded $2 million, and the New Arts Center for the Capital Region got $1.7 million. The Rensselaer County Historical Society received $1.5 million to renovate the Hart-Cluett Mansion, and the Albany Institute of History & Art got about the same to fix up its home. Creating the Saratoga Film Institute cost $60,000, and the Saratoga Children's Museum and the Albany Symphony Orchestra were each awarded $100,000.[5]

At the top of my to-do list, and the key to all the other doors I wanted to open to the future, was my desire to fix the Albany County airport, and as our negotiations were winding down, I decided to press my case. It was Shelly Silver who gave me my chance.

Shelly and I were in the governor's office, and Pataki, feeling the pressure to finalize the budget, said, "Let's get this done. What's it going to take, Shelly?"

As was his habit, Shelly hemmed and hawed as if there wasn't enough funding in the universe to satisfy him. But, as the saying goes in Albany, *Two Makes Three*, and since Shelly knew the governor and I were together in this battle, he'd have to come along, since there were appropriations he wanted and programs he had to protect for himself and his members.

At last, Shelly said, "I need $62 million for a library in Brooklyn."

"Done." Pataki said. "Is that OK with you, Joe?"

"Hell, no, it's not OK with me!"

"Why not?" the governor asked.

"I don't have one member in Brooklyn. What's Shelly got? Twenty-five? Twenty-six? I'm not going to go for that just to make him happy. They probably don't even need the library."

I think Shelly was studying the tops of his shoes when Pataki said, "What's it going to take for you?"

"How about $62 million?"

"Sixty-two million?"

"Shelly got $62 million, I get $62 million."

"For?" Pataki asked.

"To upgrade the Albany airport." I was going to need $40 million to start the work; $11 million would go to improve infrastructure on Long Island; and the remainder would be divvied up among the members of my conference.

The governor said to the speaker, "OK with you?"

Sitting in his chair, Shelly was as motionless as a drowsy owl on a perch. Rousing himself for an instant, Shelly said, "I don't care, as long as I get my library."

We stood up, shook hands, and went out and announced that we had a budget agreement, and I think *The New York Times* had it right when its headline proclaimed: *Budget Brawlers Bloody, but Smiling.*[6]

I have to admit: I felt a sense of accomplishment. According to the budget office, we reduced the personal income tax, sales tax, estate tax, corporate franchise tax, petroleum business tax, motor-fuel tax, beer tax, beverage-container tax, and the pari-mutuel tax. The top marginal tax rate on personal income tax would shrink from 7.875 percent to 6.85 percent over three years, and by 1997, among the states that had a broad-based income tax, New York's rate would drop thirteen spots, from eleventh to twenty-fourth.

The icing on the cake came at the end of June, when I got to add my name to the unanimous vote to confirm former heavyweight boxing champion Floyd Patterson, who spent much of his career after boxing helping disadvantaged youngsters, as the state's athletic commissioner.

13

THE USES OF POWER

During my tenure as majority leader I instituted one of the best practices I'd picked up in business, managing the flow of information. If you let people pop into your office with their latest problems, you'd waste hours bullshitting and be nothing more than a fireman, racing around without priorities and wasting your two crucial assets—your time and your energy. Every afternoon as I left for my rounds of speeches, dinners, fundraisers, ceremonies, and drop-bys, an assistant would give me my call sheets and my scheduler, Leslie King, would hand me the packet. I received hundreds of phone calls every day from staff, constituents, conference, members, the governor's office, lobbyists, friends old and new, and some hapless souls whom I suspected had forgotten to take their medication. Next to each call I placed a *1*, meaning I had to speak to the caller ASAP; a *2* for a callback within twenty-four hours; and a *3* for a handoff to my staff.

The packet was more challenging than the call list. Without fail, it was an inch or two thick and contained suggestions and requests from my senior staff, members of my conference, and any information that was relevant to a project or an appropriation under consideration. I'd instructed my chief of staff, Steven Boggess, and the people who worked for me that they should bring me solutions, not problems, and almost all of them did excellent work on the packet, notating the contents with a *Yes*, *No*, or *Discuss Further*. One rule I had to put in place was that no presentation could be more than one page, a limit I set because frequently I was reading until midnight while I assumed the SOB who had written me the nine or ten pages was fast asleep.

I also insisted that the Senate itself operate more like a business and less like a combination country club and middle-school student council, which was standard operating procedure when Warren Anderson and Ralph Marino were in charge. I told my conference that wristwatches had been invented for a reason and insisted that my members show up for meetings at the beginning, not in the middle with some lame excuse. Over the years, I'd gotten sick and tired of senators ignoring the bells summoning them to the chamber: they'd ring for hours in the empty hallways until I was eating aspirin like M&M's, and I let my conference know that when it was time to vote we were going to vote and not hang around until midnight because they were off eating dinner or at a cocktail party.

I used to tease my members, saying that I wouldn't hire half of them as clerks, but I wouldn't tell them which half. Invariably, they laughed when I'd say this, but they got the message: I expected them to behave as professionals. But I tried not to be unreasonable by letting them know that I was willing to listen if they ever disagreed with me, and I'd do whatever I could to accommodate their objections. Yet once a decision was made, I wanted the entire conference pulling in the same direction.

This was my biggest challenge. From the get-go, when I was elected leader, I knew that almost a third of the conference didn't want me to have the job. On top of that, Pataki wasn't done cutting budgets, and though Republicans generally ran on lessening the tax burden, constituents often wanted their load lightened by their senator getting rid of programs in other districts, not their own.

In this respect, people always puzzled me. Money from government built roads, bridges, schools, parks, and stadiums. People loved that. What they didn't love was paying taxes. The voters talked about cutting spending, yet they voted for candidates who spent, particularly if that politician could convince them that the money was coming from anywhere but their own pockets. So as an officeholder you tried to act that way, which was why you heard so much chatter about federal appropriations and grants and private funding.

This aspect of human nature, the desire to get something for nothing, presented an immense problem for the members of my conference, many of whom had campaigned against taxes and were still expected by their supporters to bring home the bacon. These mutually exclusive goals were a recipe for disaster, and I realized that the only way to keep my conference on the same page was to show them, in essence, that I was in charge. Otherwise, the conference would battle over the limited resources and splinter into factions.

So I had my thirty-five senators sit at the table in our conference room on the third floor of the Capitol, and I said that a bill was going to the floor, and we needed every vote for it to pass.

"You have to stick together," I said. "Lincoln was right. 'A house divided against itself cannot stand.'"

I saw my conference staring at me. Some of them didn't look happy.

"Now this may be unpopular for you in your district, but we need to get it done, so while you are voting no, your colleagues have to vote yes, many of them because it helps them, OK, and for other reasons, so I'm asking you to suck it up and vote, whether you like it or not. If you don't need the strength of the conference and the leader behind you, well, then you go ahead and peel off. But when you need the conference or me, we won't be there for you."

If a bill came up and I didn't need everyone to pass it and one senator would be in trouble if he voted for it, I'd tell the conference that we were letting him off the hook and asked if anybody wanted to discuss that decision. Occasionally somebody would jump up and say, "What the fuck? If he's gonna get off, why can't I?"

With more amusement in my voice than anger, I'd reply, "Because you're in a district that if you were the devil himself, you'd still get reelected, OK? He's not in the same enviable position. That's why."

I would try to be fair. Sometimes, I had to bow to their will—for instance, on the antismoking bill. I'd wanted to pass it forever. I hated smoking, and my dear friend, Lester Cole, had died from it. But the bill was so vehemently opposed by restaurant and bar owners that my conference couldn't support it, and several years went by before I could bring them around, and meanwhile I took the heat for the conference in the media. Other times, if I didn't need my members' votes to pass a bill, I'd say you're on your own, vote your conscience. On occasion, though, so many of them would've been screwed if they voted in favor of something—layoffs upstate, for instance—that I'd have to call the minority leader, a Democrat from Brooklyn, Martin Connor, and say, "Marty, you gotta find me five or six votes."

He'd do it, but his help wasn't free. I'd be called upon to pay for the favor. He'd want more staff allowance. Or bigger office space or another branch office for some of his members.

Some people will read this and say, "That's terrible, dealing like a bunch of horse traders."

Whether it's terrible or not, I can't say, but some remarkable legislation has been produced by swapping favors, often promises of jobs or funding. I got a kick out of watching that go on in the movie, *Lincoln*, seeing the president dealing with lobbyists to pass the Thirteenth Amendment before the end of the Civil War so the South, once it rejoined the Union, wouldn't get a chance to prevent the abolition of slavery. I'm told that Lincoln probably didn't deal directly with the wheeler-dealers but sent his secretary of state, William Seward, who, I'd like to add, had resided upstate in Auburn and had probably learned the art of the backroom deal as a New York State senator.

However, according to President Lyndon Johnson's biographer, Robert Caro, LBJ got his Civil Rights bill out of the House Rules Committee by buying the support of Minority Leader Charles Halleck, a Republican from Indiana. Halleck had his members stonewalling the Democratic president's bill, and Johnson knocked down the wall by getting Halleck three-quarters of a million dollars for a research facility, and more money in grants and contracts, for Purdue University, which was located in Halleck's congressional district.[1]

And this was how that political sausage got made. Anyone willing to argue with the results?

On occasion, as I tried to control my conference, things would get uglier than I liked. I remember Joe Holland, a GOP senator from a district in Rockland County, where the Democrats enjoyed a hefty advantage over Republican registered voters. I can't remember exactly what bill was coming to the floor, but we were going to require the entire conference to support it.

Everyone was onboard except Joe, and I met privately with him and said, "Joe, let me share something with you. The bill is critically important to your colleagues, to me and to you. You vote against this bill, you're gonna jeopardize your leadership position, because I can't have you voting against the conference and be a leader, OK?"

Losing his leadership position would cost Joe his stipend, six or seven grand, maybe, but he replied, "Ah, do whatever you have to do."

We were out on the Senate floor, the vote was coming up, and I sent somebody to ask Joe to vote with the conference. Joe came over and said he couldn't, and I told him this wouldn't turn out to be much fun for him or me. The bill came up, and we managed to pass it without Joe. As soon as the session ended, I invited him to my office.

I said, "I'm removing you from your position."

Joe appeared mystified. "Why?"

"Because you don't want to be part of the conference. You're still chairman of a committee, and if you want to stay chairman, then I'd join the conference when we need your vote."

"That's not fair. It's bullshit."

Joe may have had a point on both counts, but the next day I announced that the Republicans were making some changes in leadership. I wanted everyone to know that there would be a price to pay for betraying the conference.

My announcement, as I'd hoped, shook up a fair number of my colleagues. I can appreciate how some could characterize my decision as the exercise of power for power's sake. But that wasn't it, not by a long shot. If I were going to improve upstate's infrastructure, I needed the GOP to hold onto the majority, and to do that I needed my conference as a bloc. Stripping Joe of his power was designed to underscore my seriousness when it came to teamwork.

The whole business had an interesting unintended consequence. Joe eventually left the Senate to become the commissioner of social services for Rockland County. I tried to persuade him to stay until after his reelection, because we'd lost a couple of seats in the Senate in the 1996 election, and if we lost a few more it would be harder for us to shape the legislative agenda. Joe refused, and another Republican, Thomas Morahan, ran for his seat. His big campaign promise was to try to rescind the commuter tax, which for the last thirty-three years had been levied on his constituents who worked in New York City. The tax was also hated by our members on Long Island, but we couldn't get rid of it because Shelly always defeated us in the Assembly. We tried to help Tom win the election by approving some aid for a school district in his area, and suddenly Shelly decided that the time was ripe to attempt to put a Democrat in the open seat, and he announced that he was supporting the end of the commuter tax. Shelly may also have enjoyed sticking it to the city's Republican mayor, Rudy Giuliani, since it would cost the city $200 million to $300 million in tax revenue, but I didn't care about Shelly's reasons, and without too much trouble the commuter tax was gone. And Shelly's move proved to be futile. Tom Morahan won the election.

Again, I can appreciate how one could see Shelly's machinations as being pure politics, not sound fiscal policy. I'm in no position to judge. In his place, I might have tried to do the same thing. For better or for worse, that is how the game is played.

14

ROUND 2:
AUSTERITY AIN'T BEANBAG

Q uickly, it became apparent, that for us to hold onto the majority in the Senate long enough for me to help upgrade the economic landscape of the Capital Region, we needed to put together a coalition of strange bedfellows, because across the state Democrats had an approximately 40 percent lead over Republicans in registered voters. We needed our GOP stalwarts; the Independence Party, which sapped support from the Democrats and got our members in hotly contested districts the few thousand votes they needed to win; a solid working relationship with the mayor of New York City, first Rudy Giuliani and then Mike Bloomberg; and finally the support of a union, not the usual backers of upstate Republicans. In pursuit of an ally in labor, I made a lifelong friend.

It all began when I went to Manhattan to have lunch with Cardinal John O'Connor, the archbishop of New York's archdiocese with its almost 2.5 million Catholics. I had never met him and from what I could tell he had nothing specific he wanted to discuss, but he had acute political instincts and a chat with the Senate majority leader couldn't hurt. His ornate residence was around the corner from Saint Patrick's Cathedral, and as we sat down to eat, I said, "Now that you're in charge of the diocese, tell me what your day is like."

Cardinal O'Connor, peering over his wire-rim glasses, replied, "Everybody thinks I run the church, but I'm really a fundraiser. I spend seventy percent of my day raising money, mostly for Catholic hospitals."

I laughed. "Sounds familiar. Everybody thinks I'm putting together all this policy and legislation, but I spend most of my time raising money for Republican election campaigns."

The cardinal was a charming man, a great talker, and I would've liked to sit with him longer, but I had another meeting. I hate being late, probably the early training of the nuns, and I looked over at Abe Lackman and my chief counsel, Ken Riddett. Clearly, neither one of them had any intention of interrupting Cardinal O'Connor, leaving that unpleasant task to me, and during a pause in one of the cardinal's stories, I told him that I had to go, thanked him for lunch, and told him to feel free to call me if I could be of any help.

I used a suite at the Sheraton Towers on Fifty-third Street and Seventh Avenue for my meetings in the city, and we double-timed it over there to talk with Dennis Rivera, president of 1199/S.E.I.U., New York's Health and Human Services Union. Abe had put this together with Rivera's top aide, Jennifer Cunningham, and both of them were amused that I'd agreed to it, describing it as Nixon going to China, given that during my career I'd been an outspoken critic of labor. I had agreed to speak with Dennis since you never know what will come of talking to opponents, and because, truly in my heart, as I got older and reflected on how shabbily my father had been treated by his company—pensioned off for ten bucks a week after thirty-two years—my view was changing. Treating workers like that was just plain wrong, but I'd also seen the other side, greedy union leaders pressing for more than companies could afford, and in the case of public unions, demanding so much that they alienated taxpayers. I'd concluded, by the time I walked into the suite to see Dennis, that the best way to go was to find a fair balance between unions and management.

Dennis was sitting on a couch with a stuffed leather briefcase beside him and a fedora on top of the case. He was put-out that I was late and asked me where I was, his tone annoyed and seeming to suggest that there was nothing more important than being in this suite.

"I was at lunch with Cardinal O'Connor. We had a nice talk."

Dennis was in his mid-forties, with a thick dark moustache and serious expression, but at the mention of the cardinal his face lit up with boyish glee. Just then, I was unaware that Cardinal O'Connor, whose father had belonged to a union, had taken Dennis under his wing, advising and helping him for nearly a decade.

His voice warmer now, Dennis said, "The cardinal's our best friend. He does all these great things for our people."

Dennis and I began to talk. He'd been born in Puerto Rico, dropped out of college, did a stint in the slums building union membership, and came to New York in the 1970s to continue his efforts as a union organizer. He'd had a low-paying job at a city hospital, and he was destitute when he lost it. And now here he was, in charge of 1199/S.E.I.U, which he'd transformed into a political powerhouse.

I suspected, after our first conversation, that we both had new allies, and I was sure of it after I spoke to his union's executives and told them the story of my mother's nightmare journey through the health-care system. When I was done and looked over at Dennis, tears were rolling down his cheeks.

★ ★ ★

Governor Pataki wasn't overly pleased when he heard about my meeting with Dennis, but I was going to need every friend I could find during the governor's second year because in December, just six months after passing the last budget and facing a $4 billion shortfall, Pataki introduced his "austerity" budget, calling for cutting more than another 7,000 state workers, claiming most of the cuts would come through buyouts and early retirement. I had John McArdle, the excellent director of communications for Senate Republicans, tell the media that I was pleased by the news, because it had been reported that the governor wanted to lay off 15,000 people, but I knew voters in my district and the members of my conference were going to be furious, and as I considered the cuts I was thinking—*Again? You got to be kidding me.*

It was at moments like this that I was tempted to stand up and quote the old political chestnut: "Half my friends are for it. Half my friends are against it. And I stand with my friends."

Except, because of my business background, I dealt in reality—not fantasy. I brought the same attitude to my role as majority leader, and it got me in hot water not only with my opponents, which you'd expect, but also with my political buddies.

Honeymoons are short, right? That's why they're called honeymoons, but my honeymoon with Governor Pataki was shorter than the media realized.

In early February 1996, Pataki vetoed a bill that increased the salaries of police and firefighters in New York City and called for raising them to the same levels as the suburbs in the metropolitan area. I led the fight to override his veto in the Senate, which we did three days later, and Shelly followed suit in the Assembly. Mayor Giuliani was more vocal about the override than the governor, complaining that the law took the responsibility of salary arbitration away from the city Office of Collective Bargaining and handed it to the state Public Employment Relations Board, which, Rudy claimed, would cost the city hundreds of millions of dollars.[1]

Listening to that rhetoric, you would've thought the cops and fire killers were employed by hedge funds, when, in fact, they risked their lives for modest pay, and the city could be very dangerous—which the whole world got to see up close and personal on 9/11—and why shouldn't they earn the same as their brothers and sisters in the suburbs?

Meantime, as the layoffs progressed, I heard that from some of the distraught workers who were losing their jobs. One guy I never forgot called me in tears, saying that he had three children and couldn't get by on unemployment. He'd worked hard, done his job well, and he walked in one morning and was told to clean out his desk and not to come back. When he asked why, he was told, "Bruno."

"What did I do wrong?" he asked me.

"Not a goddamn thing," I answered, and then tried to talk sense to Pataki's appointment secretary, Thomas Doherty, a hard-driving, hard-hitting guy who had been active during Pataki's campaign. We had become close in the run-up to the election, but Tom was fanatically loyal to the governor. Tom told me that the governor said that we had to do layoffs, so he was going to do the layoffs, and that was the end of that.

I phoned Pataki. Almost on a daily basis he'd taken to reminding me that *he* was the governor, and I'd remind him that there were three branches of government—executive, legislative, and judicial—and I was the majority leader of the Senate and sometimes I disagreed with him and felt free to push for what I wanted.

Now, we skipped the civics lesson, and I got right to the point. "You're making a terrible mistake. Telling people they're getting fired because they're friendly with me. That fuck head Doherty isn't the governor, and he's got no right doing that. And if you're doing it because you're angry at me, this isn't how you retaliate. It's not fair to the people who have nothing to do with our disagreement—absolutely nothing."

"Let me look into it," the governor replied, which was what he always said whenever I confronted him about the shenanigans his staff engaged in.

It didn't take the governor long to call back. "Joe, we have to lay off, and we're going to lay off more. And if you want to play hardball, then we'll play hardball."

Through gritted teeth, I said, "You don't know what hardball is, and I'm going to show you."

Pataki and I came from different worlds; his was more genteel than mine, and I was confident that I'd win any street brawl with him. And he had another disadvantage. Governors read their names in the media every day, and hear all about themselves on radio and television, and this can lead to champagne of the mind. Fortunately, the State constitution made me—and Shelly—a significant counterweight to the governor.

As soon as I hung up with him, I called the Senate appointments office and instructed them to hold every confirmation that the governor sent up until I told them otherwise. This meant that Pataki couldn't get any of his commissioners or judges approved—anyone who had to be authorized by the Senate. Many of the recommendations for these job seekers came through the county chairs and my own members, so the governor responded to my move by contacting Republican senators and telling them the reason their appointees were not being put in place was because Bruno thinks he's governor, Bruno's acting out, Bruno's doing this and that. So my members started calling me and asking if I could make an exception for their appointees.

"No exceptions," I replied. "When your county chairs and the governor get in touch, you tell them, 'I'm sorry. I feel badly. I want to get it done and I'm doing everything I can. But that prick Bruno won't let any of these go to the floor.'"

At one point, I believe, I was holding up more than 150 appointments and raising holy hell within government. I got a call from Ron Stafford, one of my best friends in the Senate, and he pleaded with me to let in one of the appointees. I began to make exceptions here and there if some of my members were going to find themselves up the creek, but for the most part I continued the game of hardball with the governor.

Pataki began badgering my conference, inviting members to his office and saying that they ought to dump me because he couldn't deal with Bruno as leader; I assume that he felt I had no respect for the governor; I was nuts; I was nothing but an egomaniac.

My members would call me and tell me about their adventures in the governor's office. Some complained about the pressure they were getting from Pataki and his staff, and asked me if they should accept his invitation.

"Go ahead," I told them. "Have a ball."

At our regular meetings, I started asking my conference, "Who's been down to see the governor?"

The first time I asked, maybe seven raised their hands. The second time, ten, and the time after that, fifteen.

Chuckling, I looked around. "How come the rest of you haven't been invited? Aren't you as important as these other guys? If I hadn't been invited, I'd be calling the governor and saying 'What's the matter with me? Isn't my opinion as important as the people you're talking to?'"

Everyone was laughing now, and in the event that any of my members suffered a momentary lapse in judgment and forgot how things operated, I kept my tone light and added, "If there's anybody who wants to listen to the governor and represent his position in the conference instead of him working out things with me, when you want a bill that's important to you and your constituents to get to the floor, I'm going to tell you to see the governor. When you want to be chairman of a committee or want to increase your staff allowance, I'll sing you the same song—go see the governor."

My type of standoff with the governor is one reason New Yorkers consider their government dysfunctional, but, in view of my political goals and the desires of my constituents, I had no choice other than to make Pataki miserable until he was willing to talk.

Finally, the governor and I decided to get together in his office one-on-one—no staffers allowed, which meant that Zenia Mucha probably had a mini-stroke. During our discussion, I got quite emotional. "I'm getting calls, like you intended, from people with kids. You want to do things, do things to me. These people have nothing to do with what's going on here and what's happening here is going to hurt them and their families, that's unconscionable. How the hell do you sleep at night?"

"We've got to do the layoffs. I've got fifty more. I'll send you the list."

Pataki had the list delivered to my office, and when I got done reading it, I was seeing red and called him.

"Governor, I'm telling you now: if you want to see some bloodshed in this state, go ahead and lay off one more person. All of us will get bloody, but you're the governor so I guarantee you, you'll get the worst of it."

A few days later, we spoke again. I told him that when he rehired the people who were thrown out of their jobs, I'd start confirming his appointees. Most everyone was rehired except for a handful of folks who had already found other employment, and one guy my aides said was the most incompetent boob in New York State, so I couldn't argue his case since the workforce was much improved without him.

I took little satisfaction from winning my fight with the governor—mainly because, with my twenty years of experience in the Senate and understanding the prerogatives of the leader, I knew the battle was over before it began. What pleased me was that I had obviously done a good job as leader. My conference had supported my decision, trusted that I had their long-term interests at heart, and spoken with a single voice even though my holding up the confirmations troubled some of their supporters.

The 1996 budget restored most of the $1.4 billion in cuts that Pataki had wanted yet we also reformed the workers' compensation program and didn't touch the drop in income tax that we'd passed in 1995.

All in all, I'd say, it was a very good year.

15

FLYAWAY

One difficulty in retelling my tenure as majority leader is that writing, if it's not going to confuse the readers, has to progress in an orderly fashion, marching from one event to the next. This is the exact opposite of my experience as leader, where things happened simultaneously so that every night, as I got into bed, I felt as if I'd spent the last eighteen hours standing under a meteor shower.

My days and evenings were spent politicking among my colleagues, managing the conference, talking to the media, advocating for bills and appropriations I supported and fighting against those I opposed, dealing with the needs of the constituents in my district (Democrat or Republican, since anyone you help may vote for you next time around), mudwrestling with the governor and Shelly, traveling up and down and across the state for my members' campaigns, attending fundraisers from New York to Florida, eating enough rubber chicken to choke an elephant, shaking hands until my right arm was numb, talking to everyone who was making a serious pitch for an idea or program that would need funding, and pursuing my own agenda—improving the local infrastructure and economy.

Fixing the airport had been my one stated goal during my first campaign for the Senate in 1975, and more than two decades on, the airport was still a disgrace. Not only was it an eyesore, you could hardly get anywhere on a direct flight, which I'd learned flying off to meetings while I was at Coradian and which Victor Riley Jr., chairman of KeyCorp, would later cite as a factor in moving his corporate headquarters to Cleveland. In addition, if you were unlucky enough to land at the airport in inclement weather, you took your life in your hands coming down the slippery metal rolling stairs and crossing the equally slippery tarmac, praying with every step that you weren't going to need an orthopedic surgeon. Winter was the worst, because you were often granted the privilege of going to the outdoor lot, brushing the latest snowstorm off your car, and getting a shovel out of your trunk so you could dig out from under the ice-crusted mountains that the plows had pushed against your bumpers.

I had secured some funding, and by August 1996, the plan for the parking garage was approved, and John Egan, the CEO of the airport, who had a reputation for bringing in projects on time and under budget, had things in hand. However, there was a lot more to do. Because of the lack of competition among the airlines using Albany, the fares were sky high, and to fix that we were going to have to attract another carrier. That would require selling on my part to the airlines and to the Legislature.

After New Year's, I put together a task force of five Republican senators, three from upstate—Ron Stafford, Jess Present, and John DeFrancisco; and two from downstate, Roy Goodman and Norm Levy. My professed goal for the quintet was to collect input from the business community, airlines, and anybody who had successfully operated an airport.

As soon as I named the members, I got slammed by a Democratic state senator from Manhattan, Catherine Abate, who indicated to reporters that I was wasting time with this study group. My guess was that Senator Abate, an outspoken critic of the high fares, was afraid that I, the Republican leader, might solve the problem, and she wouldn't receive her share of the credit.

In one way, she was right. We didn't need another study. What I needed was a handful of senators banging the drum on behalf of the upgrade. The improvements were going to cost in the neighborhood of $160 million and would include a bond issue. The group's efforts would get the movers and shakers in and out government on board, generate positive stories in the media, and convince voters that something had to be done, a key factor given that a boatload of tax money would be spent.

If you're going to be an effective leader, you have to turn around on a regular basis to make sure that you have some followers, and the task force was designed to help me recruit them.

I set my sights on bringing in Dallas-based Southwest Airlines. They had been founded in 1971 with a handful of planes and their growth had been astronomical. I think they had a fleet of approximately 250 planes flying to maybe fifty cities and best of all, for my purposes, the company was renowned for its low fares. Even if their arrival didn't pressure other carriers to lower their ticket prices, you could still fly more cheaply and get to more places. Dozens and dozens of cities around the country were banging on Southwest's door, but the company only expanded by a couple of sites a year.

I got in touch with John Nigro, an avid supporter of mine who had started out in his family's supermarket business and gone on to become an enormously successful developer. John was a member of the strategic initiatives committee at the Center for Economic Growth, and I asked him to meet with John Egan, the CEO of the airport, and figure out what we'd need to attract Southwest. They got together with Colonie, New York, developer Bernard Conners, and I got my answer: a two-gate addition to the terminal that was being renovated. To do that I'd have to promise to come up with $4.5 million.

"Consider it done," I said.

The funds were appropriated. The media referred to it as a "member item," but that wasn't correct. The money came from Senate capital funds, part of the $1 billion we raised with a bond issue. The way I recall it I got about 35 percent of it to distribute, Shelly the same, and the governor got a bit less. Pataki complained that he was getting shortchanged, arguing that it should be a third, a third, a third, but Shelly and I stuck together and ganged up on him, and we got our way.

Now came the hard part. I had to sell the airport and Albany to Southwest.

For the last few months, I'd been talking to Herb Kelleher, the co-founder, CEO, and chairman of the airline. My approach to selling someone was simple: Remind myself of one of my favorite sayings, *Be bold and mighty forces will come to your aid*, then call the person and tell him why I had a good deal for him. Herb listened, not exactly intrigued, but he didn't say no.

"Herb, we're going to build those new gates for you."

"Even if you do that, I can't commit to you. I'm not gonna jump you ahead of everyone else."

"It would be helpful if you gave us the criteria you use for making the decision."

"We've got to have those gates. Some airports have already built us jetways."

"We'll do the building, Herb, and I'll be talking to you."

I had several conversations with him without getting a commitment. Then one afternoon, I said, "Come on up here, would you? Come on up and take a look at what we've got."

He agreed and arrived with a whole crew of experts to complete the due diligence. While I ate lunch with Herb I told him about how we were improving the business climate upstate and why Southwest would profit from our plan. Herb had grown up in New Jersey and had a law degree from New York University, but it seemed that his years in Texas had turned him into a good old boy. In the book I'd read about him, I learned that Herb had once avoided a lawsuit by arm wrestling his opponent instead of going to court. That took balls, because Herb wasn't an athletic, muscle-building, workout kind of fellow. Truth is, he didn't look like he could arm wrestle a nine-year-old, and his main diet appeared to be cigarettes and bourbon, but he had an infectious laugh and would throw his arm over your shoulder for no reason at all. Behind this happy-go-lucky façade, though, was a brilliant guy, who told me something at lunch that I've never forgotten.

When I asked him to explain the success of Southwest, he replied, "People. That's it. Our people. We train them and they participate in everything that happens—our profits and many of our big management decisions."

I thought our lunch had gone well, but Herb still wasn't sold, and I kept calling him, going around and around in the same circles. Kevin O'Connor, president of the Center for Economic Growth, would later claim that I was operating on pure faith. It may have appeared that way, yet during those months I was convinced that we would prevail. If faith was involved, it was a faith rooted in my business experience, where I discovered the power of positive thinking combined with a shamelessness about pressing your case. That works because occasionally when a decision maker is sitting on the fence, he is really waiting for someone to knock him off on one side or the other.

That was my approach with Herb. I got him on the phone one day and said, "We've got this thing almost completed now. That has to mean something. You're a smart guy, an experienced guy, and we're good to go. And we'll do whatever's necessary, because we need you here to attract new businesses."

Herb mentioned the fifty or sixty other cities that were in line, and I replied, "I wasn't elected to care about those places. I'm asking you, Herb, as the CEO, to make an executive decision to come here."

"I'll get back to you, Joe. And soon."

My instincts told me that Herb would do it: whether it was the sound of his voice or his willingness to keep taking my calls, I can't say—I just knew.

Southwest Airlines came to Albany in May 2000, and by August, according to the *Times Union*, 161,000 people boarded flights at the airport, "an all-time high," and 45,000 more than had flown the previous year.[1]

In my speeches, I kept referring to the airport as an economic engine. I thought it had a quotable sound to it.

And best of all, it turned out to be true.

16

ROUND 3:
FOOTNOTE TO
THE BATTLE

Sometimes you just say, "Screw it," and do what's right. That was how I felt about getting rid of rent regulation. The laws applied to 1.2 million apartments, the overwhelming majority of them in New York City, and the "sunset" was scheduled for June 15, 1997. That meant all I'd have to do was sit on my hands unless Shelly and Pataki could come up with a new program that made sense. I anticipated getting burned at the stake for suggesting it, but I had enough support in my conference that I could even let my downstate senators—Roy Goodman, Frank Padavan, Guy Velella, and Nick Spano—vote against the expiration, so as not to alienate their constituents, and the law would expire anyway.

The current form of rent control had been put in place to help veterans of the Second World War find affordable housing. Fast forward more than a half-century, and there were thousands of very wealthy people in rent-controlled apartments, all of them subsidized by the taxpayers of New York City and New York State, and other renters who didn't enjoy the same advantage. It was unfair, and I was pleased that Raoul Felder, divorce attorney to the rich and famous, had the decency to admit in public that he wasn't entitled to pay so little for the luxurious, rent-stabilized Fifth Avenue apartment he'd been renting for two decades. What few were talking about—and another reason I favored getting rid of the law—was that it was also bad for the real estate market and created a bogus housing shortage.[1]

Even before I spoke publicly against rent control, Michael McKee of the New York State Tenants and Neighbors Coalition, referred to me as "Attila the Hun" in *The New York Times*.[2] I felt like I was on firm ground assuming that this guy wasn't a Republican. What was curious about the battle was the abject hypocrisy of people like Mr. McKee. To read their pronouncements, you would've thought I was getting ready to throw poor people into the street, when, in fact, for the majority of middle-class renters, the law was making apartments unaffordable.

In early December, I traveled to Manhattan and addressed the Rent Stabilization Association, the largest landlord group in the state, and announced my two-year phase out plan. Opponents pointed out that landlord associations were generous contributors to legislative campaigns (for the record, not all of them were Republican candidates), and to the Senate Republican Campaign Committee. To *The Times* credit, they ran a letter from Don Fedorisko, a man I never met, that succinctly outlined the problem:

> The most damaging aspect of rent regulation in New York City is its squeeze on the middle class. The system creates an artificial shortage of apartments, causing renters who have market-value apartments to pay exorbitant rents, while those with rent-controlled apartments pay almost nothing. I pay $1,155 a month for a small studio on the Upper West Side. Many of my neighbors with larger apartments pay under $700 a month. I have friends with four-bedroom apartments who pay under $200 a month. If rent control were abolished, my apartment would probably rent for a reasonable price.[3]

So you see, at bottom, it was nothing more than folks whining about their ox getting gored, and once again, it struck me how readily they transformed the loss of their entitlement into a moral issue, with them perched high atop their mountain of self-righteousness and hurling accusatory thunderbolts at anyone with the nerve to suggest that they were not as entitled as they thought.

Shelly Silver, I was sure, was cooking up a countermove, most likely dragging out the budget process in the hope that I'd compromise. I had no intention of doing that, nor did I have much to worry about, since there wasn't one rent-controlled unit in my district.

Even though I'd told Governor Pataki what I wanted to do and he heard me out without responding, my announcement made him nervous, and took the position in the media that I was jumping the gun, and he preferred a more measured approach.

I wasn't in the mood for a measured approach in March when I returned to Manhattan to carry my message to the audience attending Crain's New York Business breakfast at the Sheraton. I pledged "to end rent control as we know it," and the people inside the hotel were a lot happier about the news than the people outside who I'd seen across the street as I'd entered the hotel. They were pressing against a police barricade, shouting at me and holding up signs that I couldn't read from so far away, though I doubted they were wishing me long life and much happiness.

Shortly afterward, I had lunch at Fresco, a midtown Italian restaurant owned by the irrepressibly affable Scotto family. As I was leaving, an old Italian woman came up to me and, with anger and fear distorting her face, asked, "Why you want to take away my apartment?"

I attempted to explain that I wasn't going to kick her out of her home, though given her age I didn't mention that one of the rent-control provisions that drove me nuts was that apartments could be passed on in a will, and not just to the surviving spouse, but from relative to relative across generations, which was nothing but a hustle, so for decades these units couldn't be brought into line with market rates. I had started with a radical announcement about ending the laws—a good negotiating position, I figured—but my chief objective was "vacancy decontrol," meaning that after the tenants had died or found another place to live the apartment would no longer be rent-protected.

I knew it would be a fight, but I never expected what came next. I began to receive death threats—eighty-seven of them, according to the state troopers. The troopers couldn't investigate each one, so a guard detail was sent to watch over my house and family, and I and my staff were instructed not to open any mail or packages without having them scanned. One Republican senator even had a bullet fired through his windshield, and whenever I had to go to the city, Mayor Giuliani would provide with me with a police escort in front and back, and they would go right through red lights, saying that to stop would make me a sitting duck. The mayor even asked that I cut back on my trips to Manhattan, because the extra security was costing a fortune, and I did the best that I could to limit my visits.

One trip I'll never forget, the trip that underscored for me that I was trapped in the middle of this insanity, was to the World Trade Center. My motorcade had to go up on the sidewalks to escape traffic. It was a harrowing ride, and I was relieved when we drove into the underground garage. As all of us headed toward the stairs, I noticed a line of policemen with automatic weapons.

I asked someone if they were expecting a top diplomat or if the president were in town, and he replied, "No. They're here for you."

Negotiations ground on between Pataki and me, with Shelly claiming that he wouldn't give an inch on rent control. His statements to the media were pure theater, because I could wait everybody out until June 15, the sunset date. The governor was pushing me hard, a result of a poll that showed a precipitous drop in his approval rating in New York City and a meeting he'd had in early June in Bay Ridge, Brooklyn. The people there had been big supporters of his run for governor, unlike most of the city, and now they let him know how displeased they were with the potential changes to rent control, displeased enough to go shopping for another candidate the next year when Pataki had to run again.[4]

On June 14, a Saturday, the son of Bill Powers, the state Republican chairman, got married in Columbia County, and I sat at a table under a tent with Pataki and Senator D'Amato, and in between drinks and dinner we talked rent control and reached a tentative agreement. It wouldn't be the bill I wanted, but it was a start, and we left the wedding on a wave of good feeling, and I told Pataki that I'd see him tomorrow.

Sunday morning negotiations continued at the governor's office, and I thought everything had been worked out when I went home for a Father's Day lunch. I was eating with my family when the phone rang, and one of my staff informed me that I'd better get downtown pronto because Shelly was meeting with the governor alone. I hopped in the car, and as I arrived, Shelly was walking out of Pataki's office, and he extended his hand as if we were supposed to make peace. Forget it, I thought, and walked in to confront the governor.

"What are you doing? Meeting with Shelly behind my back? What kind of deal did you cut with him?"

He explained that he'd been talking to his staff and to D'Amato, and they felt that if rent control was drastically altered he'd lose his next election.

"Make these concessions, Joe. Please. Please understand the bind I'm in. We need a new bill."

"I don't get it. Yesterday, you tell me one thing, and this morning you say we're going forward, and now I need a new bill?"

"I'll lose next time out. You've got to help me with this."

That moment permanently altered the political dynamics between us. I had used up a lot of political capital in this fight, and if the governor had told me early on that he couldn't support me, I would've recalibrated my position. Instead, I felt he'd sent me straight into the fight and retreated when the going got tough. I still liked him enormously, though now I had a clearer picture of his political strengths and weaknesses.

I stood up, and Pataki came around the desk and hugged me, and somewhere in the midst of asking me to help him avoid a train wreck, he worked in that his mother Maggie wanted me to back him up. That was a low blow. Pataki knew that I adored his mother—she was a wonderful woman—but I wasn't convinced she was mixing into the rent-control controversy.

Sometimes in order to move forward on other fronts, a leader has to step back, and that was the judgment I made. Figuratively speaking, I closed my eyes and held my nose, and agreed. Then I went to bring my conference up to date.

Most had supported me throughout the ordeal, though several of them had paid a political price. I gave them the news and went to my office to get in touch with some of the leaders of the landlord associations, but none of them were around. I later learned that Pataki's people had them in rooms in the Capitol, where they could pressure them into concessions and keep me from talking to them. It was a smart play that served to isolate me, and I comforted myself with the handful of changes in the Rent Regulation Reform Act—some vacancy decontrol, removing nieces, nephews, aunts and uncles from those who could inherit the apartment, and limiting the right of free succession to one generation.

The following day, a New York City tabloid ran a cartoon that captured how I felt at that time—a picture of a knife sticking out of my back while Pataki stood there grinning.

The good news was that in July we agreed to a budget that contained $5 billion in tax cuts, a record, I believe. More than $2 billion was dedicated to property-tax relief, which would later become the New York State School Tax Relief Program that still exists today.

17

BODY POLITICS:
A BRIEF EXPLANATION

All the bravest dreams politicians dare to dream won't come true unless they can get elected. This truth is multiplied for leaders in the Senate and Assembly because they not only have to worry about their own districts, but the districts of their members. And while I've discussed the desire of constituents to see tangible proof that their tax dollars are being spent on their behalf, they also demand something less tangible from their elected officials—a sign that in their hearts they agree with them on deeply personal issues, which is why the subjects of abortion and gay rights are elevated to crucial electoral touchstones.

Truthfully, I wish it wasn't so, but there is no avoiding it. I was eager to introduce a bill requiring parental notification for a girl under sixteen who wanted an abortion. Speaker Silver lambasted me for it, saying that it was the first step in rescinding a woman's right to choose. That wasn't how I saw it. I thought it was bizarre that a doctor couldn't put a cast on a child's foot without permission from a parent, but he could perform an abortion. Also, in a society that bemoans the breakup of families, the existing law further undermined the status of parents, removing them in a profound way from their daughters' lives.

I knew the bill wouldn't go anywhere yet I felt strongly about the issue, and it was shrewd politics. Regarding abortion, I had first run as a straight pro-lifer and received support from those groups. They were less supportive when I announced that I approved of abortion in the event of rape or incest and to save the life of the mother. In truth, I did my best to evade debates about abortion. At bottom, I thought it was a matter of individual conscience, and being pro-life in a pro-choice state was no help to Republicans and served only to hand a club to the Democrats, which they used to beat on our overall agenda, as if our stance on abortion cast a pall of suspicion over any legislation we wanted to pass.

Gay rights was even trickier for me. How could anyone believe that gay men and women weren't entitled to the same legal protections in housing, employment, public accommodation, education, and credit as heterosexuals? Yet, for years, I had to back away from the question until finally, in 2002, after spending months behind the scenes whipping up support for the Sexual Orientation Non-Discrimination Act, I proudly voted for it in December. Still, it only passed in the Senate 34 to 26, an indication that my members in more conservative districts were unable to join the majority.

The most painful issue for me was same-sex marriage. I had gay members of my own family who had been in loving, committed relationships for decades. In 2007, the Assembly passed a bill legalizing same-sex marriage, but I refused to bring it up in the Senate, not because I opposed it, but I couldn't press my conference to get behind it. Some opposed the bill outright, and others believed if they voted for it, they'd lose their next election.

Two years later, when I was no longer in the Senate, Governor David Patterson pushed the Senate to bring his same-sex marriage bill to the floor, and he enlisted my help. I spoke about it on Fred Dicker's radio show, and I gave Empire State Pride Agenda a statement they could use: *This is America and we have unalienable rights. Let everyone decide how to pursue their own happiness. I understand that this issue stirs great passion in many people...[but] homosexuals who wish to enter into the union of marriage are just like the rest of us and they ought to be free to enter into it.*

The bill never made it, and at last, in 2011, under Governor Andrew Cuomo, same-sex marriage became law. I was gratified that I'd played a small part in pushing for its passage, phoning my former colleagues and telling Fred Dicker, state editor of the *New York Post*, on the radio that the benefits married couples receive shouldn't be denied gay men and women, and the time had come to allow people free expression.

I wish that I could've passed the antidiscrimination and marriage bills sooner and helped to make the lives of gay New Yorkers easier. Truthfully, though, if I were put back in the same place and time, I wouldn't have done things differently. I couldn't. It was a tradeoff, and I knew it then. Citizens seem to believe that officeholders pay no price in regret or guilt or disappointment. They are dead wrong, but defying the voters is the last thing you want to do if your goal is to improve the future.

After all, losers don't get to govern.

18

CITY AND STATE

Mayor Mike Bloomberg, one of the smartest guys I ever met, was in love with the grand gesture, possessed an unshakeable faith in his own abilities, and brought a single-minded devotion to any project he wanted. We shared an impatience to get things done, and I hated disagreeing with him because I respected his judgment. Contrary to his image in the media, he was usually respectful when we disagreed, saying quietly, "Joe, I respect your right to be wrong."

As dedicated as I was to resuscitating upstate, New York City was the economic engine of our state, so I'd go out of my way to be helpful to Mike, but he came up with two major projects I couldn't back—approving plans for a new United Nations office building and funding a stadium on the West Side of Manhattan.

The UN project was an office tower that would connect to the main Secretariat building via a tunnel. Once the tower was finished, the plan was to move employees out of the headquarters and give the HQ a pricey face-lift. The reason Mike came to me was that the construction would swallow up some of the Robert Moses Playground, and he couldn't build on public space without an OK from the Senate and Assembly. The whole project was budgeted at $1 billion, and I seem to recall that Mike was going to need some guarantees on the loans, but the specifics are hazy now, and that wasn't my major objection.

To start, I was not inclined to help the United Nations. A lot of the member nations skipped out on their dues and owed hundreds of millions of dollars; their diplomats blocked traffic by parking illegally and refused to pay their fines; and my impression was that they weren't especially polite guests in our country. On top of that, I objected to the UN taking the playground from the neighborhood, and the tower was going up over a section of the Queens-Midtown Tunnel, which could be dangerous.

Mayor Bloomberg wouldn't leave me alone about that tower, and the issue was getting increasingly political. I had a couple of members in the city, and one of them, Marty Golden, told me absolutely not to do it— the community surrounding the park was adamantly against the tower, and he had no shortage of Jewish constituents who were angry about the anti-Semitic leanings of the General Assembly. Mike had George Klein call to persuade me. A Brooklyn native, George's family had owned Bartons candy company, and George became a real estate developer and threw his considerable energy into Jewish causes. He was also a generous backer of the Republican Party, and a sweetheart of a guy. I hated saying no to him, but I did.

Mike made a final try.

"Joe, if it weren't for New York City, the rest of the state would be bankrupt. And the UN adds hundreds of millions to the economy, and if we don't do the tower, they'll move."

Moving was a standard threat when a group in Manhattan wanted funding, and I'd been hearing it from the stock exchange folks for years. Even so, I had to admit that the tower wasn't the worst idea that ever landed on my desk. I could've flipped a coin, and if it came up in favor of building, I imagine life would've gone on. Yet the politics of the situation made it impossible, so I ended the conversation by saying, "If they can get a better deal somewhere else, then maybe they should move."

That disagreement with Mike was a day at the beach compared to our discussion of the West Side stadium, which would sit on a platform over the rail yards and cost the city in excess of $1 billion. Predictably, the argument was that the money spent would create jobs and revenue that would make it a wise investment and spiff up a large swath of the city.

I knew that one of my longtime supporters, Charlie Dolan, was against it. Charlie was a sharp fellow about my age, and I invariably learned something whenever I spoke to him. The Dolan family, among its other holdings, owned Madison Square Garden and a stadium so close to the Garden was unwelcome competition. On the other side of the debate was another of my allies, Woody Johnson, who owned the Jets and wanted his team to play in the West Side stadium. Over the years, I'd become close to Woody. He was personable, charismatic, and the opposite of a showoff. I was impressed with wealthy people who were also kind and gave generously to charity, because I'd met more than my share who would've embarrassed Scrooge.

Woody was at the Upper East Side penthouse for a $25,000-a plate dinner with Pataki and me when I took a spill on the terrace and spent the evening with blood on my face, an icepack pressed against the goose egg on my forehead, and two black eyes. The worst of it came the next day when someone leaked the story to the media, and the hostess was livid because she hated seeing her name in the papers. I had to call her and apologize, and that was her last fundraiser. "Hey," I told Woody later. "She's lucky I didn't sue her."

That headache was minor compared to how I felt when the Dolans and Woody went to war over the stadium, taking ads on radio and television. The governor, Congressman Charles Rangel, and Mayor Bloomberg jumped in on Woody's side. Shelly Silver didn't want the stadium, because he—and his constituents—believed that the expense of the West Side project would hurt the redevelopment of Ground Zero. Shelly wasn't wrong, and I remembered how heartbreaking it was for me leading a delegation of senators through the blackened ruins of the site. Mike Bloomberg wasn't indifferent to the needs of Lower Manhattan, but he saw the stadium as an opportunity to alter the face of the city for the better, and he was hot to bring the 2012 Summer Olympics to Manhattan. To do that, he needed a new, modern stadium.

I wasn't necessarily opposed to helping with megaprojects. You couldn't generalize and had to make a judgment pro and con on the merits—namely, does it improve the quality of life for a meaningful number of New Yorkers?

For instance, the Buffalo Bills aren't as flush as the downstate teams, and I thought it was worthwhile to keep them upstate, and thus I was willing to be helpful whenever they asked.

Bloomberg made a strong, legitimate case, though at first I sided with Shelly, in no small part because if the speaker wouldn't go for it, funding for the stadium wouldn't pass in the Assembly, and I tried to avoid politically exposing myself and my members for a losing cause. Furthermore, we had some polling done that showed 62 percent of New Yorkers were opposed to the stadium, believing that it was a waste of tax dollars and that the congestion would be unbearable. Before I knew it, celebrities were phoning and saying that Manhattan just had to have the Olympics. Then Mike set the labor unions on me. Tens of thousands of jobs were at stake, and the unions are experts at turning up the heat.

Finally, I told Mike, "OK, you bring the Olympics to New York, I'll pass the bill for the stadium."

"That won't work," Bloomberg replied. "The Olympic Committee has to see the venue."

"That's your perception. If those guys want to choose New York, you tell them you have a guarantee from the leaders."

Shelly hadn't altered his opinion, and actually he was plenty nervous. If I went for the stadium with the Olympics as the prize, Shelly would in all likelihood have to hop onboard, for as I frequently reminded him and the governor, "What goes around, comes around, so remember what you're doing now when one of you needs me to do something I don't necessarily want to do."

As I remember it, a member of the Olympic Committee called and reiterated Mike's pitch. I told him that he had to put the cart before the horse: get the deal done, commit to bringing the Olympics to New York, and he'd get a stadium. Then I offered to put my promise in a letter.

No, I was told, get us the horse, the buggy will follow.

I made up my mind during this conversation. When I'd spoken to Herb Kelleher about bringing Southwest to the airport, I had a positive feeling about him and his approach to making decisions. When I said to him, "If we build those gates, will you come?" Herb wouldn't say yes, but the way he answered me I was sure that if we extended ourselves, he'd reward us. I had the opposite reaction talking to the Olympic Committee member. I sensed that he tended to stick his finger in the air to see how the wind was blowing, and he was politically unreliable. And even if we put up the stadium, I'd still have no idea where the Olympics would wind up.

Convinced that the West Side project was neither in the interest of the residents of New York City nor the Senate Republican conference, I sided with Shelly and the stadium wasn't built.

No one was more disappointed by my decision than Woody Johnson, who hoped that his Jets would be playing in Midtown. Woody had lobbied me hard, which I understood, and I didn't care because I enjoyed talking to him and felt bad that he didn't get what he wanted. At the beginning, Woody took the position that he'd only consider returning his team to New York if they could play on the West Side. Then there was talk that maybe a new stadium could go up in Flushing Meadows-Corona Park. I told Woody I could get him $200 million or $300 million to get him started. He said OK—if I could persuade Silver and Bloomberg to agree.

I spoke to Shelly. He was reluctant, but we'd both angered the labor unions by shutting down the other deal, and the unions didn't give a damn about location as long as their members were working.

I phoned Bloomberg. Mike didn't want to do it, claiming that replacing the parkland with a stadium would be a political headache for him. That sounded more like he still had his dander up about not getting what he wanted on the West Side, a type of pettiness that was rare from the mayor.

The cure for it was easy. I said, "Mike, you have a lot of things you want to get done. A stadium in Queens helps us, it helps you, it helps everybody. Work with me, and I'll work with you. You don't work with me, I don't work with you. Life becomes difficult."

Mike agreed, and before I had a chance to discuss the deal with Woody, I read in the papers that he'd reached an understanding with the governor in New Jersey to keep the Jets there.

I got Woody on the line and told him that I'd gotten Shelly and Mike to sign on, and I was disappointed that he'd used my offer as leverage to put together a package across the river.

Woody stunned me with his reply. "You're one of the most despicable people I've ever dealt with in politics. I'll never give you one more cent of support, and I'll never take another one of your calls. I want nothing to do with you."

"I'm sorry to hear that, but I don't think you handled this situation very well."

I hung up and felt terrible. I sincerely liked Woody, and had he come to me and said that he wanted to stay in Jersey that would've been fine. Instead, he let me use up a lot of credibility with Mike and Shelly for no other reason than to cut himself a better deal.

I never spoke to Woody Johnson again.

19

Take Me Out to the Ball Game

Thinking back over my career, I feel blessed by the recognition I received for my work. Nevertheless, as time goes by, it is difficult for me to separate the grander shows of appreciation from the more modest ones. I'd be a liar if I didn't admit to a great sense of satisfaction when a few hundred movers and shakers, Herb Kelleher among them, gathered at Albany International Airport for the unveiling of a bust of my mug, done by *Times Union* political cartoonist Hy Rosen. The bronze sculpture was a thank-you from business leaders, and I'm glad they didn't wait until I was dead. I felt the same way—thrilled to be up on the fun side of the grass— on a Friday evening in June 2002, when the sold-out crowd cheered as I threw out the first pitch at Joseph L. Bruno Stadium.

It's still hard for me to believe that a poor kid from Glens Falls has had the chance to meet every president since Richard Nixon, discuss legislation with Sophia Loren, Martin Sheen, Lauren Bacall, and Sam Waterston, introduce Senator John McCain to an audience of veterans, kick around ideas with Jack Welch and other captains of industry, and sit in the owner's box with George Steinbrenner to watch the World Series. It was in that box that I had one of my greatest thrills, meeting Joe DiMaggio, a hero of mine—and every Italian I knew—for as long as I could remember. DiMaggio was sitting next to me, and I'd been warned that he hated signing autographs, but I did have a program in my hand and we were chatting, and finally I worked up the nerve to say, "You know I was told not to ask, but—" and before I finished my sentenced, DiMaggio smiled at me, took the program, and signed it.

Perhaps the most political being I ever met was Hillary Clinton. As I recall it, shortly after she was elected to the United States Senate, she phoned my office and requested that we have a private meeting. I met with her, and she assured me that the campaigns were over. It was time to govern, she said, and we had work to do for the people who depend on us. It was a pleasant and productive conversation, and she hugged me before leaving.

Then Hillary stepped outside my door, where thirty or forty reporters were waiting. My staff later told me that when she was asked how the meeting had gone, she said fine, but added that she hoped to swing the majority in the New York State Senate to the Democrats.

An hour later, I phoned her on her cell. She answered, and I said, "I'm very puzzled. I thought we had a great meeting, and you go out and talk to the press about replacing Republicans. You told me the campaign was over, and we're going to govern. So which did you mean? When you talked to me or the reporters?"

"Oh Joe," she said. "You know how it is. I'm a Democrat and I made a political speech."

As it turned out, we did work together, and she was always very gracious toward me. I remember seeing her at an event after my wife died, and Hillary broke away from a group and took the time to offer her condolences, a kindness that I've never forgotten.

Without question, the most unforgettable character I ever met was Donald Trump. Not only did he raise substantial campaign funds for Senate Republicans, he was endlessly amusing and, despite his over-the-top personality, a very decent guy.

When I first met him at his apartment, I walked in, shook hands, and before I even sat down, he led me over to the window and said, "See that big building over there? That's mine. See that building? That's mine." When he was done pointing out his collection of high-rises, he began showing me his collection of autographed baseball bats, and I reached an inescapable conclusion: Donald had an ego as big as any of his buildings but he was so affable and charming, it was easy to like him.

I remember we played a lot of golf in Florida at the Mar-a-Lago club, and after taking the time to introduce me to a group of big fundraisers, Donald continued pointing out his ability to cut deals.

"See that clubhouse," he said. "The builder wanted $27 million to put it up. I did it myself for $7 million. See all of those palm trees? I would've had to pay tens of thousands for them. I think I paid twenty-five hundred. I bought them from a company that went bankrupt. And that waterfall. Isn't it a beautiful waterfall? I had that built, and I don't want to tell you how little it cost me because we brought in the rocks from around here."

Despite the display of ego, he was a straight dealer and considerate. I remember one year there was a fundraiser planned at Mar-a-Lago. Donald called and said to me, "I'm in a real bind. I've got an appointment in New York City at eight tomorrow morning that I can't miss. So I can fly down to Florida and introduce you, but then I'd have to fly back that night. You know, it's going to cost me twenty-five thousand to fly down. How about if I just donate the twenty-five to you on top of what we're already doing, and I let my wife introduce you and be the hostess instead of me being there as the host?"

I kidded him, saying I was probably better off with his wife in charge, since everyone liked her, but my point here is that it gave me some insight into how he made deals—the constant search for the win-win compromise.

In all honesty, I feel just as honored when I recall the well-wishers shaking my hand on opening day of the Saratoga racetrack or those little girls in their Brownie uniforms waving to me as I rode past them on my pinto Apache in the Saratoga Flag Day Parade or the phone call I received from the family of an elevator operator at the Capitol after she passed away and heard that the woman had mentioned how much she had appreciated the concern I'd shown for her over the years.

The same holds true with sifting through my accomplishments, because doing anything to improve the lives of people gives me tremendous pleasure. I can't help but smile when I think about how important the five grand was to the Hoosic Valley Stampede youth football and cheerleading program or the $25,000 that went to renovating a VFW post, even though it was peanuts compared to the $10 million I had to get from Governor Pataki's 2001-2002 budget to finish the new train station in Rensselaer. I'd thought we'd secure the funding in 2000 from a multibillion dollar transportation bond act, but the act was rejected by voters. And unlike the airport project, the train station was mired in problems, chiefly misman-agement by the Capital District Transportation Authority, and I had to threaten the CDTA with withholding financing. This fight played out in the media, and in the end, when the station opened in the fall of 2002, I ignored the mess and checked another task off my to-do list.

I suspect, and here I will make a prediction based on my more than thirty years in politics, that nothing I've done will be remembered longer and with more reverence by upstaters than the Joseph L. Bruno Stadium on the campus of Hudson Valley Community College. The stadium is the home field of the Tri-City ValleyCats, a minor league affiliate of the Hous-ton Astros, and baseball is tailor-made for collecting joyful memories of balmy summer evenings spent with friends and family. And The Joe, as it is known locally, is a gem of a ballpark, modern and not so big that it loses that old-fashioned feel, with 4,500 wide, comfortable seats, ten luxury suites, a picnic pavilion, bar and grill, a children's playground, a huge video scoreboard, reasonable ticket prices, and free parking.

Ironically, my reaction when a stadium was proposed for the site wasn't positive. John Buono phoned me. I knew John well. He'd been the Rens-selaer County Executive, and Pataki had appointed him the director of the New York State Dormitory Authority. In 1998, John was named president of Hudson Valley Community College, a position he was proud to accept, because he'd graduated from HVCC before going on to complete under-graduate and graduate degrees. John was an unabashed booster of Hudson Valley, and he told me that his school could use a new stadium. That might be the case, I said, but it was unlikely that I could come up with the $5 million or so to finance it, given the educational needs around the state. Eventually, I'd find millions to pour into Hudson Valley for high-tech edu-cation—more about that later—but for a stadium? No way.

Shortly after that call, I heard from Bill Gladstone, a former co-CEO of Ernst & Young, one of the largest professional services firms in the world. After retiring, Bill, a baseball aficionado, bought a Class A minor league team affiliated with the New York Mets. His agreement with the Mets was finished after the 2000 season, and Bill was searching for another team and venue. Currently, his club played in Wahconah Park in Pittsfield, Massachusetts, and the city refused to replace the 81-year-old stadium.

"I'd like to bring a team to Saratoga," Bill said.

The wheels started turning in my head, and I suggested that maybe we could build him a nice home in Troy.

"How about Saratoga?" he asked.

His mind was made up, so I got in touch with the chamber of commerce in Saratoga. Guess what? They weren't interested. The racetrack and the performing arts center were all they could handle. I delivered the news to Bill.

"So where's this place in Troy?" he asked, and we were off.

In early May 2000, I announced that the state would spend $12 million to put up a minor league baseball stadium on the campus of Hudson Valley, and that Bill Gladstone would bring his team to play there. The college would also use the stadium, and students at HVCC would have opportunities to gain some real-world experience by interacting with the business side of a professional sports team.

Baseball fans in the Capital Region were tickled pink. We had lost the Albany-Colonie Yankees, a minor league club, because before I was majority leader the state Urban Development Corporation hadn't ponied up a couple million bucks to make the improvements to Heritage Park that management wanted, another example of upstate being shortchanged and suffering because of it. The Diamond Dogs, which weren't affiliated with any major league team, had taken over the park from the Yankees, but they were struggling financially, and I heard rumors that they were going to fold.

One baseball fan who was less than enthusiastic was Mayor Jerry Jennings of Albany. A month after my announcement he claimed that a group from New York City was ready to buy a Class AA team, which was a step closer to the majors than Class A, and build them a stadium in Albany.

Jerry had talked to me about it and, I guess because my parents couldn't afford a nickel pony ride for their kids, the first question I asked myself was how much it would cost a family of four to take in a game. When I found out that tickets for Double A could go for twenty a pop, I added in the price of hamburgers, hot dogs, and sodas, and a beer for mom and dad, and I concluded that it would be too expensive an outing for a lot of families. Class A tickets went for five or six bucks, and I liked the sound of that, and I told Jerry that I wasn't interested.

Jerry continued talking about it in public. I had no idea if he had a group lined up, but I did know that the minor leagues prohibited two teams with major league affiliations to dip into the same fan base, so his plan was going nowhere. When reporters asked me for a response to Jerry, I replied that I had a done deal, and everything else was pie in the sky.

In March, three months before the baseball season began, the trustees of Hudson Valley Community College voted to name the stadium after me, an honor that choked me up and still does whenever I attend a game. The final price tag was about $14 million, and it was money well spent. John Buono and the kids at HVCC got a new stadium, complete with an exercise-physiology lab that can be used by students. And the Capital Region got a professional baseball team that year after year keeps breaking its own attendance records.

20

FUTURE GAINED

Not long ago, a journalist asked me if, while I was in the Senate, I'd had a master plan. That was flattering, as if I were a soothsayer, but it was more accurate to say that I had a bottom line—a pair of questions that I continually asked myself. If the state was going to allocate tax dollars to an undertaking, how would that expenditure create a job? Or how would it enhance the quality of life for people?

I knew that for the first time since New York State had started keeping records, we had gone under fifty thousand smokestack jobs. Environmental constraints prohibited us from competing with countries like China and Mexico, so where did that leave us? My staff and I consulted with experts. Our basic question never changed—how do we stop losing jobs? Our best bet, we were informed, was more scientific research, which could be tied to the surrounding universities and colleges, and high tech, which was neat and clean.

Getting $5 million to help the University at Albany Foundation to buy the Sterling-Winthrop site with an eye toward creating a medical park was a no-brainer. Less obvious was what to make of a meeting I had with Dr. Alain Kaloyeros, a physics professor from the University at Albany. I had some friends and neighbors who knew him, and I brought Kaloyeros in at their recommendation. He was seeking a $15 million investment for nanotechnology, which he said was the future of high tech. Listening to him was compelling, though what he was talking about was mind-boggling. Everything would be more powerful and smaller—the smaller, the better. The state university could become a world-renowned center for this research, and his ultimate goal was to see the Capital Region become another Silicon Valley.

Since my days in the intercom business, I'd been intrigued by technology. Even so, my experience selling a newfangled alarm system that had, for no detectable reason, started going off in the middle of the night and startled half the population of Glens Falls, had taught me to be wary of grand claims about technological advances. Kaloyeros was obviously a brilliant guy, and I'd soon discover that he had keen political gifts, an instinct for who could actually help him and the ability to make that person feel as though the success or failure of a project hung on his decision, and his decision alone.

I suspected that his assertion that we could replicate the success of Silicon Valley was designed for me, because my dedication to improving the upstate economy was a matter of record. I don't begrudge a salesman for tailoring his pitch, but I was skeptical. Yet if I'd learned anything in this life it's that you've got to take a first step to reach the end of the journey. Later, my friend, John Nigro, would kid me that I supported nanotechnology before I could spell it. John wasn't wrong. I just took a leap of faith and signed on for the file.

Before I even had a chance to talk with Shelly, Kaloyeros paid him a visit and impressed me with his savvy. He was seeking $15 million, and he shrewdly asked me for five, the speaker for five, and planned to ask Pataki for five. By doing this, Kaloyeros allowed each of the three men in the room to believe that he was crucial to realizing his vision.

Later on, Shelly claimed that he had climbed aboard before I did. That was revisionist history, but the speaker wasn't far behind me. The challenge, it turned out, was the governor.

No one should underestimate the role that George Pataki played in bringing high tech to upstate New York. He cut a deal with IBM to keep that venerable corporation in the state and championed the cause of bringing technology companies to the Capital Region, understanding that if people lost their jobs due to budget cuts and there was no employment for them, they'd leave, and the exodus of talent would make a bad situation worse, depleting both our labor pool and tax base.

Nonetheless, at the outset, when I spoke to him about funding Kaloye-ros, he was hesitant.

"I met with my staff," he said. "And it was unanimous—everybody thought it was unrealistic to invest in technology. That we're not going to be Silicon Valley East."

I waited a couple of days and called him again. "I've gotta get this off my desk. Let's do something constructive. Shelly's on it, I'm on it. And we need your $5 million."

"If you and Shelly want to do it, use your own money."

The following afternoon, I made another try. "You gonna come up with the five? It's the right thing to do."

"No, I'm not."

"Why not?"

"I told you. My staff doesn't think it's real. Not one of them. And we're not going to waste the money."

We had two or three more conversations. There is a fine line between persistence and being a nuisance, and by now I had crossed it, and Pataki was getting annoyed with me, especially when I asked him whether he or his staff were running the state and suggested that a lot of funding he'd approve would be for stuff that wound up in the shithouse. Still, he kept taking my calls and was very congenial, and I continued pestering him without mercy.

"Joe," he said. "Forget this thing. I'm not doing it."

"Well, I'll forget it. But when you need me to buy into something that I don't fully agree with you on, I'm gonna say, 'I can't. My staff's against it.'"

The next afternoon, Pataki called me. "Maybe it's not so crazy," he said. "It's only $5 million. The budget's what? Sixty-five, sixty-six billion?"

So, contrary to the urging of his advisers, he did it, and this slice of the story has an ending that shows how generous George Pataki could be.

In June 1997, the Center for Environmental Sciences and Technology Management opened up on Fuller Road and Washington Avenue across from the main campus of the University at Albany. This 70,000-square-foot white, glass-sided structure resembled an ocean liner capable of sailing through outer space.

Before the ribbon cutting, I went to the mansion with some of my staff for a celebratory lunch with the governor and his people. We were eating hamburgers and kidding around while Pataki reviewed his remarks for the ceremony.

I grinned at the governor. "What a great occasion, huh?"

"It sure is."

"Do you remember the game that went on over this?"

"I do. I didn't want to do it. My staff didn't want to do it. We were wrong and you were right. No question about it."

That admission was rare in politics, and the truth is once he got behind high tech he was a remarkable leader. "Thank you for saying that." I paused, then added, "I'm betting that's not in your speech," and everyone at the table broke up laughing.

At the end of that year, we pledged another $35 million for jump-starting semiconductor manufacturing and research at the University at Albany and Rensselaer Polytechnic Institute. Our long-term goal was to bring a plant here to make semiconductors, which could net us $2 billion in additional investment.

By then, because of numerous discussions I'd had with John Kelly, a senior vice president at IBM and an expert in microelectronics, I was convinced that this was the wave of the future. IBM was considering a chip-fab facility in East Fishkill, and I believed it was possible to build one here as well. I respected John Kelly: he was an IBMer from head to toe, but he was objective. Whatever we were discussing generally concluded with my asking John the same question: "Would this funding increase our ability to attract high tech companies?" John understood the potential of the Capital Region, having earned his undergraduate degree from Union College and his doctorate from RPI, and when he assured me that we were on the right track, I believed him.

My father had passed away in 1982 at the age of eighty-six. Vitaliano Bruno had lived an exemplary life, raising eight kids by himself after his wife died. He did remarry, though his new wife eventually went to live in Italy while he remained in Glens Falls. His children made certain that he wanted for nothing, which isn't as noble as it sounds because he rarely asked for anything. To honor him, every Father's Day since his death, we visited his grave at St. Mary's Cemetery.

Following one of these visits I recalled the morning that I'd gone with Pa to the factory where he worked. He'd been there for decades, and he showed me how he no longer had to shovel coal into a furnace, a blessing because the glowing coal flakes didn't burn and pockmark his face. Instead, he had to operate the heating system via a series of gauges and levers, and someone had to draw him a diagram so he could manage it. I felt bad for Pa, watching his struggle, and to make matters worse the equipment had instructions and warnings written on it, and Pa couldn't read. This accounted for the company encouraging him to retire.

Now, as the state began investing heavily in technology and the area was being referred to as "Tech Valley," I remembered Pa. When most people think of high tech, they imagine rich brainiacs, visionary entrepreneurs, and software and hardware engineers. However, the companies that we hoped would come would require technical workers—the blue-collar men and women of the future, if you will. Muscle wouldn't be of any use to them. Training, that was the key to a decent-paying career.

Furthermore, workforce development, I was told, would be instrumental in bringing a semiconductor facility to the area, so I decided to adopt Hudson Valley Community College. I liked that the overwhelming majority of its students came from the Capital Region, and while half of HVCC's graduates entered four-years schools after completing their associate degrees, the other half went to work, and I figured they'd stay if there were jobs in Tech Valley. It bothered me that the first-rate education offered by the SUNY system didn't fully benefit the taxpayers who funded it. You could find our graduates flourishing across the United States. I understood that young people moved away for lots of reasons, yet it was galling that many of them left because they couldn't get employment. Bottom line— New Yorkers were footing the bill for states that didn't dedicate the same extraordinary resources to higher education.

Gradually, I began directing funds to HVCC, sometimes in dribs and drabs, other times sizable appropriations. By 2005, the community college was training students for jobs in semiconductors and nanotechnology, and five years later, with $13.5 million in funding, HVCC opened a Training and Education Center for Semiconductor Manufacturing and Alternative and Renewable Technologies in Malta.

I didn't know how this would play out, yet of one thing I was certain. Unlike my father, these young men and women would retire with more than a ten-dollar-a-week pension.

I wouldn't want to leave the impression that my days were swallowed up by my obsession with attracting companies to Tech Valley. To be an effective majority leader, you have to keep your hand in every game, and those games are often political. I did my share of battling with the governor, though none of it was personal. I'm not sure his communications director, Zenia Mucha, saw it that way in the late winter of 1999, when I praised Rudolph Giuliani during a dinner at the Rensselaer County Regional Chamber of Commerce. I stated that Rudy had done great things in the city, and if he decided to take a run at the U.S. Senate, I'd back him.[1]

Rudy had endorsed Mario Cuomo and not his fellow Republican, George Pataki, in the 1992 governor's race. I had publicly criticized Rudy for his "betrayal," a bit of pro forma politicking. I was philosophically opposed to holding grudges, not seeing see how that benefitted New Yorkers or me. Apparently, Zenia didn't buy into my anti-grudge philosophy, and she cornered me at a fundraiser soon after the chamber of commerce dinner and read me the riot act for cozying up to Rudy. In her mind, I suppose, Zenia was protecting her boss by preventing another Republican—yours truly—from overshadowing the governor. I wasn't aiming to do that: Rudy was very popular and, if he ran, would bring out Republicans in droves. I wasn't worried about me; my district was secure. But increased turnout would benefit the members of my conference in tight races.

Zenia was in fine form, and I wouldn't have been surprised if she'd tried to bite me. Not wanting to offend her by acting as though I didn't take her seriously, I fenced with her for a while, then returned to circulating through the crowd. Andrea Bernstein, a reporter from the *New York Observer*, questioned me about the interchange, suggesting that Zenia and I were fighting. I considered that type of gossip more appropriate for *Entertainment Tonight*, and I said that she shouldn't confuse Zenia's zest for politics with anger.[2]

Truthfully, I thought, Zenia was shortsighted when it came to forging alliances, and to some extent her views had an impact on the governor. Both of them had been upset with me when I began getting close to Dennis Rivera, president of 1199/S.E.I.U., a union with more than 200,000 members, millions of campaign dollars to hand out, and the ability to put thousands of volunteers into neighborhoods to get out the vote on Election Day.

I had argued that Republicans could become allies of labor if they could find common ground, and in my estimation health-care workers were woefully underpaid and deserved our assistance. In January 2002, we put together a package of $1.8 billion in raises for members of the union, and two months later they endorsed Pataki's reelection, an endorsement that stunned the Democratic contenders for the governorship, former HUD Secretary Andrew Cuomo and State Comptroller H. Carl McCall.[3]

It was in my interest for Pataki to win reelection, and he won easily. Still, during his third term, we frequently clashed. I saw this as a natural state of affairs if the leader and speaker functioned as the State constitution intended. All the same, I liked George immensely: he was smart and reflective and funny (and today he remains a good friend.) We disagreed face-to-face, refusing to backstab each other in the media, and he didn't hesitate to defend me if I was unfairly attacked.

I remember a late-night meeting at his office in June 2003. We were discussing the Rockefeller drug laws with their draconian mandatory sentences. Something had to be done. My staff had passed on a number of stories to me like the one about a poor mother who'd been locked up for fifteen or sixteen years for a single drug arrest. That was bullshit, and expensive, taxpayer-funded bullshit at that, to say nothing of how the woman's family must have suffered. The sticking points were whether district attorneys or judges would shape sentencing and what we'd do about violent drug dealers and those who recruited children. The governor was there with

Shelly and me, and Russell Simmons, a hip-hop mogul who had been lead-ing a campaign to change the laws. Simmons had arrived in Albany with an entourage and a woman—his wife or his girlfriend, I can't recall.

The way I understood Simmons, he wanted every nonviolent drug offender to be released, and for the state to offer new offenders treatment in lieu of punishment. I wasn't against treating drug users, but politically the course Simmons was advocating was a heavy lift, since it amounted to decriminalizing hard drugs, and my conference—and a large segment of the state—wouldn't go for it.

Somewhere after midnight, while I was wondering why this get-together had dragged on for hours, I explained that to the mogul. Evidently, Simmons was dissatisfied with my explanation, because he snapped at me, "Just do it."

My patience was almost gone, and hearing a tagline from a sneaker commercial didn't replenish it. "Look," I said angrily. "Changing laws doesn't work that way."

Simmons jumped up and suggested that we step outside to finish our conversation. I was in the mood for him to take a swing at me, and the governor must have read that on my face, because he stared at Simmons and said, "You better find out who you're talking to before you get hurt."

We didn't reach an agreement that night, and the next morning I received a phone call from the woman who had accompanied Simmons. She apologized for his behavior and sent flowers to my office.

That was thoughtful. Better yet, before the year was out, the Legislature voted to reduce some of the mandatary sentences.

During George Pataki's third term it felt as if we never stopped battling over the budget. The governor and I were intent on controlling spending and we knew that there was no way of doing so without some New Yorkers losing their jobs or funding for their communities. The difference between us was that the constituents in my district—and the districts of my con-ference members—were only willing to endure so much pain. Pataki had a statewide view and wasn't as distracted by the ground-level disruptions that the cuts caused. That was fine for the governor, but not for the Senate majority leader if he hoped to continue to be the leader and not lose the majority to the Democrats.

I never wanted any position other than leader, which was essential in light of my economic goals for the Capital Region. Pataki, I believed, was contemplating a future outside the state. He was very involved in President George W. Bush's reelection campaign, traveling the country, raising money, and getting to know the major players in national Republican circles. I doubted that he'd seek a fourth term as governor and figured he was wondering if, someday, he'd have a shot at the White House. This also explained his insistence on slashing the budget, which would burnish his conservative credentials. He'd need to put a real spit shine on his résumé, because he was pro-choice, and that would hurt him in the presidential primaries.

In 2003, New York was facing a massive deficit of some $11 billion. Pataki wanted to cut education and health care, and borrow. Shelly and I agreed with the borrowing, but given the bind the state was in we wanted to levy a temporary, income-tax surcharge on high earners so we could still offer help to communities. I realized this reversed the earlier gains we'd made cutting overall rates, but I didn't see that I had a choice, either economically or politically. The governor stuck to his guns, and the Assembly and Senate wound up overriding 120 of his vetoes.[4] One of my staff mentioned that that this hadn't been done in more than two decades, ever since Hugh Carey was governor, and it was small potatoes compared to three years later, when, in what must be a world record, the Legislature overrode 207 vetoes.[5]

In 2006, our proposed spending was some $113 billion, an eight or nine percent jump, not an increase that thrilled me. The governor, who wasn't running again, felt free to take a meat cleaver to the budget. I felt no such freedom. Half of my conference was going to be on the ballot, and for me to hang onto the majority I had to override his vetoes. At best, this was a compromise, and I understood why some conservatives attacked my decision to restore funding for property-tax relief, hospitals, nursing homes, and urban rebuilding. However, ever since becoming leader I had decided to play long ball, believing that I could help to reinvigorate the upstate economy. The trouble with long ball was that my majority was up for grabs every two years. That meant I had to focus on the future while doing what was politically expedient in the present. For instance, that was why I'd fought the governor when he vetoed raising the minimum wage. Fact is, I could have taken either side of that argument in a debate, but given the political atmosphere I wanted to be on the side of the angels on Election Day. And it worked—the Republicans held their majority in the Senate. And everything came up roses again in 2006. After nine long years of effort, the budget contained $1 billion in cash and tax incentives to help Advanced Micro Devices build a computer-chip fabrication plant in the Capital Region.

Not too long after becoming leader, I got a quarter of a million dollars of seed money for the Center for Economic Growth. Their representatives used the funding to travel around the country and to Germany to learn about chip fabs and to drum up interest in putting one of them here. Meanwhile, in 1997, the state had established a program to locate and pre-permit potential sites for a plant, so if a company wanted to build, it wouldn't face the daunting task of going through the local zoning and other related headaches. Albany, Rensselaer, Saratoga, and Schenectady counties were being mentioned as possible sites, and by the winter of 1998, I thought we had a shot to build a chip fab in North Greenbush, where Rensselaer Polytechnic Institute had its technology park.

I supported the idea, and the pre-approval process began. It didn't hurt that RPI's park was in my district, but Rensselaer County was in need of an economic boost. Bill Leitch, my deputy director of district operations, was keeping track of the progress, and right away he saw trouble. Environmentalists—Bill told me a bunch of them were from out of state—started scaring the residents of North Greenbush. They did this by focusing on the cleanroom suits, the so-called, "bunny suits," the white coveralls, caps, and boots that people wear in the rooms where computer chips are produced. They distributed fliers in the community that showed people in bunny suits with big skulls and crossbones next to them, as if the suits were worn to protect technicians from the chips when the reverse was true—the chips had to be protected from the skin and hair of people.

Our response was to gather the business leaders of the community and the presidents of hospitals and colleges, and have a big public meeting to rebut the false claims and spell out the benefits of a plant. That was a no-go. The town board voted to halt the pre-approval process.

I was annoyed, which made me even more determined, and at the annual meeting of the Center for Economic Growth I assured the audience that I was going to make sure that if a chip fab was built in the United States, the Capital Region would be first in line.[6]

Now, as I reflect on that time, I see how organizing my thoughts into words distorts an eight-year process by compressing it and making it seem as though GlobalFoundries arrived here in the blink of an eye. The truth is that along the way there were fits and stops, but my desire to bring a chip fab to the area buzzed around my head like a fly that wouldn't go away. Whatever I was doing—and my schedule was filled from morning until night—I kept thinking about it, pushing my staff to somehow get to the next step. The New York State Energy Research and Development Authority owned close to 300 acres in Malta, and there was plenty of housing available nearby in Luther Forest. I encouraged the town board to rezone the acreage for light industry, and in December 1999 they did just that. Less than a year later, we offered $500 million in state assistance so IBM could build a $2.5 billion chip fab in East Fishkill, believing that would spur growth upstate, and by the following summer, Big Blue was announcing plans to invest $100 million in Albany NanoTech.[7]

Still, I wanted a plant in the Capital Region, and toward the end of May 2002, I got the Saratoga Economic Development Corporation, the owners of the Luther Forest Technology Campus, a $1.4 million grant to pay for the permitting process. This was the beginning of tens of millions of dollars in grants and loans I directed to SEDC over the next three years to make the site shovel-ready and to buy additional property. By the summer of 2002, IBM's chip fab opened in East Fishkill, so I knew it was possible to build one of these behemoths in New York, and now all I had to do was bring one a hundred miles north.

Let's jump ahead to 2005. By then, representatives from the Center of Economic Growth had been talking to Intel and Advanced Micro Devices. Intel's attitude was that if we were talking to AMD, they wouldn't talk to us. My response was, "Fine, then I'm not going to talk to you." There was bad blood between the companies, and in June, AMD sued Intel for allegedly offering PC manufacturers in Japan cash rewards for scaling back on their orders of AMD processors.[8] Charlie Gargano, chairman of the Empire State Development Corporation, and some of his people had broached the subject of building a chip fab in Luther Forest with Samsung. In September, the governor led a trade mission to China and Japan, and Charlie went with him.

Before Pataki left I suggested that he add South Korea to his itinerary and talk to some of the Samsung principals at their headquarters in Seoul. My recollection is that either my staff or someone at the Center for Economic Growth set up an appointment for him. I spoke to the governor shortly after he landed in Albany, and he told me that he didn't stop in South Korea.

"It didn't make any difference," he said. "We were late. We were sidelined."

I was ticked off. I'd been a salesman most of my life, and I knew nothing could be more crucial than an important government official or executive going out of his way to meet someone for a face-to-face on their home turf. It was both a sign of respect and an indication of seriousness.

By October, when Samsung announced that it had decided to build a chip fab in Austin, Texas, I was talking regularly on the phone with Hector Ruiz, the CEO of AMD. The governor's office wasn't involved. I wanted to keep this a one-on-one relationship, like I'd had with Herb Kelleher when I was trying to persuade him to bring Southwest to Albany. I invited Hector to send a team up to inspect the Capital Region. I met with them personally and wined and dined them. They had a list of criteria the area had to meet, and I recall showing them public and private schools, the University at Albany, RPI and Hudson Valley Community College, and taking them on a tour of Albany Med, where they spoke to a few people about the new pediatric unit I'd helped to fund. Proudly, I showed the team the train station and airport and the Palace Theater and the Saratoga Performing Arts

Center. As we drove toward Luther Forest, the team leader asked me if there would be enough housing for the chip fab's employees, and I crossed my fingers and replied, "You come and they will build."

To pursue research in nanotechnology, we needed a $100 million super-computer that could do 70 trillion calculations per second. I couldn't even comprehend that number, but I didn't have to. John Kelly at IBM assured me that the supercomputer would help us bring a computer-chip fabrication plant here, so all I had to do was cobble together a partnership with IBM, the state and Rensselaer Polytechnic Institute, and secure funding for what Shirley Ann Jackson, president of RPI, said would be the fastest computer on any college campus in the world. Once we got that locked down, I returned to a debate I'd been having with Shelly Silver.

Shelly thought a chip fab was swell. He just didn't think it should be in Luther Forest, which happened to be in my district.

"Where should it be Shelly?" I asked.

"I'm thinking Utica."

"RoAnn's district?" RoAnn Destito, a long-time Democratic Assem-blywoman, was a rabid ally of the speaker, and it was understandable that Shelly would want to reward her.

"You have a senator there," Shelly said.

I did, and Ray Meier was top-shelf, a bulldog on veterans' issues, property-tax relief, and Medicaid reform.

Shelly asked, "What's wrong with putting the chip fab in Utica?"

Philosophically speaking, not a thing. The city of Utica, an hour and a half west of Albany, had been suffering economically since the 1960s, losing 40 percent of its population and now had more than a quarter of its residents living below the poverty line. Utica could've used the economic jolt, and the SUNY Institute of Technology was nearby in Marcy. All the same, even had I wanted the facility in Utica, which I most assuredly did not, I doubted that we could persuade AMD, accustomed to operating out of upscale communities in California and Texas, to go there.

I expressed my view to Shelly, who replied, "No plant in your district."

I was tempted to propose that he plant a kiss on my ass, and I may have done that in so many words during a tug of war over the location. Then I figured my smartest move was to quit banging my head against the wall and to get in touch with Hector Ruiz and fill him in. Hector sent a team to Utica to scout for a site. The team reported back that the area was a distant second to the Capital Region and, if that was the location the state was offering, AMD would choose to expand their existing operations in Dresden, Germany.[9]

I trumpeted that news to the media. Whether AMD had adopted its stance as a ploy was impossible to know, but the company had dealt me a heck of a hand to play against Shelly. If New York State missed out on joining the major leagues of high tech—and the increase in jobs and tax revenue that went with it—the voters could thank the speaker. In pursuit of his agenda, Shelly was willing to take a jab or two, a black eye and a swollen lip, though I doubted he'd want the public thrashing that I, the governor, the chambers of commerce, and upstate business executives would give him—and the Democrats in the Assembly—if the AMD deal collapsed.

I don't know what convinced Hector Ruiz to build in Luther Forest—if I had to guess, it would be the financial commitment the state was willing to make to technology in general and to AMD in particular, and that his site team came away believing that the Capital Region offered all the amenities that employees would want.

In my memory, at least, it was a warm blue May afternoon, and I was scheduled to be the keynote speaker at the New York State Investors Conference at the Marriott on Wolf Road. I'd gotten out of the car and was crossing the parking lot when Hector called to tell me that AMD had decided to build a chip fab in Luther Forest. He wanted to speak to the governor, to make sure that he was onboard, and I told Hector that Pataki would be in touch. I got the governor on the phone and told him what was going on, and then he hung up and called Hector.

That should've been the moment to break out the champagne, but the governor, Shelly, and I were warring over the budget. Shelly had stopped fighting me over where to stick the chip fab, but he was performing his turtle routine, tucking his head into his shell and refusing to sign off on the

$1.2 billion package we'd discussed for AMD—$650 million in grants for construction, equipment, and research and development. The remainder of the funding—from the feds, the state, and localities—included tax incentives and improvements to the roads and utilities around the site.

AMD had hired an Albany lobbyist, Harold Iselin, and Harold started phoning me in the evenings at home to ask if the Legislature would approve the package. I didn't have an answer for him, nor did I know if I'd ever get one. Shelly told me he wasn't going near it, and by Thursday, June 23, as the session was breaking up, I started worrying that Shelly was serious.

I remember glancing at a shelf that held an award I'd been given by Nassau County, a bust of one of my heroes, Ronald Reagan, and glancing out my office window and seeing that it was dark. I'd been so busy in meetings to close down the budget that I'd lost track of the time. I checked my watch and saw it was past eleven. Figuring that I'd better do something, I got Pataki on the line and asked him to intercede with Shelly. His response, I assumed, was the result of twelve years-worth of headaches fighting the speaker's passive-aggressiveness.

Pataki replied, "Shelly's a miserable son of a bitch, and I'm done talking with him."

Then I phoned Shelly and suggested that he speak to the governor. "No," he said, and hung up.

There I was, wondering what my options were given that two of the men in the room weren't speaking to each other. Amy Leitch, my executive assistant, came into my office. Her husband, Bill Leitch, had been overseeing our AMD effort, and Amy said that Bill had called and needed to see me immediately. Bill had an office across the street at 90 South Swan, and I assumed, at this late hour, he was probably somewhere in the Capitol. He was, as it turned out, and he wanted to bring AMD's lobbyist over to deliver a message.

"Fine," I said, and prepared myself for some bad news, because Amy, normally cool and calm under fire, had a hint of panic in her voice.

Bill brought Harold into my office, and Amy sat on the couch, ready to take notes.

Bill said, "Senator, you better hear this."

Harold told me that Hector Ruiz had a plane ready in Austin, Texas, but he had no intention of flying to Albany until the deal was official, and if the Legislature didn't stop dillydallying, AMD would take its plant elsewhere. Harold had been instructed by Ruiz to call in twenty minutes to give him my answer. As a rule, I wouldn't let a lobbyist stay in my office while I was finalizing a budget, but the clock was running out, and I wanted Harold to hear our discussion, since I knew he'd report back to Hector.

I phoned Pataki and relayed the information. He still didn't want to talk to Shelly, so I asked him to hang on, put him on hold, and got Shelly on the other line. Then I hit the conference-call button, and said something on the order of, "Shelly meet George Pataki, Governor meet Shelly Silver. We have an important matter to discuss."

I was trying to keep it light, but the speaker and the governor reacted with a spate of grunts and grumbles, and neither one would talk directly to the other. Tired of screwing around, I said, "Spit it out, Shelly. What do you want?"

Shelly was silent.

As if he were talking to no one in particular, Pataki said, "This chip fab is important as hell. It's the only one being built in the country."

"Joe," Shelly said. "Resurrect New York."

That was a worthwhile program we'd never been able to fund. The money would be used to return properties to the tax rolls by renovating substandard buildings, or tearing them down if they were beyond fixing, or cleaning up rubble-strewn lots and preparing them for new construction.

"How much?" I asked.

"Five hundred million."

"Can you get real now?"

"Joe, it's a great program."

"A great, great program. But $500 million is too much. It'll never happen."

"Three hundred million."

I said, "How about it, Governor. Are you OK with $300 million?"

"You get the plant, Joe," Pataki replied, "Shelly gets his program. Where does that leave me?"

My parents, Rachel Catherine
and Vitaliano Bruno.

*The boxing tournament was a big deal among
the soldiers because we were in the 25th Division,
which had been partially formed from the
division in the huge bestseller, From Here to
Eternity, and one of novel's main characters,
Private Robert E. Lee Prewitt, was a boxer.
And I thought: This is a good opportunity to get
a break from digging up the dead. In the end,
I became the division light heavyweight
champion. South Korea, 1953.*

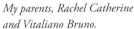

With my friend, Horace Jackson. South Korea, 1953.

With my wife Barbara. We were married on March 25, 1950, in the rectory of Saint Mary's Church in Glens Falls.

State senate hopeful Joe Bruno [second from right] brought his campaign to East Greenbush last week, here visiting residents [from left] Peter Loirumento and George Anderson. With Mr. Bruno is Anthony Carpinello, his local coordinator. [Photo by David

My first campaign for the Senate during the fall of 1976.

In the Senate chamber. I loved every minute of it, no matter how frustrating.

On Apache in the Saratoga Flag Day Parade.

Nothing made me happier than breaking ground on a new project.

Bringing in a new airline was crucial to upgrading the Albany County Airport. Southwest Airlines came in May of 2000, and by August, according to the Times Union, 161,000 people boarded flights at the airport, "an all-time high."

Downtown Manhattan, post-9/11. The worst sight of my life. Left to right: Governor George E. Pataki, President George W. Bush, Senator Joseph L. Bruno, and Mayor Rudy Giuliani.

(Inset) *What a thrill. Throwing out the first pitch at the Joseph L. Bruno Stadium.* (Left) *That first pitch was so much fun, I try to do it every year!*

Even before I was elected to the Senate, I was determined that the Capital Region would have an upgraded airport and a train station. In 2002, the new rail station opened in Rensselaer.

(Above) *Press conference. I look a lot happier than I was. Left to right:* Silver, *Senator Joseph L. Bruno, and Governor Eliot Spitzer.*

(Left) *Wedged between Governor Eliot Spitzer, the self-described "Steamroller," and Attorney General Andrew Cuomo. If I think about that time long enough, my blood pressure still goes up.*

Illustration: John Corbitt, DuetStudio.com

With Donald Trump, one of my biggest supporters and always willing to raise money for Senate Republicans.

(Right) *One of the best decisions of my career, providing seed money to bring nanotechnology to the University at Albany.* (Below) *Toward the end of May 2002, I got the Saratoga Economic Development Corporation, the owners of the Luther Forest Technology Campus, a $1.4 million grant to pay for the permitting process, and this was the beginning of bringing Advanced Micro Devices and a computer-chip fabrication plant to the Capital Region.*

My mantra. And I believe it! Always have, always will.

In June 2008, I said good-bye to the Senate. Governor David Paterson gave a speech about me and my tenure. I was invited to speak, and the Senate stood and gave me an ovation for four or five minutes. When it ended, I was so emotional I could hardly get the words out. Almost fourteen years gone in the blink of an eye.

(Above) Talking to the press during my first trial on the steps of James T. Foley United States Courthouse in Albany. (Below) With my lawyer, E. Stewart Jones, after being acquitted at my second trial.

Same day, with my son, Ken. I am one happy man.

Kay Stafford and I walking to Jack's Oyster House for lunch. People stopped me on the street to shake my hand and wish me well, and after a bus driver waved to me and I waved back to him, I had to stop and wipe the tears out of my eyes.

Before I could answer him, Shelly, to his credit, decided the moment had come to behave like a responsible, straight-thinking leader. "Governor, you can pick where the money is spent. Joe and I will sign on to whatever you decide."

And that was the closer.

The lobbyist ran for the phone as if his tail was on fire, and the next afternoon, as the package moved through the Senate and the Assembly, Hector flew in. I picked him up at the airport and we went to the University at Albany's nanotech research and development facility and announced that, with the assistance of the biggest corporate investment New York State had ever made, AMD would build a $3.2 billion chip-fab plant at the Luther Forest Technology Campus in Saratoga County.

In the midst of the hoopla, nobody mentioned that our approval of the package didn't bind AMD, and the company retained the option to walk away. AMD was facing some severe financial challenges, and privately, Hector had told me that he was talking to investors in Abu Dhabi, and he thought that they would bankroll the plant, but nothing was signed and sealed.

From bitter experience I knew that a deal wasn't done until all of it was done. Had AMD been ready to go, I would've announced my retirement then and there. I was 77 years old, exhausted from the budget fight, and anxious to devote my energy to business. Yet to leave before I was sure that the chip fab would be built in Luther Forest was to risk losing one of the greatest economic achievements of my career. If problems came up, who would ensure that the plant opened upstate? Odds were I'd be replaced as leader by a downstate senator, and he wouldn't share my commitment to the Capital Region.

My life would've been far easier had I stood up in the middle of the news conference and belted out a chorus of "So long, It's Been Good to Know You!"

But I didn't. I buried my worries a hundred miles deep, smiled for the cameras, gave some quotes to the reporters, reveled in the notion that one day our area might rival Silicon Valley, and once again appreciated the wisdom of Ronald Reagan, who observed that he didn't know how anyone could serve in public office without being an actor.

21

BOY WONDER

I first became aware of Eliot Spitzer in 1994 when he was in his early thirties and entered the Democratic primary for attorney general. He had an undergraduate degree from Princeton and a law degree from Harvard, and from what I could tell from reading the newspapers, he appeared to be immersed in the details of the issues. His father Bernard was a real estate developer who, among other properties, owned the luxurious apartment building where his son's family lived, and whose fortune would one day be pegged in the neighborhood of $500 million. During primary season, Spitzer managed to pick up the endorsement of some New York City papers, but neither the blessings of editorial boards nor his dad's money could carry the day, and he finished last in a field of four.

In 1998, Spitzer tried again. Although his opponents accused him of trying to buy the primary, he won, and proceeded to put the Spitzer fortune to good use in the general election. He lambasted his opponent, the Republican incumbent Dennis Vacco, a lawyer from Buffalo whom I had helped with both of his runs for attorney general. In speeches and interviews, Spitzer accused Dennis of ignoring the political cesspool in Albany. Spitzer reveled in challenging his opponents' ethical standing, though he himself got caught in a deception about his campaign finances. He had claimed that he had paid for his 1994 campaign with his own money, but finally, with reporters hot on the story, admitted that it had been his father who had supplied the funds. That was a problem because while a candidate is free to spend as much of his own money as he wants, there were legal limits on the kind of assistance Bernie had doled out to his son.[1]

This revelation hurt Spitzer, but he squeaked by Dennis. As the Senate majority leader, I kept tabs on what the attorney general was doing, primarily Spitzer's assault on the finance industry, and on occasion I gave him a call to share my concerns. Earlier in his career, Spitzer had worked for the Manhattan District Attorney and successfully pursued members of the Gambino crime family, and I had the feeling, once he was elected attorney general and I heard about his slash-and-burn exploits, that he considered all the Wall Streeters he was chasing to be no more than mobsters with fountain pens.

When we talked I acknowledged that some wheeler-dealers deserved whatever he could do to them. But I was concerned about the media the AG was garnering, because it added to the perception—the reality, as far as I was concerned—that New York State was hostile to business. Would it be possible, I asked, to go after the abusers without so much noise?

His answer was noncommittal but, from his overblown statements to reporters, lowering the volume wasn't on his agenda. I had the sense that he relished, perhaps a little too much, being referred to as "the Sheriff of Wall Street."

Still, our relations on the phone were collegial. He easily won reelection in 2002, and in December, two years later, he announced his intention to run for governor, stating that he intended to clean up Albany. As if to underscore his rhetoric, shortly after he made his announcement, State Comptroller Alan Hevesi resigned for using a state employee to chauffeur his wife—and later went to prison for a pay-to-play scheme he concocted with some characters who wanted to handle a piece of the state pension fund.[2]

Throughout his gubernatorial campaign, Spitzer teed off on Albany, which even though I was a visible target of his criticism, didn't bother me for I had come to believe what has been said by a number of people that government in New York is systemically dysfunctional.

Unlike the critics, though, my criticism doesn't just take in the legalized shenanigans in the Assembly and Senate, but extends to city and town governments and school districts across the state, where conflicts of interests are so common that the watchdogs rarely bark at them anymore. In my view, all of this is part of the greater American dysfunction—the notion that everybody has to look out for number one while the idea of the common good is something you vaguely recall being mentioned in some class in college.

Throughout my years in the Senate, it frustrated me. I'd bit my tongue so often negotiating in my office and in the chamber that it was a miracle I could still talk. Yet I'm in no position to point fingers. I was a major feature of this dysfunction, though hardly its poster boy despite the charges that the feds would bring against me. As I saw it, my job was to be pragmatic and function as best I could in light of that dysfunction and perhaps to change some of it if I got the chance.

And during the campaign, as Spitzer and I spoke on the phone, I figured that my chance might be coming—proof that no matter how much experience you have you can always be the victim of idealism.

"We're going to get along fine," he said. "We're going to do great things together. I think I have more in common with you than I do with Shelly."

I thought he was right, and we talked about some things we could do—budget and ethics reform, straightening out worker's compensation, and passing a civil confinement bill for sex offenders, which I'd been trying to pass for more than a decade but couldn't get past Shelly and the Assembly.

I was running unopposed in my district. The lack of opposition was far more satisfying than mere flattery. It was a relief. By this election season, I'd been in the game for thirty years, and while I'd be the last to deny that men of a certain age can list toward the cranky side of the ship, in my view campaigning has degenerated into a nauseating, soul-crushing, twenty-four-seven, kill-'em on TV, eviscerate-'em on the Internet (no courage required, you can sign your post, *Anonymous*) exercise in which each candidate tries to convince the voters, during the 4.3 seconds a day they have to spare, that he or she is less lazy, stupid, incompetent, corrupt, and greedy than his or her opponent.

Forgive my cynicism, or write it off to a faintly jaundiced sense of humor. However, polls reveal that voters are chronically disappointed by the officials they elect. Some of their disappointment is fair, some of it is due to unrealistic expectations—read no taxes, please, and don't forget to increase my services, and I wouldn't mind if you sent me a rebate check or two. And with all their disappointment, coupled with the rocky economic situation, the pressure on working families, the confusing changes in health care, escalating college costs, the threats of terrorism, and the increasing complexity of almost everything, I understand why the public might be in the mood to witness some bloodletting from summer to fall, especially since they had to remove bushels of political mail from their mailboxes and listen to robo-calls on their answering machines that made chalk scratching across a blackboard sound like the young Sinatra.

Anyway, without a campaign of my own, I had the time to help other Republicans, and to talk with Spitzer, who, after telling me we were going to be partners once he was in office, pledged that he wouldn't campaign against our majority, a move that I thought was designed to show he was serious about working together. I should've drastically revised my opinion of him downward the morning I picked up a newspaper and saw that he was campaigning against a Republican candidate for the Senate. By no means was this unusual, except that Spitzer had promised me he would lay off, so I called to remind him.

"Joe, what do you want me to do?"

"How about what you said you would?"

He laughed.

I didn't think it was funny, but hey, we hadn't even gotten past the election yet. It was too early to start fighting.

22

LANDSLIDE

Spitzer won the governorship with 69 percent of the vote, and the Republicans came away with a 34–28 majority in the Senate, which assured that I would be reelected leader.[1] As if to celebrate his record-setting plurality, Spitzer bought a farm and 160 acres of land in Columbia County, where he had been renting a weekend retreat for him, his wife, Silda, and their three daughters.

Shortly after that the governor-elect phoned and invited me to lunch at his new home. He was very charming and gave me a tour—the grounds and buildings were magnificent. Silda was elegant, friendly, and palpably intelligent and made us a wonderful lunch, which I thought was above and beyond the call of duty. As we ate, Spitzer spoke about his desire to rein in the budget and his commitment to improve public education and the business climate in the state, sounding as if he wanted to implement the agenda of the Senate Republican Conference, and he reaffirmed that we would be partners and accomplish great things together—starting on day one.

I remember sitting there watching him, this clean-cut man in his mid-forties, in great shape and good health, and listening to him talk—his passion for the issues and his comprehension of the smallest details, both of which were coupled with a naked ambition that was as pungent as coal smoke. I thought about the name he'd made for himself as AG, and his lovely, photogenic wife and daughters, his huge margin of victory in the election, and the enormous personal fortune at his disposal. I had heard him and his father referred to as a Jewish version of the Kennedys and, on the surface, that wasn't a far-fetched comparison. During a lull in the conversation, I glanced out the window, saw the last flames of autumn in the trees, and I believed that I was seated across from a future presidential candidate.

In retrospect, I have wondered if Spitzer believed it, too, or if he realized, down deep in the darker part of himself, that the country would soon see and be snickering at along with the late-night TV hosts, that he was an actor starring in an absurdist comedy, enjoying putting something over on everyone while knowing that his days were numbered, that the endgame had already been determined by invisible scars, and no reprieve was possible, that he would be forced to walk the plank and it was a long way down, and he would have no one to blame but himself.

Lunch was over, and I thanked Silda and the governor-elect for their hospitality. As I got up to go, I said to him: "What's important to me is communication. To relate, to talk, to be straightforward, to tell it like it is. We don't have to agree on everything, but we ought to know why we're disagreeing and we should have a right to disagree without it being a big deal and blowing up in the press."

He stiffened, as if I'd slapped him across the face. Later, much later, when he was gone from the Governor's Mansion, I understood that he was showing me a flash of his true colors. In a voice laced with the resentment of a surly teenager responding to advice from his father, Spitzer replied, "You don't have to tell me that. I know that."

Then he was palsy-walsy again, and I departed, not giving it a second thought. Mainly what I had seen that afternoon was a book-smart man who had done his homework and a politician with a covetous eye on the White House. Degrees from the Ivy League weren't necessary to realize that, however unwilling I might be, I could help him on his way to 1600 Pennsylvania Avenue by demonstrating to the state and country that he had passed meaningful legislation in Albany, and we agreed on several bread-and-butter issues that appealed to voters. And when it came time for Eliot Spitzer to enter the presidential primaries, the record created by the Senate and the Assembly and the governor would become his record alone. No one would mention the contributions of Joe Bruno or Shelly Silver—the kudos would belong to the candidate—and it was hard for me to believe that he didn't see this and that he would waste such an opportunity.

I'm a pretty good judge of character. *Pretty good.* Not perfect.

Even during one of Spitzer's first political moves he was considerate toward me. Senator Michael Balboni was a Republican who represented a district in Long Island that included Great Neck, Hicksville, Roslyn, and Westbury. In that district, Democratic registered voters already outnumbered Republicans, and I was relatively sure that the seat would go to a Democrat if Mike, who was popular and had been elected to the Assembly and then the Senate, decided to leave. I was very fond of Mike and knew, after Spitzer left the AG job, that he had his heart set on becoming attorney general. Mike would have been an excellent one, too, but I didn't want him to go. Believing that when the news is going to be bad the food ought to be good, I took Mike to lunch at the venerable Jack's Oyster House. The state was being swallowed by the Democratic Party, I said, and we needed to maintain our majority in the Senate, so the big GOP donors wouldn't be funding any campaigns for him. I knew Mike was disappointed, and I felt terrible about it. I preferred to help people get ahold of their dreams, not lose them. True, Mike staying benefited me and the majority. Nevertheless, I was convinced that one-party rule would not be in New Yorkers' best interest, especially for those upstate and on Long Island who were being flattened by property taxes and had lower social-service needs than the state's major cities.

Next thing I hear Mike has resigned from the Senate and accepted a job as a deputy secretary for public safety, becoming New York's homeland security czar. The Monday-morning quarterbacks among a coterie of journalists and politicos who, as a rule, are profoundly in love with their own opinions and possess an insatiable hunger for intrigue—real or invented it doesn't matter because it feeds their propensity to concoct those magnificent opinions the world awaits—concluded that Spitzer, prior to being sworn-in, was going to war with me.

That wasn't close to true. Mike planned to resign and join the private sector until he was offered a job for which he was eminently qualified. And when I spoke to Spitzer after the offer had been made, I asked him if Mike could remain in his seat until our conference voted for leader, because I knew Mike supported me. Had Spitzer wanted to poke a stick in my eye, he would've refused my request.

"No problem," he said.

So much for intrigue.

Eliot Spitzer was sworn in as the fifty-fourth governor of New York at a private midnight ceremony in Albany on January 1, and by dawn he was running through the cold and rain of Washington Park with reporters trailing behind him, a show of vim and vigor formerly associated with the glory days of the 1960s, when John Kennedy was in the White House and exhorting American youth to exercise. Prior to his inaugural address, to demonstrate that he was serious about ethics reform, the governor issued a handful of executive orders forbidding state workers from accepting gifts and top officials from getting into the lobbying game until they had been gone from their state job for two years. In a jab at outgoing Governor Pataki—a jab that would, in short order, become a roundhouse punch—Spitzer prohibited elected officials and candidates from taking part in any ads that are paid for with state dollars, which had been SOP for most governors.[2]

For the first time in more than a century, the public swearing-in ceremony was slated to be held outdoors at noon, in West Capitol Park, a patch of green wedged between the impressive stone of the Capitol and the Alfred E. Smith Building. Due to the weather, which called for freezing rain, the ceremony was delayed an hour. Spitzer appeared without a coat just like JFK (who had the sense to wear long underwear). As the governor launched into his speech by thanking his family and greeting the assembled dignitaries, I half-expected him to recite a redo of JFK's famous Inaugural, so I was less than shocked when he worked in the word "torch" and recycled the ask-not line by saying that we shouldn't ask of the political process what's in it for me, but what's in it for us.

I'm hardly qualified to criticize anyone for practicing the theatrics that goes with politics like mustard on a hot dog, but gee, Spitzer shouldn't have been so blatant when the image he was trying to conjure up was that of a murdered president who has, for many, joined the pantheon of American saints.

Yet this would be the least of my objections.

Spitzer spoke about this being a new day for New Yorkers. I should've guessed what was coming when he spoke about Teddy Roosevelt and the reformers who fought corruption, but like almost everyone else in the audience I was busy shivering. I heard him touch on crushing property taxes, expensive health care, vanishing jobs, and failing schools—the subjects he and I had discussed at lunch. Then, after claiming that the current government of the state was operating for the benefit of "those who hold office, not those who put them there," he uncorked one of the least gracious lines a governor has ever uttered in a formal address:

He said, "Like Rip Van Winkle, the legendary character created by the New York author Washington Irving, New York has slept through much of the past decade while the rest of the world has passed us by."[3]

My first thought was, how could this fellow, as bright as he is, begin his term with a nasty crack that was guaranteed to alienate the people he'd need to assist him with his agenda? He'd won by a landslide, and now that he was required to govern, the canny political move would've been to be magnanimous. My second thought was that Spitzer could kiss my ice-cold ass, and I leaned over to Governor Pataki and said, "We don't have to listen to this. Let's get the hell out of here. I know my conference will follow."

"No, no," George said. "We'll make the front pages—the guys who disrupted the inauguration."

That would've been shrewd politics, for it would've underscored the governor's pettiness, and some Republican senators did leave, but I sat there until the end.

Spitzer's remark wasn't lost on Danny Hakim, the Albany bureau chief of *The New York Times*. Danny, who knew his business and was adept at stirring the pot, asked for my opinion about it. I replied that in my view the last twelve years had been productive and we'd be judged on our accomplishments, not some small-minded rhetorical flourish. Then Danny got a quote from Shelly, noting that the leader had, along with George and me, been in charge of the state during the dozen years we were alleged to be snoozing. Shelly claimed that he wasn't offended, because the governor was talking about Pataki.[4]

That gave me a laugh. Shelly knew that he'd been referring to him as well. So did I, because in private Spitzer had said far less kind things about Shelly to me.

Later, there was a concert at the Times Union Center, where James Taylor performed. Taylor had written a song called "Steamroller Blues," and it would become part of Eliot Spitzer's sad little tale.

23

SYSTEMICALLY CORRUPT

Here's a bit of hard-won wisdom that I've tried to practice. When you're getting to know someone you have to do business with and he takes a swing at you, act as if it never happened. Ignoring it gives him room to back up without losing face and provides him with the chance to make it up to you. That was my approach with Governor Spitzer. At the beginning, it appeared to be working. We agreed to budget reform legislation which would, among other things, put member items in the budget, where they would be subject to the governor's veto, and required the Senate and Assembly to pass a balanced budget every year. Spitzer had also promised to enact ethics reform, and we spoke privately about that in his office.

"That's easy," I said. "The real way to be transparent and eliminate conflicts is to make legislators list every cent of outside income and who's paying them. Put it up on a website and let the people take a look at the potential conflicts of interest and weigh in when they vote."

"Shelly's a lawyer. He'd never report the names of his clients. That's privileged."

Shelly Silver was of-counsel to Weitz & Luxenberg in New York City, which has an impressive record in personal injury cases. Shelly raked in hundreds of thousands of dollars a year from the firm. As far as I could see, his major focus was on snuffing legislation that would limit the money involved in litigation, notably the size of awards. Outrageous awards are one of the reasons medical malpractice insurance is so expensive, and has contributed to the skyrocketing cost of our medical care. In February 2015, Shelly would be indicted for fraud and extortion.

"Governor, I can get you that ethics bill through the Senate tomorrow. Shelly's your problem. He's a Democrat. You make him fall in line."

Spitzer wasn't wrong when he indicated that Shelly would fight that proposal tooth and nail, so I suggested a second approach. Make the Legislature a full-time job, drastically increase the salary, which would have the added bonus of enticing more accomplished candidates from outside government to run for office, and prohibit legislators from earning one penny of extra income.

"It'll take two, three years to get everything together," I said. "I'll pass what we need in the Senate—no problem. Let's do it."

"That's wonderful, but I don't think Shelly will go for that either."

I had never mentioned this idea to Shelly, though I doubted that he'd see anything in it for him, because the state couldn't match what he earned with the law firm. However, it would be popular among voters, and Shelly never had any trouble detecting political wind direction.

At the moment, though, sitting across from the governor in his office, it occurred to me that Eliot Spitzer was more enamored of newspaper ink than accomplishment. His proposals, nipping here and there at the arrangements legislators make, were not a global solution, but more of the same, more of figuring out how you could adhere to the new rules and do what you had been doing under the old rules. I was as involved as anyone in trying to function in light of existing ethical guidelines, and I knew there was no shortage of gray areas. I would've have been happier with less gray, with tighter lines drawn in bolder colors. To pass that kind of legislation would've been one of the great accomplishments of my career. It would've reassured citizens that legislative decisions were on the up and up, and it might have saved a future legislator the grief that I experienced during my trials.

As a governor allegedly serious about ethics reform and a potential candidate for the presidency, Spitzer was being stunningly short-sighted not taking me up on the idea of a salary increase and the prohibition against outside earnings. Corruption concerns voters at both the state and the federal level, and even if he fought a valiant fight and lost, which was not a foregone conclusion, it would make him more appealing to a nationwide electorate.

Instead, by the end of January, Spitzer cobbled together a bunch of proposals that had been around for a while, including a gift ban that the Senate had passed eight years back but was opposed by the Assembly and Governor Pataki. My view of anti-corruption measures—unless you made critical changes to the system, the reason I favored cutting off any external income—mirrored my view of gun control legislation. A person who is intent on robbing a bank or murdering someone isn't going to sweat an illegal firearms charge. By the same token, an official who wants to accept bribes or steal funds isn't going to be overly worried about breaking some rules.

Well, Spitzer got his newspaper stories—and one of them will most likely trail him to the grave.

A news conference was scheduled to trumpet ethics reform, a bit of pro forma stagecraft because, when push came to shove, Spitzer didn't have the fortitude to confront Shelly and attempt to make any meaningful changes. What he did do, in an effort to earn himself a pat on the head from editorial writers by insinuating that the three-men-in-a-room approach to negotiating legislation was over, was to invite Malcolm Smith, the Senate minority leader, and Jim Tedisco, the Assembly minority leader, to stand up with us in front of reporters.

Whatever one thinks of journalists, they are not quite that easy to fool, but the governor's biggest problem was that Jim didn't want to participate in the phony extravaganza. To urge him to attend, Spitzer called and reached him in his car. According to Jim, he expressed his reservations to the governor. Spitzer decided the most effective method for persuading Jim was to scream at him with a reference to a James Taylor song: "Listen, I'm a fucking steamroller, and I'll roll over you and everybody else."

In the event that berating Jim didn't do the trick, Spitzer chose to inform him of his own greatness by observing that he'd accomplish more in less than a month than any governor in state history.

Looking back at Spitzer's brief governorship, commentators would highlight his steamroller remark in neon. As I reflect, it was his observation that he'd done more in a short span than any previous governor that reveals the troubled chambers of his soul. Spitzer did have a dazzling early record, but clearly the governor believed that his accomplishments were his alone, as though Shelly and I, and by extension, the Assembly and Senate, had no role to play. Spitzer had backed Shelly into a tighter corner than Pataki had done. Nevertheless, Shelly had his areas of flexibility and less flexibility, and when Spitzer tested his less flexible side—over the selection of a replacement for Comptroller Alan Hevesi—Shelly would dance to the governor's tune right up until he stalked off the dance floor and sided with his conference. In the end, the most important revelation during Spitzer's bullying of Jim Tedisco was his unwarranted self-regard, and his inability to accept the imperfect horse trading that was the essence of governing. It was these two qualities, more than the uncontrollable rages that detached his brain from his mouth that would make Eliot Spitzer unsuited to be a leader in a democracy.

I suspect Jim was anxious to get off the phone, and he agreed to go to the news conference. He also repeated his conversation with the governor to John McArdle, the director of communication for the Senate Republicans, and John passed it on to me and to Fred Dicker, the state editor of the *New York Post* who also hosted a radio show in Albany. I assume Dicker verified the story with Jim, and the blow-by-blow was recounted in the *Post*, along with mentions of earlier Spitzer eruptions, under the headline: ELIOT SPITZ FIRE.[1]

In his book, *Client 9: The Rise and Fall of Eliot Spitzer*, the governor's college friend, Peter Elkind, wrote that the humorous aspects of the situation escaped Tedisco and that the story was leaked to Fred because I "wasn't about to pass up an opportunity to embarrass the new governor."[2]

Ah, yes, Eliot Spitzer—another one of the world's victims.

First off, there is nothing funny about a governor bullying a legislator—it's an unfair fight. Bullying a leader was more sporting, but that wouldn't turn out to be as much fun for the governor, and I attempted to indicate that to him when the media asked me to comment on his steamroller reference. I said that once, on a spring afternoon, I'd tried to use a steamroller in one of my hilly pastures at home, and I learned, much to my regret, that a steamroller just spins and spins when you try to get it going uphill. If the governor knew anything about heavy equipment, he wouldn't have compared himself to a steamroller.

The reporters began laughing. I wasn't trying to embarrass Spitzer with that anecdote, only to encourage him to stow his crazy act and focus on what we could accomplish. I can't say that it worked, though embarrassing someone for sport was neither my style, nor in my interest. I still believed that if Spitzer got his temper under control, we could do more together than I'd done since arriving at the Capitol.

We did pass another bill in February, this one improving the state's workers' compensation system by increasing benefits and the ability to make sure employers were buying the insurance—to name just two of the improvements. The bill was a feather in everybody's cap not only for the particulars, but that it was applauded by business *and* labor.

At the same time, the governor and I were working on a civil confinement bill, which would make it possible for the state to hang onto sex offenders when their sentences were finished if they were judged to present an ongoing threat. Republicans in the Senate had been trying to pass this sort of bill since 1993. Shelly opposed it on philosophical grounds, telling me that it was wrong to imprison an individual after he had paid his debt to society. Fair enough: I understood his objection and respected it, but I wanted these predators locked up, and the issue was now front and center. On a summer afternoon in 2005, Concetta Russo-Carriero had gone to her car in a public parking garage next to the upscale Galleria mall in White Plains. There, she was stabbed to death by Phillip Grant, a convicted rapist who had served more than twenty years in prison. People in Westchester were outraged and frightened, and they—along with citizens across the state—wanted something done about these violent habitual criminals. By the fall of 2005, a proposed bill was being referred to as "Connie's Law," and I was sure that with bipartisan support and the governor's approval, we'd finally pass it.[3]

Observing these accomplishments, *The New York Times*, in an uncharacteristic burst of optimism about Albany, asked: DYSFUNCTION JUNCTION NO MORE?[4]

24

WAR GAMES

If my honeymoon season with the governor sounds too good to be true, it was, and that was gradually becoming clearer. Spitzer was not just fighting with me, he was simultaneously going after Democrats. He may have been telling himself that he was battling the evil Albany dysfunction, but were that true the dumbest move he could make was to disregard the law and try to steamroll the Assembly and Senate.

And that's what he did.

By law, once Alan Hevesi resigned as comptroller, a joint session of the Legislature was supposed to vote for his replacement. Given that Democrats far outnumbered Republicans, it was their call, and they wanted one of their own, a well-liked Nassau County man, Tom DiNapoli, who had applied for the job. Spitzer had other ideas. He wanted a professional, top-drawer money manager. On the merits, that made sense. In reality, it was ludicrous, and again demonstrated Spitzer's inability to comprehend process. No branch of government ever—and I mean ever—willfully relinquishes its power to another branch.

This is not dysfunction. It is how the system was designed. Evidently, Spitzer was under the impression that this reality didn't apply to him. Shelly tried to avoid fighting with the governor by agreeing to a committee to interview candidates. That was a stalling tactic to appease both sides and, as I watched from the sidelines, I knew that it was destined to fail. And it failed spectacularly. No member of the Legislature was recommended for the post, which infuriated Shelly's conference, and the speaker wouldn't stand for that.

In the joint session, DiNapoli was elected comptroller, and Spitzer reacted like an almost well-adjusted two-year-old.

He bludgeoned Assemblyman William Magnarelli in his own district, a rather egregious no-no; he backed out of a fundraiser for Democrats, and excoriated his own party in the media; and, worst of all, Spitzer seemed not to care about the ill will he was engendering on his own side of the aisle.

Then he set his sights on me.

I don't accept that Eliot Spitzer planned to go to war with me from the beginning. With the dubious wisdom of hindsight, I believe that he started to fall apart emotionally—and his political judgment, overrated beyond belief by me and an army of politicos, began failing him—shortly after taking office. Why else would he go to war with the Assembly? That made less sense than attacking me. I suspect that the drumbeat in the papers about the Spitzer-Bruno battle served to inflame him and gave credence to his most destructive impulse: that the essence of governing was treating your opponents as if they belonged behind bars for the crime of daring to disagree with you. I also think there was a more specific and psychologically complex dimension to his problems with me, which didn't become apparent until later.

Spitzer's first opportunity to go after my scalp was the special election held to fill the seat vacated when Spitzer appointed Republican Senator Mike Balboni to become deputy secretary for public safety. It was a hotly contested race and the most expensive in state history for the Senate, with spending surpassing $5 million.[1] We had run a fine candidate, Assembly-woman Maureen O'Connell, who was a lawyer and a nurse, but she lost to Craig Johnson, a Democratic member of the Nassau County Legislature.

Much was made of the fact that the Republican majority in the Senate was down to 33–29. Malcolm Smith was spreading the rumor that a couple members of my conference were going to start voting with the Democrats, and we'd be cooked because David Paterson, the lieutenant governor, would be casting the tie-breakers. Malcolm was full of shit, and everybody knew it. There were Democratic senators who were eager to work with us and, to make this point, a few weeks after the special election I tapped one of them, Carl Kruger, who represented a district in Brooklyn, to be chairman of the Committee on Social Services, Children, and Families. To reporters, Malcolm indicated that I had made the appointment because he'd been urging me to share power with the minority. We both knew that was nonsense.

What annoyed me most about the special election wasn't that we lost a seat: it was the role Spitzer played in the race.

After assuring me he was going to lay off the politics and focus on getting things done, the governor threw himself into Johnson's campaign, giving speeches, starring in radio and TV ads, and personally donating to his war chest, and I started hearing rumblings around the Capitol that he wanted me out as leader.[2]

So I phoned him. "Why are you doing this?" I asked. "We've done some good stuff together, and we can do a lot more. Why don't you want to govern? Why do you want to fight?"

"Ah, c'mon, Joe, it's fun. And it's not personal."

"It's not fun, and it is personal."

"No, that's the game. It's war."

Spitzer said this as casually as if he were announcing a luncheon we would be attending together.

"I . . . ," I said, "And people get hurt in a war. Remember that."

"Fighting is healthy. That's the way life is. And I think I'm going to win."

Recalling my boxing matches in Korea, I replied, "You might win. But sometimes when you're in a fight even if you win, you get bloody and your nose gets broken and you'll regret the fight. There are always winners and losers, but when it's over it can be hard to tell the difference between them."

I hung up and that was the first time I felt as if Spitzer had more than a few screws loose. He was too angry, too confrontational, and appeared totally ignorant about the compromises inherent in governing. For a while, I couldn't understand what the rational part of him—if such a part existed—had in mind. Was he going to run for the White House by declaring, "Vote for me, I beat up Joe Bruno!" and in one loud, confused voice the nation would reply, "Who the hell is Joe Bruno?"

Later, his thinking was made clearer by an anonymous source, obviously an ally of Spitzer, who spoke to Geoffrey Gray while he was writing a profile of me for *New York* magazine.

The source said: "The way legislative bodies around the world have worked is that in one room you're trying to collaborate, and in the other room you're trying to fuck the guy.... So if Joe feels hoodwinked by that, he's dumber than I think he is."[3]

That's me—the dumb country bumpkin in his coonskin hat. If it had not been so damned pathetic, I would've laughed.

Still, I held out hope that I would be able to turn the governor in a more constructive direction. I kidded him about our differences. One day, I was walking past his office and saw him leaning in the doorway.

"You look good," he said. "You still working out?"

"Chores around the farm. And I hit the heavy bag. What'd you weigh?"

"A hundred and eighty-seven. Why're you asking?"

"I'm a hundred and seventy-five. I wanted to see if we were in the same weight class." I smiled to let him know I was joking. "Just in case."

He didn't return the smile. "I play tennis," he said.

In attempt to demonstrate that we could all be friends, I led a group of Senate Republicans down to his office and presented Spitzer with a bouquet of roses on Valentine's Day. He seemed friendly enough and thanked me, but noted that there weren't a dozen in the bouquet, and he'd need three more so he could give them to Silda. Then we went over to see Shelly and gave him a bouquet as well.

My light-hearted approach didn't pay off, but you can't blame a guy for trying.

★ ★ ★

I love the Capital Region yet I must admit that March can be a rough month, cold and dreary and capable of shaking your faith that spring will ever come. March 2007 was among the worst I can remember. And it had nothing to do with the weather.

It was silly season in Albany, the deadline to pass a budget drawing near. The vast majority of our annual spending is mandated by the federal government, the State constitution, and laws enacted by the Legislature. The remainder of the money we're allocating is normally about three percent of the total, and based on a projection of taxes we hope to collect and needs we may or may not have. This section of the budget is akin to a wish list, and now and again, it has reminded me in its interminable requests and questionable realism of the letters children write to Santa. But above all else it is a method in dollars and cents to stake out positions, and to allow negotiations to begin. So far, so good, except this assumes that the two leaders and the governor are willing to do business, each of them keeping in mind the needs of the others.

With respect to the budget, the governor faces a different challenge than the leaders. He has a constituency of two—the great mass of all New Yorkers, not the singular constituents who call your office with heart-breaking problems or tug on your sleeve during the July Fourth parade. And himself. If the budget is cut and the governor can announce that he's reining in spending and controlling taxes, he gets a standing ovation. On the other hand, when the services are cut or local taxes rise because the state passed out less money, it is generally the legislators who take the hit even if they fought like hell on behalf of their constituents.

Governor Spitzer preferred dictating the terms of the budget, and he seemed surprised when that didn't work and became increasingly frustrated about it. Shelly saw it as well, but he was willing to go along to get along, playing the wimp, as I described it to reporters, because he saw some political advantage in what the governor was advocating, namely hundreds of millions of dollars in cuts to health-care spending.[4] The advantage was that he was going after me by putting pressure on Dennis Rivera, the leader of the healthcare workers' union and among my strongest supporters.

Rivera had his union run TV commercials with an elderly woman asking Spitzer to remember her and the other workers, many of whom earned just north of seven bucks an hour, asking him why he was coming after their jobs—a tug on the heartstrings that seemed to imply that millions of struggling New Yorkers were difficult to spot from the windows of a Fifth Avenue apartment overlooking Central Park.[5] Spitzer fought back with his own ads, using something like half a million bucks of his own money. And health-care workers weren't the only ones objecting to the budget. Mayor Bloomberg complained about more than $300 million in cuts to state aid to the city and the closing of corporate tax loopholes that would encourage corporations to go looking for a more tax-friendly location. Then Congressman Charlie Rangel, a New York Democrat and chairman of the House Ways and Means Committee, weighed in, observing that the governor bludgeoning people who disagreed with him was not an effective method of negotiation.[6]

Really?

Because this disagreement led to the ugliness that ensued, I have to pause here to recite some numbers. The governor had proposed a $120.6 billion budget; the Assembly wanted it to be $121.2 billion; and the Senate was asking for $123.8 billion.[7] All this blood spilled for three percent of the budget, and Spitzer, Shelly, and I knew that we would haggle and in all likelihood be closer to the Assembly's number than to the Senate's.

So why the war? Looking back at the papers I saw this short piece by Danny Hakim from *The Times*. At the signing of the worker's comp bill, Spitzer "needled" me by saying, "Did I hear somebody say 'profligate'?" and then introduced me as his "good friend." As Danny noted, I went along with his ribbing, but afterward I told Danny that the budget won't "get done by any one individual, or several, getting it all their own way."[8]

Shortly thereafter, I was a guest on Fred Dicker's radio show. I like Fred, and Fred likes political gunfights. He challenged me, saying that like everyone else I was afraid of Spitzer. I laughed and basically explained that I would keep at it until the governor understood that the final budget was a negotiated document, not a royal decree. I also worked in that I thought Spitzer was a spoiled brat with a chip on his shoulder. I knew this was the most incendiary charge I could make against him, because I suspected at some level that he believed it about himself. But I hoped it would make him more cooperative if for no other reason than I'd stop saying it. When I finished the show I went back to my office, and my press secretary, Kris Thompson, told me that while I was on the air he'd received a call from

Darren Dopp, the governor's communications director. Spitzer had tuned in to Fred, and he hadn't enjoyed the show.

Gee. What a shock.

The day after my appearance on Dicker, I was scheduled to attend the signing of the civil confinement bill in the Red Room. The family of Concetta Russo-Carriero, who had been murdered by that convicted sexual predator in White Plains, would be attending, and I was looking forward to offering my condolences to them and to the ceremony because I had worked so long to get the legislation done. The governor had been quite helpful, pushing Shelly to get onboard, and it should've been an opportunity for smiles and handshakes. It wasn't.

I got a preview of what was about to happen at a quarter to eight that morning when I was in my kitchen drinking a cup of coffee and reading the paper. The phone rang, I picked up, and the governor said, "You have to get over to my office immediately. We need to talk."

I prided myself on being punctual, and I had something like ten meetings scheduled and a speech to give, and I wasn't about to delay or back out of any of them to witness a tantrum. "I'm not getting over there," I replied. "I'm busy until our press conference. I'll see you there."

"If you don't fucking get your ass over here, I'll knock you down."

"Well, I've been knocked down before."

"When I knock you down, you'll never get up."

He went on in that vein until I broke in, saying, "Why don't you go fuck yourself" and hung up. I'd heard a story that he'd threatened to cut a Republican senator's throat. I'd found it nearly impossible to believe. Until now.

I got to my office about nine-thirty. Amy Leitch, my executive assistant, said that my hotline, the direct line that connects the governor and the leaders, had been ringing off the hook. I knew it was Spitzer, but I had no intention of answering the phone. Why bother? I could call myself names.

When it was time for the press conference, Kris and I walked downstairs to the Governor's Hall on the second floor, where a state trooper stood guard outside the governor's office. Usually, before a signing, there was a pre-meeting in the governor's inner office to finalize the details of the rollout. Except the trooper told us that he'd been ordered to tell me I wasn't welcome at the meeting. I'd have to wait in the Red Room.

This wasn't a strategy unfamiliar to anyone who has attended third grade: *I'm mad at Joey, and he can't come to my birthday party!* I remember thinking that while Princeton and Harvard were among the finest institutions of learning in the world, they must not offer a course on political common sense. Forcing me to wait in the Red Room was a thousand miles shy of shrewd. The media was waiting there, and the reporters knew about the pre-rollout meetings, so they asked me why I wasn't with the governor. I indicated that temper tantrums were not just an ineffectual method for boys and girls to get their bedtimes extended, they were also useless as a negotiating tactic for the budget.

Kris was the first to see Spitzer walk into the Red Room, and he later told me that his face was flushed and the veins were popping out in his neck. I joined the signing and made a few comments. Spitzer wasn't overly friendly toward me, but he didn't act like a junior hitman. Shelly was telling the press that the state had plenty more to do regarding sex crimes. That was his way of sharing the credit for a popular bill that he had opposed. I didn't care; I did the same thing to him. While I was standing off to the side chatting with a reporter, I saw Darren Dopp talking to Kris, who then came over and said the governor wanted to see me—ASAP.

"No," I said, and left the Red Room.

A group of Spitzer's staff streamed out into the hall as I was passing by his office to inform me that the governor needed to see me. Jesus, would this stuff never end?

This isn't going to be fun, I thought, and went in. Spitzer, visibly upset, was sitting behind his desk, and I sat across from him. He began fidgeting like he had to take a leak.

"What the hell is wrong with you?" he asked.

"Nothing. What's wrong with you?"

"Missssssster Bruno," he said, dragging out my name. I wasn't sure why and guessed it could be a method of insult among private school boys. "Do you realize you're speaking to the governor of New York?"

"And you're talking to the majority leader. You better recognize that there are three branches of government— legislative, executive, and judicial. Equal branches, OK?"

"Misssssssster Bruno," he repeated, his voice louder. "I am the governor."

"Then why don't you start acting like it? Because guess what? You're not a prosecutor any more. You can't prosecute anybody here. You should go to CEO school and learn how to be a governor."

He demanded that I apologize for saying that he ought to learn how to be a CEO, and I said, "Grow up."

"Misssssssster Bruno, don't you know who you're talking to?"

"I don't give a fuck who I'm talking to."

Spitzer jumped up out of his chair. "Get out of here."

I watched him as he bolted out of his office and wondered where he was going and figured that he was going to get the troopers to arrest me. I was imagining the headlines when Spitzer returned, gaping at me as though I were a ghost and shouting, "You're still here!"

"Settle down."

"Get out of my office," he replied, and ran out again.

Holy shit, I thought. The governor is running out of his own office.

The third time he returned, I was standing up, and before I knew it, we were standing almost nose to nose. His face was purple and he seemed to be on the verge of having a stroke while he yelled that he was going to knock my head off.

I shouted, "I've been threatened by mobsters—professionals. And I've dealt with thugs and bullies like you my entire life. I know how to deal with them. Don't bother threatening me. You're an amateur. And I'm not scared."

I walked out and, heading upstairs to the Parlor to attend a meeting with my conference, I wondered why Spitzer thought if he could pound me into a grease spot he'd be able to feed the hungry, clothe the naked, and bring peace to the world. The complete answer was beyond my skills, but I have raised four children—two of them sons—and I did feel that the governor frequently responded to me like a little boy competing with his dad and losing control of himself if he didn't win. I also sensed that Spitzer had the respect—and contempt—that some people raised in unimaginable privilege have for those of us who, through our own efforts, escape poverty. He obviously struggled to accept that I considered myself his equal, but I did, and I had the New York State Constitution to prove it. Furthermore, I knew in a way that Eliot Spitzer never could, with the protection provided by his father's wealth, that I was a survivor, that I had seen far worse than Spitzer's infantile fireworks, had been through far rougher patches in my own life—including, at the moment, Bobbie, my wife of fifty-seven years, being carried away from us by Alzheimer's. These challenges didn't make me tough; they made me confident. Spitzer had survived nothing. Underneath his bluster you could almost see the scared kid standing in the corner, frustrated, resentful, raging. His only move was to use his position to berate people and to shove them around, and if there was one thing I knew for sure it's that when you pop a bully's balloon, you get just what you'd expect—hot air.

In the Parlor, I told the senators the story and they laughed as if I were recounting a Laurel and Hardy routine.

"It's not funny," I said. "I think the man is unbalanced, certifiably crazy. I'm telling you now. He'll never finish his four years."

It was around then that I started dreaming about Spitzer taking a swing at me. He took his swing, and then I got my chance.

That was one beautiful dream.

25

For of All Sad Words of Tongue and Pen

Leaving aside his psychological affliction, the governor's biggest challenge was his inexperience and his belief that intellect is a substitute for experience. In plain English, some folks think they're so smart they don't have to bother knowing anything and can figure everything out. Spitzer was one of those.

This put him at a disadvantage negotiating the budget with me, because I didn't accept that there was something inherently wrong with a late budget. Had Spitzer bothered to bone up on past budget battles, this would've been apparent to him. Instead, he chose to treat the April 1 deadline as if it were the key to the Promised Land, and once he staked so much political capital on that date, I knew I'd be able to restore some health-care cuts and the aid to schools I wanted—aid that would offer some relief from the crushing property taxes on Long Island. All I'd have to do is threaten to stall and wait him out. I can't claim to have invented this tactic, nor was I its lone practitioner. Old Stonewall Shelly Silver was a master at it.

That was how it went. The governor convened a meeting in his office to finalize a deal. He invited Shelly and me along with the two minority leaders, Jim Tedisco and Malcolm Smith. I assume this was his lawyerly side in action, his bending the truth with technicalities, because he could claim that the era of three-men-in-a-room was over: the number had increased to five. Of course, neither Shelly nor I had any intention of revealing our strategies to our respective minority leaders, whose goal was to switch places with us, and the notion that the views of our own parties' minority leaders would supersede our positions was preposterous, so despite the Day One changes Spitzer had promised, nothing had changed. We negotiated for six or seven hours, and all of us got something we wanted. The government do-gooders—Common Cause, the League of Women Voters, and others—weren't thrilled with their fair-haired boy, and some took to beating the stuffing out of him in the newspapers. This enraged the governor, though in lieu of explaining to these folks the realities of governance as spelled out by the State constitution, he appeared to stew about it, and despite the momentary post-budget glow, I had the feeling that things between Spitzer and me hadn't improved.

I never guessed how bad they were about to become.

Spitzer had promised to enact campaign finance reform, and no issue was worse for our relationship, because it threw into bold relief our vastly different lives. Acting as if he were occupying the moral high ground, Spitzer proposed scaling back the amount limited liability companies were permitted to give, a proposal that Shelly objected to as much as I did. Shelly, being a Democrat, was happy to let me do the fighting with the governor in the media. I couldn't blame him for doing precisely what I'd done to him when Pataki was governor.

The nuts and bolts of the debate weren't as important as the fact that such limits favored the wealthy, who could finance their own campaigns. When I pointed that out in public, Spitzer blasted me at a meeting with the editorial board of the *Troy Record*, my hometown paper, and launched a statewide tour excoriating Republican senators. It was a dumb political move, but by then I believed that the governor was losing his grip on reality, and I responded to his tour by telling reporters, in essence, that rich kids had trouble understanding how most people lived.[1]

Spitzer and some of his staff behaved as if I were too stupid to comprehend his proposal, dismissing my concerns by saying that it had a provision to deal with wealthy candidates. If they pumped cash beyond the limits into their campaigns, then their opponents could get double donations from their contributors.[2]

This was Grade-A horse manure, and Spitzer was able to peddle it because most citizens haven't run for office. A candidate receives money throughout the campaign, frequently in dribs and drabs. *When* you get the funds is as crucial to victory as the total. Producing campaign literature, buying inserts in newspapers or advertising on radio and TV doesn't happen by snapping your fingers—there are lead times involved, everyone working for you needs to get paid, and the threat of running out of cash is a constant headache. A candidate with deep pockets doesn't worry about any of this: he writes checks. The other guy has to get on the phone and cancel appearances, which hurts during a race, or slap together an emergency mailing so he can pester contributors, who have already come through for him and are often less than thrilled to be asked for more money.

While Spitzer and I were duking it out, I heard that he was contacting Senate Republicans to inform them that I was a senile old shit (OK, I was old), and to see if he could persuade them to dump me as leader. Again, this struck me as bizarre. It hadn't worked when Pataki, a Republican, had tried it; how could any governor believe that my conference would side with a Democrat. The answer, I suspected, was that Spitzer wasn't behaving rationally, and not only did my conference refuse to revolt, they told me what was going on. I also heard that someone had cooked up another wacky scheme—attempting to talk Malcolm Smith into reporting me to the IRS for some made-up tax evasion. Malcolm refused.

By spring, the governor and I hadn't spoken in months, and perhaps it was his inability to steamroll me that led Spitzer to get involved in a nutty plot that would become known as "Troopergate."

The plot was ill-conceived, banal, and an indication, I thought, that Spitzer had taken up permanent residence in crazy land. The governor had tried to discredit me by having Darren Dopp, his communication director, enlist the State Police to help him gather my travel records on state-owned aircraft and claim that I'd used them solely for political purposes, which was against the law. This was absurd. I worked constantly to shore up my conference, and whenever I flew to New York City on state business I always tried to do some politicking, which is a big part of the majority leader's responsibilities.

The full story about the origins of the scandal wasn't spelled out until the winter of 2008, when Albany County District Attorney David Soares offered Dopp immunity if he'd be placed under oath and tell the truth or face criminal prosecution. Dopp agreed and told the district attorney that he wanted to give my records to James Odato, a reporter at the *Times Union*. Before doing so, he went into Spitzer's office to get final approval.

"Yeah," Spitzer said. "Do it."

"Are you sure?" Dopp asked. "Joe probably will be pissed."

According to Dopp, Spitzer was red-faced and "spitting a little bit," when he replied, "Fuck him. He's a piece of shit. Shove it up his ass with a red-hot poker."[3]

The story was splashed across the front page on Sunday, July 1, and I believed Odato had done his best to bury me. The governor denied that he'd had anything to do with it. I didn't believe him. Most interesting to me, Spitzer and his staff seemed miffed that I didn't roll over and play dead, further proof that the boss and his minions had lost touch with reality. I had told the governor in January that fighting was a waste. Maybe he interpreted that to mean I didn't know how. What Spitzer & Co. were discovering was something anyone who knew me could've told them. By inclination—emotionally and strategically—I'm a counterpuncher, a lesson I learned in that long-ago schoolyard in Glens Falls. No reason to start a fight; every reason to finish one.

On Monday, I hammered away at the governor on Fred Dicker's show, saying that he was out to destroy me. Fred checked into it, and four days later he told his readers what had happened in the *Post*. The governor had set in motion an "unprecedented State Police surveillance program" to discredit me.[4] Meantime, Odato published more stories, one of them stating that I had used state aircraft on April 8 to go to New York City, where I had a whole series of meetings, most of them political, which was an inappropriate use of state resources. Odato seemed to imply that I was breaking the law. Yet, perhaps because Odato was lazy, he didn't check his facts and thus failed to discover that April 8 happened to be a Sunday—Easter Sunday, actually, and my birthday. I'd spent the whole day at home with my family, not on a helicopter going back and forth to New York City.[5]

That type of shoddy journalism is just plain wrong, and though I'd been the target of it for my entire political career, I never made my peace with reporters like James Odato, who appear to care less about uncovering the truth and more about making headlines.

I phoned Rex Smith, the editor of the *Times Union*, to point out the error. I do not recall ever seeing a retraction. However, an ad salesman for the newspaper contacted my office and asked if I'd like to respond in a paid ad. Then Rex wrote a column defending his reporter and denying there was any connection between the coverage and the request that I purchase space.

I'm not making this up. I'm not nearly that creative.

Before July was out, Attorney General Andrew Cuomo issued a report that said my use of the aircraft was perfectly legal and criticized the governor's staff for their foray into the spy business. The governor's own inspector general approved the report's conclusion, and Spitzer told the media that he had phoned me to apologize. Perhaps he spoke to a twin brother I didn't know I had, because I have no memory of that call. Darren Dopp paid the price for Troopergate, being suspended without pay; eventually being fined $10,000 by the Commission on Public Integrity for "using his official position as the governor's communications director to obtain an unlawful benefit;" and spending, from what I hear, more than a hundred grand to fight the fine, a case the judge threw out of court.[6]

In my opinion, Darren fell on his sword for his boss, but Spitzer didn't escape unscathed.

By the end of 2007, he discovered what any experienced politician knows. When you go negative on an opponent, you do suppress his approval ratings, but you also hurt yourself, and in December a Siena Research Institute poll showed, for the first time, that Spitzer was underwater with New York State voters. Fifty-six percent wanted a different governor; only one-third of Democrats said they would vote for him again; and the poll ascribed much of this statewide disapproval to Troopergate and his ongoing war with Republican senators.[7]

★ ★ ★

On January 7, my wife died. My grief was strange and terrible, a mix of sadness and fear. I'd known Bobbie for more than sixty years, and I felt that once she passed away, the memories would go with her, and I'd stop being who I was. Gratefully, as the worst of my mourning receded, I found that the memories remained, but still I had trouble believing that the touchstone of my life was gone.

We held a memorial service for Bobbie at St. Pius X Church in Loudonville. Cardinal Edward Egan, the archbishop of New York, and Albany Bishop Howard Hubbard presided, along with the Reverend Michael Farano, the pastor of St. Pius X. Hundreds of people filled the church, many of them friends Bobbie had collected over the years, and a flock of politicians: The governor, lieutenant governor, and attorney general; Shelly was there with the comptroller, Tom DiNapoli; Mayor Bloomberg; City Council speaker Christine Quinn; and former Senator Al D'Amato.

Originally, my daughter, Susan, was going to speak, but I was thinking how much Bobbie had hated politics and yet I would never have gotten involved without her help, so I owed it to her to say something.

I spoke off the cuff, and I'm grateful to Danny Hakim for recording some of what I said and to *The New York Times* for publishing it, because I was never able to remember it.

"Her father and her mother, who was a beautiful, beautiful, caring lady, her sisters, did everything and anything they could to get to Bobbie, to keep her from marrying me. And who could blame them? Think about it. I was a kid, literally, with no prospects.... They would have voted me as the boy most unlikely to succeed. Every year. But Bobbie...saw something and stuck with me, literally defied her father.

"Bobbie really disliked politicians. I say that, because Bobbie always thought there was kind of a phoniness, that instead of us dealing with the merits, we dealt with the press. My Lord. But that was her attitude.... Bobbie taught me English. You know, I was a kid. Everything was 'Ain't, yous guys, yous guys ain't gonna do this,' and Bobbie subtly corrected me and corrected me. When you say she was elegant, she was gracious, she was caring, she was loving. She brought me along, really. Honest to God, I think she felt sorry for me…. I can tell you this. If Bobbie wasn't there, I never would have wanted to go to college, I never would have done much more than exist, because she showed me a better life…without being presumptuous. We had our peaks and our valleys like anyone who lives together for fifty-eight years…but you know what, Bobbie was always there. And I say this now publicly because I never said it enough to her."[8]

My battle with Eliot Spitzer ended in March when it was revealed that the governor had been involved with call girls, and he sent the following letter to Shelly and me: "I am writing to advise you that I am resigning my position as Governor of the State of New York effective at 12:00 noon on Monday, March 17, 2008."

I'd be a liar if I said that I wasn't glad he was leaving. Perhaps because it had all happened so close to Bobbie's death, I felt sick watching Silda Spitzer go through that public humiliation, and for days I found myself thinking about their daughters, how horrible that it had to be for them, young women who never hurt anyone, being surrounded by such sordidness.

I hoped that Spitzer would get the help he needed, though I wasn't optimistic. As the media rehashed the story day after day, nothing in this world seemed uglier to me than the rock-'em-sock-'em game of politics, and ironically, soon enough, I'd have my own introduction to the worst moments of this game.

26

MOVING ON

Early in 2006, I began to hear rumors that the FBI was looking into my dealings with Loudonville businessman Jared E. Abbruzzese. I'd done some consulting for Jerry and we owned a horse together, but I knew there was nothing to find. By law, legislators are permitted to conduct outside business; before signing on for any undertaking, I'd cleared it with lawyers; every cent I'd made was on my tax returns; and I'd filed the required financial disclosure forms with the State Legislative Ethics Committee.

Still, you can go nuts listening to rumors. As a gossip mill, Albany is only behind Washington, D.C., and Hollywood, and when I kept hearing about an investigation, I wondered if maybe I'd overlooked something: I was a businessman, not a lawyer, and different rules applied to us with respect to clients. I checked and rechecked with my counsel, Ken Riddett, but I was told—and believed—that my arrangements were on the up and up. I asked some sources I knew who had contacts with the office of Glenn Suddaby, the then-U.S. Attorney for the Northern District of New York, if there was anything going on that I should be aware of. The answer was no—there was nothing going on.

Fast forward a few months to December, and John McArdle, the communications director of the Republican conference, informed me that he'd heard Fred Dicker was going to break a story that the FBI had been asking questions about me. To prevent the inevitable feeding frenzy, where journalists would inflate a federal hunting expedition into the juiciest scandal since Watergate, John recommended that I call a news conference and disclose the information before Fred had a chance.

I talked to the press and, momentarily, the molehill became a mountain, partially because of the way the feds operate and how their remarks, on and off the record, get reported in the papers. When *The New York Times* asked Paul M. Holstein, a chief division counsel in the Albany office of the FBI, for a statement, he replied, "We have no comment on any pending investigations or even about whether there is an investigation ongoing on Senator Bruno."[1]

To the average person this sounds above-board, but politically astute observers would suspect that the media would never have gotten any story unless someone was breaking the law by leaking information about a federal investigation. So the denial makes the target of the inquiry appear guilty. Then *The Times* dug up every association I had with Jerry Abbruzzese, none of it illegal. Yet if you read the story, it seemed as nefarious as hell, especially that I'd "steered state money to a business linked to [Jerry]."[2]

The paper was referring to Troy-based Evident Technologies. In 2001, the state had given a grant to the company for $400,000. This was before I did any consulting for Jerry, and neither my contract with him nor our friendship had anything to do with the grant. In fact, I didn't even know about the money until much later.

Fred Dicker was spitting bullets that I screwed up his scoop, and I can't say that I blame him. During the following year, I was crazy busy, fighting with the governor and spending as much time as I could with my wife. I had engaged outside counsel, Bill Dreyer, a former chief assistant to the U.S. Attorney for the Northern District of New York. Bill checked with their office and was told that I wasn't the target of an investigation.

Somewhere during this period—I don't recall the exact timing—Bill got in touch with the FBI in Albany.

Since I hadn't done anything wrong, I asked Bill if there was any reason I shouldn't go talk to them as a sign that I had every intention of being cooperative.

Bill is a cautious, meticulous attorney, and I don't believe he would've permitted me to speak to the FBI if he thought it would get me in hot water. He and my Senate lawyer, Ken Riddett, accompanied me to the interview. Both of them cautioned me about offering any information that I wasn't asked about, because it could be twisted to appear as if I were lying, and it's a crime to make fraudulent statements to the feds.

I had a congenial conversation with two agents. They were curious about my flights to Florida with Jerry Abbruzzese on his private plane. Yes, I said, we had played golf at the Mar-A-Lago Club. Donald Trump, who owned the club, held a fundraiser for us every year. Jerry had taken me and four of my staff to Palm Beach. The law permitted the total cost of the round-trip flight to be categorized as a campaign contribution, and that was what I did. Totally legal and not uncommon for elected officials.

I finished the interview, and as I was walking out, one of the agents asked, "Do you work for Jerry Abbruzzese."

"No," I said. That was the truth. Jerry was helping out a company in Texas, and the new CEO had asked him, "Who is this Bruno? Does he report to work on a daily basis?" Jerry explained that I assisted him on an as-needed basis, and the CEO told him to get rid of me. So he did.

Outside, I said to Bill Dreyer, "I wanted to tell him that I'd worked for Jerry until three or four months ago, but his question was do I work for him, meaning now, and I don't."

"Perfect," Bill replied. "That's perfect."

"You know damn well that he knows I'd worked for Jerry. Or he wouldn't have asked me about it."

"Right, but you don't offer information to these guys."

Subsequently, I'd hear that the FBI claimed that I'd lied during my interview. That was a crock, and a God-awful one at that, but by then I believed that in my case the government wasn't especially interested in the truth. I had many sleepless nights considering the fact that people had the right to malign me, my personal life, and my professional life, but I resolved to keep fighting, as I couldn't let them define me or my legacy.

Life returned to normal—almost. The rumors persisted, and in December I decided to quit working for Wright Investors' Service. Wright had been doing a first-rate job for its clients since the early 1960s, and I didn't want the negative publicity surrounding me to muddy up their image. Wright managed millions of dollars for labor unions in New York, and I'd suggested that pension managers talk to the company and consider if their services would be a good match for them. Again, this was legal: I'd been at Wright for thirteen years, beginning before I became leader, and I never, ever hid my role or pushed a union into hiring Wright.

Yet when *The New York Times* wrote about it, the story contained a healthy dose of innuendo:

> *An examination of state records and tax documents also reveals that several officials at the unions that invested with Wright also intersected with Mr. Bruno, whether by making political donations, by lobbying or by receiving state money disbursed at his discretion. Three of the unions' political action committees contributed to Mr. Bruno's campaign fund. Four trustees at the unions, who help decide how to invest the unions' money, were longtime political supporters of Mr. Bruno and some had endorsements listed on his campaign Web site.*[3]

It wasn't until the end of the piece that *The Times* revealed that a number of union officials admitted that "they did not know Mr. Bruno worked for Wright," and one union official whose pension fund had used Wright, added that he knew I worked for them, but "he had never been solicited by [me] for investments."[4]

The next few months passed in a blur. Bobbie died, and Spitzer resigned. I began thinking that I should leave the Senate. Hector Ruiz was making progress on securing funding for a chip fab, and once that was in place, I could go. For much of my adult life I wanted to become the CEO of a growth company in which I'd have an equity stake and earn $1 million a year. It wasn't a plan, more like a prayer, or a vision that I could see just over the rainbow, and I never thought the opportunity would come my way.

★ ★ ★

My friend and colleague, Senator Ron Stafford, passed away in the summer of 2005. I'd known his wife, Kay, for many years, but I hadn't spoken with her for a while when she phoned me a few months after Bobbie died. Kay wanted to talk about some legislation, and I took her to lunch at the Fort Orange Club.

Kay owned CMA Consulting Services, one of the most successful woman-owned companies in New York. Her firm specialized in information-technology consulting, systems integration, training, and software development, and that was why Kay had contacted me. The Assembly was supporting the use of red-light cameras, and she wanted to know if the Senate would vote for it. On the merits, it was a no-brainer, but I told Kay that I doubted the state was ready for it, because whenever a municipality passed it, people went nuts about the traffic tickets that arrived in the mail.

We spoke several times following our lunch, and Kay demonstrated that she paid attention to politics by telling me that I shouldn't pass the bill—it was too controversial. Kay also mentioned that she had stacks of logs in her backyard that she wanted cut up.

"Do you have a pickup truck?" I asked.

Yes, her company had several of them, and I suggested that she have someone throw the wood in the back of the truck and bring it out to my house and I'd chop it up for her.

On a Saturday morning, she showed up without a truck or the wood, because her backyard had been flooded.

"Well, Kay, did you ever split wood with a log splitter?"

She had grown up on a farm, but her father didn't have a splitter. I split wood for exercise and invited her to hang around. She agreed, and we walked to the woods with a chainsaw. I began to cut down a tree.

"Lookout!" she shouted, and a branch, falling from the top of the tree, glanced off my helmet and shoulder.

The branch was long and thick, the kind they call a widowmaker.

Laughing nervously, I said, "I guess you saved my life," and finished knocking down a couple of trees.

"Can I cut those?" Kay asked, and though unfamiliar with chainsaws, she caught on quick, and we finished sawing the wood into logs.

On the way back to the house, Kay asked me what I did on weekends. After the loss of a spouse, Saturdays and Sundays were the toughest because everyone, except you, seemed busy with their families. I told her that I did a lot of exercise, starting with a walk, then going inside to use my workout machines and hit the speedbag.

Kay had wanted to get on an exercise regimen, and the next morning we walked the big ski hill on my property. I'd been doing it for years, and I was surprised how easily she went up and down. I taught her how to use the equipment in my workout room and laced the boxing gloves on her and gave her a lesson. Soon, she asked if we could do this on weekdays, and I was amazed by her discipline. She lived in Clifton Park, and in order to be at my place by six, Kay had to get up at four, then she stopped to open her office in Latham before driving to Brunswick.

Most of all, I think Kay enjoyed the boxing, and we began to spar, with me instructing her on the art of the jab and pulling your punches. Then one morning, while we were boxing, she popped me in the face, and my nose spurted blood.

"Jesus Christ, Kay, you're not supposed to hit me."

With wide-eyed innocence, she said, "I wasn't trying to hit you hard."

Some mornings, after we exercised, Kay and I would have coffee and chat. As a rule, I read a prayer book every day before leaving for the office. I found it comforting, and Kay seemed surprised by it.

She said, "You never mention it to reporters."

"Some things are none of their business." Besides, I could imagine the headlines: *Majority Leader prays to God—Will the Lord Receive a Member Item?*

Kay was easy to talk to, and I found myself telling her that I was worn out by politics and ready to retire from the Senate. Kay said that she'd been looking to hire a CEO and had been interviewing candidates, but nobody had been the right fit for CMA. Would I be interested?

Interested? It was an answered prayer. We discussed it for a week. I told Kay that there was talk about an investigation, and I didn't know what was in store for me.

"Oh, don't worry about it," she said. "I know you, and I'm not worried about it."

In June, we drew up a two-page agreement and signed it. Kay told me to take my time finishing up at the Senate—the end of the session or the end of the year, whatever I decided was fine with her. Over the weekend, I phoned Frank Luntz, the political consultant with a talent for choosing the right words. I told him what I had in mind, and he gave me a statement. It sounded too formal for me, and I spoke to a close friend of mine, John Combs, a brilliant businessman who was the president and CEO of Shore-Tel, Inc. John suggested that I simply speak from the heart. Good advice, I thought, but there was a problem. When I woke up on Monday, June 23, I wasn't sure I was ready to leave.

That morning, I met with Shelly and Governor David Paterson, and we went through a list of unresolved matters. It was awe-inspiring to watch the governor, who was legally blind, deal with legislation. Paterson had no notes or any aides whispering in his ear, and he seemed to know the bills by heart and dealt with them without missing a beat. We came to agreement on sending the bills to the printer, and our meeting was done.

Back in my office, I phoned the governor and told him that I was leaving. He was in a state of shock. I tried to explain my reasoning, but there was a lump in my throat, and I had other calls to make. I phoned Shelly, Mayor Bloomberg, Dennis Rivera, and some other people, though I can't remember all of them. On Mondays, I usually held a conference for my members, and I walked in and said I was resigning.

Complete silence.

Finally, someone asked, "When?"

"Almost immediately."

Steven Boggess, my chief of staff, stood up and began to clap. Then everyone was standing and clapping, and I broke down. When I regained my composure, I told the conference that their efforts would have to be focused on maintaining the majority in November, and I asked them to sit still, because I needed to talk to the two senators who were in contention to replace me as leader, Dean Skelos from Long Island and Tom Libous from Binghamton.

Once the three of us were seated, I said, "If we have a battle over this, it'll be a disaster on Election Day. Tom, I think Dean has the votes. He's got the Island behind him. I'm asking you to join Dean, become his deputy, and shake hands, and after November, when we hold onto the majority, the leader job will be up for the grabs."

Tom stuck out his hand to Dean, and I started crying again. I went back to see my members and asked them to support Dean.

I announced my decision to reporters on Monday evening, and on Tuesday, I discovered that some of my members weren't pleased. I was operating out of the lieutenant governor's office, because with Spitzer's resignation I had become next in line to the governor. Six or seven of the older senators came in and told me that they wouldn't support Dean. I had to stay—at least through December.

I talked with them for a half hour. It wasn't that they disliked Dean, it was that they preferred that I didn't go.

"I have to," I said. "It's not fair to my family, it's not fair to you. I've been told I'm not a target, but who knows what'll happen. It'll get all mixed up in politics and it'll be a mess."

That seemed to do the trick—for the moment. Then I got a message that Tom Morahan, a crusty GOP senator from Rockland County, wanted to see me. It didn't start out too well.

Tom said, "I'm not voting for that fucker."

"Dean's going to need every vote."

"I'm not voting for him. I don't give a shit what you say. I voted for you. You're going to be the leader and you're going to stay."

I felt miserable listening to Tom, as if I were abandoning my friends. "Please, please, understand. We've got to have your vote and I've got to leave. Will you talk to Dean if I bring him in here?"

"No, I don't want to talk to him."

We went around in circles, and at last I was able to bring in Dean. Fifteen minutes later, Tom agreed to vote for him.

We went into session, and Dean became leader. Dean asked me to go up front and preside, and Governor Paterson came in, and I introduced him. He gave a speech about me and my tenure. I was invited to speak, and the Senate stood and gave me an ovation for four or five minutes. When it ended, I was so emotional I could hardly get the words out.

Almost fourteen years gone in the blink of an eye.

But the day also had huge upside. Hector Ruiz had visited Albany and assured me that the financing would be available for the chip fab in Luther Forest. I decided to leave in July, and to nail down my district for the Republicans, I dipped into my war chest and donated $400,000 to Roy McDonald, who would go on to win the election.

I took some comfort flipping through the pages of *Site Selection* magazine. When I became leader, the magazine rated New York forty-ninth out of fifty states as a place to locate a technology business. When I left, we were number one.

While I'd been preparing to leave, the FBI was carting away fourteen years' worth of my records from my Senate office and delivering the boxes—more than thirty of them, according to one of my assistants—to the U.S. Attorney for the Northern District.

I told reporters what I honestly believed. "I've never been accused of anything and don't expect to be accused of anything because I haven't done anything wrong. It's totally proper for authorities to take a look at what people do, especially when they're in higher offices. But they've been at this for three years and I am confident that absolutely nothing has been done wrong."[5]

Rumors were flying around the Capitol that I was retiring as part of a plea bargain, but I said that wasn't even close to true, and reporters kept pressing me to admit that I'd resigned due to the investigation. Again, untrue, and while I'd maintained my cool talking to the press, I was shocked by the FBI grabbing my files.

I phoned Bill Dreyer. "What's going on? Jesus, you told me I'm not a target."

"You're not a target."

"Isn't it pretty strange, the feds spending all this time and money investigating me if I'm not a target? The FBI wanted every piece of paper I touched since becoming leader."

"Good," Bill said. "That's good."

"How can that be good?"

"They'll be buried in paper."

Bill was an excellent lawyer, and if he wasn't worried, I wouldn't worry. He couldn't have known what was to come. I left the Senate in July, and I started work at CMA. I loved being there, learning the ropes, talking to potential clients. I was invited to appear before a grand jury, but Bill laughed, saying that the government would force me to incriminate myself in some inadvertent way through a series of Have-You-Stopped-Beating-Your-Wife type questions, and I'd be royally screwed at trial. He added that Sol Wachtler, the former Chief Judge of the New York Court of Appeals, was right on the money when he observed that a grand jury could indict a ham sandwich.

The FBI kept suggesting to Bill that I come in and tell them which legislators were breaking the law. The feds' attitude was that I knew where the skeletons were buried, and if I'd help them dig some up, they'd leave me alone.

"I don't know any individual who is breaking the law," I told Bill. "Had I known about it, I would've corrected the situation."

I offered to sit with the FBI and explain how the system worked, the serpentine process of functioning within guidelines that were more gray than black and white, how right and wrong were generally in the eye of the beholder, not some rules etched in stone tablets. Frequently, the view of a legislator's behavior was based more on his political alignment than his ethics. The chief challenge faced by part-time legislators was the mixing of politics and business, which made it almost impossible to avoid conflicts— starting with the fact that we often voted on legislation that affected us. In my case, for instance, I voted to increase benefits for veterans, and all of us would wind up voting for laws or backing programs that had an impact on our political supporters.

Not surprisingly, I don't think the FBI or the U.S. Attorney were interested in hearing from me.

I knew there was a grand jury impaneled and subpoenas had been issued in November, but I was occupied at CMA and the legal threat was like a bird warbling outside my window—off-key.

I remember it was on a freezing cold afternoon that Bill Dreyer stopped by the office. He sat with Kay and me and delivered the good news.

"It's over," Bill said.

"What do you mean?" I asked him.

"They need sixteen for a grand jury, and I heard one of them is sick and not even showing up. The feds are going to close it down. They have nothing on you. There's nothing there."

That was a relief and, if hadn't have been the middle of a workday, I would've popped the cork on a bottle of champagne.

However, Kay wanted to make sure, and she had a contact that put her in touch with William M. Welch II, an assistant U.S. attorney in Washington, D.C.

"Where is this coming from?" Kay asked him.

Not from Washington, he replied. It was being pursued locally. Then he gave her the number of the acting U.S. attorney for the Northern District of New York and suggested that she phone him. His name was Andrew T. Baxter, and he had filled the post when Glenn Suddaby was appointed a U.S. District Judge. Baxter would later be replaced by Richard S. Hartunian—whose ineptitude, in my opinion, would only be exceeded by his vindictiveness. For the moment, though, Baxter was overseeing my case, and Kay called him and asked who was pressing to indict me.

Baxter told her that it was coming out of D.C.

"That's not what I was told," she said. "He's our CEO now. Do you know how many people here depend on him?"

"Didn't you hear about what was going on?" Baxter asked. "Don't you read the papers? Why did you hire him?"

"Because I believed he was innocent. He left the Senate. They can change the rules. Didn't you think it was worth a conversation before you started with this?"

Baxter passed the buck back to Washington and told Kay that he'd look into the matter and call her back.

The next morning, at seven o'clock, Baxter phoned and told Kay that I was going to be indicted. Kay was flabbergasted, and when she told me, I felt as if I'd been sucker punched. Later, Bill Dreyer came up to CMA.

I said to him, "For three years you've been telling me I'm not a target, and you tell us a week ago it's over. Now they're moving to indict me? How can that be? And on what charges? Who can be accusing me?"

"Nobody—you don't need an accuser. It's the 'theft of honest services' law."

"The theft of what? Like I didn't do my job for the people?"

"Yes."

"I'm one of the hardest working guys they ever had in the Senate. And probably the hardest working leader ever. I've accomplished so many things. And the feds are saying I didn't do my job?"

"That's exactly what they're saying."

"It sounds like they could indict anyone."

"They could."

Bill told me he was confident that I'd be exonerated—the honest-services statute was horribly vague; the courts had been fighting over it; and sooner or later he thought the Supreme Court would get involved.

When he was gone, Kay said that I was staying at CMA until the case was finished. I was grateful for her faith in me.

On Friday, January 23, 2009, accompanied by Kay and my lawyer, I went to the federal courthouse on Broadway in downtown Albany. The U.S. Attorney had produced an eight-count, thirty-five-page indictment that claimed I had defrauded the people of New York by, in effect, pursuing my business interests.

I pled not guilty and was released without bail. I'd be damned if I was going to be attacked—and that was what I believed this was—without fighting back. So outside the courtroom, I gave the journalists my take on the proceeding, calling it "a three-year fishing expedition" that stunk to high heaven and the result of a "politicized" U.S. Attorney and an "overzealous" FBI.[6]

Getting into the car, I was convinced that I'd win my case, but I had no idea how much of my life would be devoured by it.

Between my indictment and the beginning of the trial I felt like I was living in suspended animation. I met with my lawyers, went on working at CMA, and made preparations to pay for my defense, thanking my lucky stars that my friends had started a fund to help me.

The strangest experience, and the most painful, would be a preview of how I'd come to be treated even after I cleared my name.

AMD had finalized a deal for a chip fab with investment from the Emirate of Abu Dhabi, and on Friday, July 24, 2009, ground was finally broken on the GlobalFoundries plant in Malta. I attended the ceremony with hundreds of politicians and business leaders. I was given a seat in the front row yet I felt like a skunk at a lawn party. People were polite, and reporters spoke to me, but there was a palpable distance between me and the others in attendance, as if they were reluctant to get too close or else their own reputations would be tarnished.

Senator Chuck Schumer made some remarks and credited me with getting him behind the idea of a chip fab. Governor Paterson was awarded a plaque and broke up the audience by saying, "This award is ironic. I was against this project from the beginning. Bruno had to convince me to do it."

My sense of satisfaction ameliorated my disappointment that I hadn't been asked to speak, but that was nothing compared to how I felt in September when I got a look at just how ugly politics could be.

President Barack Obama was coming to the Capital Region to laud our high-tech resurgence. He planned a stop at Hudson Valley Community College to cite their new programs as an example of how to prepare students for the economy of the future. Shortly before his visit, I received a call from a young staffer at the White House who told me not to attend Obama's speech at HVCC. The White House also phoned the president of Hudson Valley and told him that if Bruno would be there, Obama would cancel his visit.

It was the small-mindedness you'd expect from the mayor of a one-horse town, not the president of the United States. But there it was, and I hadn't even been convicted of a crime.

Right before the ceremony began, my cell phone rang. It was Attorney General Andrew Cuomo.

"I'm waiting for Obama," he said, "and standing here looking at the Joseph L. Bruno stadium."

"Nice, isn't it?"

"Joe, it's a tragedy you're not here. It's just plain wrong."

That was a classy thing for Andrew to do, and I appreciated it. Later, while the president was giving his speech and I was doing the commentary for a TV station, I wondered if Obama knew how that high-tech infrastructure and technology programs made it to upstate New York.

Probably not. And I doubted that he cared.

27

THE INTANGIBLE RIGHT
OF HONEST SERVICES

The ten months between my indictment and trial gave me ample opportunity to review the thirty-five pages of charges against me. There were eight counts, all of them related in one way or another to my consultancy agreements, and charging that between 1993 and 2006 I accepted $3.2 million in fees from groups and individuals and traded the payments for "official action on legislative, funding, contract, and regulatory issues."[1]

I didn't hide anything—some people knew, some didn't. I cleared my work with the New York State Ethics Committee, filed the obligatory state disclosure forms, and every penny was on my tax returns. Furthermore, state law didn't require me to tell anyone, and finally—and this frosted me—as the jury ultimately found, I didn't swap one official action for money.

The acting U.S. Attorney Andrew Baxter conceded that I had a right to pursue business interests outside my Senate duties, but contended that I had "improperly exploited [my] official position," and this deprived New Yorkers of the intangible right of my honest services.[2]

I told reporters that I was eager to "get this case out from the cloak of secrecy, out from the prosecutor operating behind closed doors, and in front of a jury who will look this case in the eye and then determine that this is a three-year fishing expedition that smells really, really bad."[3]

196

To the best of my ability I followed the ethics rules—I had attorneys go over every deal before I signed on—yet even if there had been a mistake, why was I in federal court?

Nor, for the life of me, could I see how I'd deprived the citizens of the state my honest services, though I was pleased to learn that the statute disturbed some of the finest legal minds in America.

Justice Antonin Scalia had written that although the law "consists of only twenty-eight words," it has been used "to impose criminal penalties upon a staggeringly broad swath of behavior," and since it didn't define "the intangible right of honest services," the statute was an invitation to "abuse by headline-grabbing prosecutors in pursuit of…state legislators."[4]

Scalia's observation wasn't news to government lawyers. Patricia Pileggi, a former prosecutor, admitted that the vagueness of the statute was catnip to prosecutors, since they didn't "have to prove loss of money," a standard that had to be met if they prosecuted a defendant for extortion or bribery.[5]

Another former prosecutor, Bennett L. Gershman, later a professor at Pace University Law School and an expert on prosecutorial and judicial ethics, agreed with Pileggi, stating that the honest services theory was convenient for prosecutors who pick someone they want to try and then locate a law to try him under.[6]

Why these specious prosecutions were clogging up court calendars was no mystery to me, and Professor Alan Dershowitz, among our country's foremost legal scholars, properly diagnosed its cause. "We have politicized the role of prosecutor," he wrote. Federal prosecutors are "appointed in a generally partisan manner," and "the job is a stepping stone to a higher office," and so "winning becomes more important than doing justice, because voters vote for 'winners' not 'justice doers.'"[7]

Opposition to the honest services statute continued to gather steam on both sides of the political aisle. One brief eventually submitted to the Supreme Court commented that the statute was so "opaque" that "an insincere sermon at Sunday religious services" might be covered by it.[8] Justice Steven G. Breyer noted that more than ninety percent of American employees could be charged under the law and speculated that a worker flattering his boss so his boss would leave his office and he could return to reading a newspaper was a deception that could be deemed a federal crime.[9]

The happiest news I received during this period was on October 13, 2009, when the Supreme Court agreed to hear the appeal of former Enron CEO Jeffrey K. Skilling, who had, in part, been convicted under the honest services law for what amounted to poor business judgment—a civil, not a criminal, matter. There was talk that my trial might be postponed until the Court issued its ruling. My natural optimism returned, and it lasted until November 2, 2009, the first day of my trial, when I got out of a car on Broadway in Albany, passed through security in the lobby of the James T. Foley United States Courthouse, and entered Courtroom 6, where in short order I'd discover that overzealous prosecutors were half my problem. The other half was occupying the bench.

28

OPENINGS

I watched the jury being selected with some interest, but I wasn't concerned about the jurors, believing that the average person, without any emotional or personal stake in the verdict, would decide that I'd operated within the law. But the judge, Gary L. Sharpe, worried me. He was about sixty with a perpetual expression of blunt rage and a haughtiness that seemed to rise off his robes like smoke from a block of dry ice. Sharpe was a career prosecutor, spending most of those years with the U.S. Attorney's office for the Northern District of New York, and his son worked there as well, a fact that I felt should've led Sharpe to recuse himself. He didn't, and it would soon become clear to me that Sharpe wasn't going to rein in his prosecutorial zeal because he'd become a federal judge.

What most of the public doesn't understand is that it's nearly impossible to become a judge in district court without doing some aggressive politicking. The difference between being elected senator and being appointed to a district court judgeship is that the voters get a look at their senate candidates' warts and all, while many district court hopefuls stick to back rooms, barrooms, and out-of-the-way restaurants, where they can curry favor with politicos in private, hoping to win their chance to ascend to the bench. I don't believe that all judges are as flawed as I thought Sharpe to be, as arrogant and resentful and eager to take a turn in the limelight, but if they are and a high-profile defendant comes before them, the opportunity to punish these unfortunate souls must be irresistible—payback, I suppose, for being forced to cozy up to power brokers to get their robes.

Assistant U.S. attorneys must be as politically adept as district court judges. They often require political connections to get their position—ironic, if you ask me, since the feds were trying to convince the jury that profiting from political connections was a crime. After they're appointed, the budding prosecutors have to get past the competition in their offices. If they're not worshipful enough toward their superiors or if at trial they don't win the U.S. Attorney the worshipful headlines he likes to read, then instead of being assigned high-profile cases like mine, they'll be prosecuting strip-club owners for bribing aldermen with lap dances.

As Assistant U.S. Attorney Elizabeth Coombe addressed the jury, I had no doubt that she could elbow her way up the career ladder. Coombe was neat, efficient, with light hair and freckles, an all-American type who amazed me with her ability to keep such contempt in her voice, as if she wanted to persuade the jurors that fining me $250,000 for each of the eight counts of my indictment and imprisoning me for twenty years was the best she could ask for, though a lethal injection was more fitting and would save the state a nice chunk of change.

Still, Coombe's disdain wasn't my most vivid memory from the start of the trial; it was Judge Sharpe's preliminary instructions to the jurors. He said, "Honest services fraud occurs when a public official deprives the public of its right to have its affairs conducted free from deceit, fraud, dishonesty, conflict of interest, or self-enrichment.... Honest services fraud is not concerned with the wisdom or results of a legislative decision, but, rather, with the manner in which officials make their decisions."[1]

These instructions revealed how nebulous the charges were and how, equally as frightening, the jury would be instructed to gaze into my heart and reach a conclusion about my motives—a determination that is thorny enough with a spouse or a child, let alone someone you meet via the thrust and parry of witnesses and attorneys.

And that wasn't my only problem. Even though I hadn't been a party to deceit, fraud, or dishonesty, I knew that if you were going to convict public officials for "conflict of interest or self-enrichment," you'd need a prison the size of Australia. How many state legislators involved in the insurance industry voted on legislation favorable to insurers? How about legislators with real estate interests? Or lawyers who voted against limiting awards in lawsuits? All conflicts that enriched the person casting the vote. And why stop at legislators? What about a town councilman who votes to spend tax dollars on sidewalks for his neighborhood, an expenditure that increases the value of his home? And let's not forget school boards. Spouses of district employees are permitted to serve, and they routinely vote to increase their families' income and medical benefits. And they do this why? To benefit students?

Thus, from the outset, I was scared because conflicts of interest were almost inherent in the position of Senate majority leader. I was legally permitted to pursue outside income, and yet countless businesses competed for a share of the state's tax pie, and my decisions had impacted all of them. Reporters observed that I appeared at ease, my usual personable self, saying hello to people before court and during breaks, chatting and asking after their families, as though the trial were a legislative hearing, and afterward we'd all go out to dinner. My real feelings were less pleasant. Most days, my stomach contracted into a hard knot as I listened to the prosecutors spin their grotesque fables about my life, and I worried that the jury wouldn't see through their fabrications, and I'd wind up in prison.

Bill Dreyer was still working on my case, but in addition I'd retained Abbe D. Lowell, a white-collar defense attorney from D.C., primarily known for representing Democrats, including a stint as the chief counsel on the House Judiciary Committee during President Bill Clinton's impeachment proceedings.[2] (Abbe had also successfully defended Joseph M. McDade, a Republican congressman from Pennsylvania, who had been indicted by the feds for bribery and had endured a six-year legal battle before his acquittal.[3]) Early in his career, Abbe had worked for the Justice Department, so he was familiar with the games played by U.S. attorneys, and he impressed me as having a healthy disrespect for the honest services statute.

I sensed, however, that Judge Sharpe, who seemed to suffer from the deep insecurity common to bullies, was intimidated by Abbe, and he was intent on proving that he was smarter than the famous, younger, legal star from Washington. Even before my trial began, Sharpe chewed out Abbe for telling the media that the honest services statute was "squishy," which could explain why the U.S. Attorney's office was so "defensive" about the staggering amount of resources that had been expended chasing me.[4] Sharpe had warned the lawyers to refrain from talking to reporters, but Abbe didn't say anything that hadn't been widely reported. Stories about the Justice Department investigating me had been around for years, and the Supreme Court agreeing to hear the Skilling case had made headlines, a course the Court wouldn't have taken if at least four Justices—the minimum necessary for the Court to review a law—didn't see the statute as problematic.

The *Times Union* reported that Sharpe "had reviewed the comments made by Lowell and that they may violate a local court rule that prohibits the parties from making statements that could interfere with a fair trial."[5] This was low-grade fertilizer. Anyone who kept current with the news would've been familiar with what Abbe was saying, and I guessed that his comments embarrassed the judge for proceeding to trial while knowing that odds favored the Supreme Court throwing out the law and making Sharpe look like a fool for wasting so much time and money.

Abbe apologized in a written filing to Sharpe and the prosecutors, and he didn't directly attack either of them again.[6] During his opening statement to the jury, he focused on the most onerous feature of the government's approach to prosecuting me, producing a blizzard of paperwork and a virtual conga line of witnesses that proved nothing more than that I'd drummed up business; gone to meetings with clients and spoke to them on the phone; consulted with state lawyers about potential conflicts and the dos and don'ts of my reporting requirements; and received payment for my services.

I thought the government's approach had a dual purpose. The first, prior to trial, was to pressure me (or any defendant) to plead guilty by burying my legal team in paper and forcing them to prepare for an army of potential witnesses. The U.S. Attorney had a huge budget and workforce, I did not, and my skyrocketing legal bills were discouraging, though not discouraging enough for me to plead to a crime that I hadn't committed. The second purpose, during the trial, was directed at the jurors. Through the sheer volume of documents that the assistant U.S. attorneys ordered their IT specialist to put up on the monitors and the hour upon hour of questions they asked the witnesses, the government attempted to persuade the jury that I must be guilty of something. This ruse sounds silly, but seeing it in action is anything but, and I could readily understand how a juror could be suckered by it.

Put yourself in his or her place. You're sitting in the jury box; you're a good person, honest, trusting, and it would be perfectly reasonable for you to ask yourself why in God's name would the government bother dedicating such enormous resources to prosecuting this guy if he hadn't broken the law? Therefore, he must be guilty.

Without overtly accusing the U.S. Attorney of bad faith, Abbe told the jury that the government's evidence was meaningless. He said, "After all the exhibits Miss Coombe told you about, all the documents, all the number of witnesses who have been interviewed and will come before you, all the people that have been spoken to by the government, all the massive amount of evidence that has been acquired, you will not find…one document, not one event, not one check, not one letter, not one phone message, not one note, nor a single witness who will say anything about being in a scheme to defraud, trying to hide information, not disclosing what they thought was proper, not taking money improperly. Not one. Instead, the only document that you're going to see that talks about fraud, schemes, and wrongdoing is the document that the prosecutors wrote themselves, the indictment."

It was a skillful rejoinder to the government's deception. Even so, reflecting on my first trial and imagining myself as a juror, I wished that Abbe had attacked the U.S. Attorney's motives and with the strongest language he could muster. This would've recast the mountain of paperwork and parade of witnesses in a far less persuasive light, and it would've provided a rationale to the jury for the government's mammoth effort to convict me.

29

NIGHTMARE
ON BROADWAY

In trying to recreate my experience at this trial, I'm overwhelmed by the official transcript, which runs 4,239 pages. Seventy-two witnesses were called, and I can't possibly go through all of them, so I've chosen to give some a brief mention based on the information they introduced and to focus on three—Mark Congi, Patricia Stackrow, and Jared Abbruzzese, who would be crucial to the outcome of both trials. This trio also captures how I felt sitting at the defense table and watching the government's attempt to mislead the jury.

The first witnesses called by Assistant U.S. Attorneys Coombe and Pericak were James Featherstonhaugh, a well-known Albany lobbyist; Timothy McGinn, head of the Albany investment firm McGinn, Smith & Company; and Francis Collins, my former chief executive counsel who had gone on to become a Court of Claims judge.

In the main, here was what the jury learned. I'd known James Featherstonhaugh since the 1970s. In 1992, Timothy McGinn had asked Feathers to set up a lunch where he could talk to me. The three of us had lunch, and I listened to an offer from McGinn for $2,000 a month to "assist in the development of money management relationships with labor unions, pension plans, corporate accounts, and wealthy individuals." The reason that he'd made the offer was because I'd been "elected nine times," and I was "held in high regard" for my "work ethic" and "integrity." McGinn testified that I told him I'd have to run the offer by my counsel and the ethics people. Then Francis Collins said that he that he'd gone to a meeting at McGinn, Smith to gather some information in order to prepare a letter for the committee. Collins sent the letter on my behalf, and the committee gave me the OK to go ahead.

During these first few days, Elizabeth Coombe got real worked up, introducing one of my old W-2 forms from McGinn, Smith, saying that I was an employee but also had a "doing business as" name that I'd filed with the Rensselaer County Clerk and listed on my financial disclosure forms. Coombe showed the jurors some canceled checks and said that they'd been mailed to my residence on Bulson Road. You don't have to be a master criminal to know that if you want to hide payments you probably should avoid sending a W-2 to the IRS and discourage the company paying you from sending checks to your house.

I listened and prayed that no one on the jury would be taken in by her tactics.

★ ★ ★

A journalist would learn, through "multiple impartial sources," that before the trial "the FBI privately expressed doubt that the U.S. Attorney's Office had enough evidence to convict Bruno."[1] No surprise there, at least not for me, because I'd done nothing wrong. So, absent proof, prosecutors have to construct the appearance of guilt, and the linchpin of their game plan is innuendo. I'd been working for Wright Investors' Service since 1994, suggesting to some labor unions that they evaluate Wright, with its excellent track record handling pension funds, and consider if they could be of some assistance. Soliciting unions wasn't a crime, and you would be hard-pressed to find a union with any sizable membership that doesn't lobby the Legislature. Two years before my trial, the media had been all over the story and found zip. A number of union officials didn't know that I worked for Wright and those who did had never been approached by me.[2]

To create the impression that I was up to no good, the government began by calling three witnesses: Howard Bennett, a former president of

Teamsters Local 294, and John Bulgaro, who took over Local 294 after Howard retired; and Norman Seabrook, president of the New York City Corrections Officers Benevolent Association.

These witnesses confirmed that I hadn't pressured anyone and explained that unions have professional, independent analysts who help choose pension managers—none of these men could simply pick Wright. Elizabeth Coombe didn't appear to like those answers, and she tried to get Bennett to say that he'd received legislative favors for choosing Wright. Nope, he told her, there was no quid pro quo, and I had promised him nothing.

Apparently, this wasn't the caricature of corruption that Coombe hoped to sketch for the jury, so she asked Bennett: "All things being equal, to the extent Wright's numbers were adequate, did you prefer to give the business to Wright because of Senator Bruno's affiliation with Wright?"

Bennett replied, "We would be pleased that he got the work because we know his track record as a legislator."

In other words, I helped unions. That wasn't exactly breaking news. You couldn't improve the business climate in the state without them.

In a blow to the government's fable, Bennett said that if Wright didn't put up good numbers for the fund, they would've been let go, and his successor, John Bulgaro testified that when the union terminated Wright, it had no impact on their legislative agenda. "They were two separate issues," Bulgaro said.

The government made other union members testify and put Leonard Fassler, a telecom executive, on the stand for hours. I'd known Len for more than thirty years, and I'd done some consulting for him and his companies. My sense was that the jury wasn't overly interested in those arrangements, a perception that was proved correct when the verdict was rendered.

The prosecutors, perhaps anticipating the numbing effect of repetitive testimony containing no bombshells, had a treat in store for jurors, a witness who could entertain them while giving the government a chance to paint me as a co-star in my very own Mob movie. His name was Mark Congi.

★ ★ ★

Mark Congi, a beefy man with a goatee, had traveled to Courtroom 6 from the federal penitentiary in Lisbon, Ohio. Once upon a time, Congi had been the president and assistant business agent for Laborers International Union of America Local 91 in Buffalo. His career was cut short when he was arrested in 2002, plead guilty to racketeering, and received a fifteen-year sentence.

To establish that Congi was an honorable man, Elizabeth Coombe had him inform the jurors that he hadn't been promised anything for testifying, but an assistant U.S. attorney in Buffalo would be told about his testimony and would consider some reduction in his prison time "depending on my cooperation."

Coombe had Congi discuss my relationship with Michael Quarcini, who had been the business manager of Laborers Local 91 for thirty-eight years. He had also been indicted for racketeering, but he passed away in 2003 before his trial. Quarcini was among the most powerful labor leaders in New York. Every upstate legislator knew him, and many of us helped the unions in the Buffalo-area due to the struggling economy. I had pitched Wright to Laborers Local 91 at a special investors meeting that included their lawyer and financial experts, and it was decided that Wright should be considered, and subsequently they were given a piece of the pension to manage.

The government had a much more nefarious vision of how Wright was selected, and I must say Mark Congi was quite cooperative in assisting Elizabeth Coombe with that story.

Coombe asked, "Who decided to include Wright Investors' Service in the search?"

"Michael Quarcini."

"Did you have any understanding about why?"

"Yes. He informed me that Senator Bruno had business with Wright Investors, and it would be to our benefit to invest money with this company."

"Did Mr. Quarcini elaborate on what benefit it would be to the union?"

"He felt that—"

Abbe interrupted with an objection, but before he could explain, Judge Sharpe overruled him. It seemed to me, as my trial progressed, that Sharpe had become increasingly antagonistic toward Abbe. He criticized him in front of the jury for supposedly making speeches when he had a witness on the stand, and he was just as harsh when the jurors weren't around. I recall Sharpe warning Abbe that if he gave the jury his take on the Public Officers Law, Sharpe would "chop your feet out from under you," a phrase that struck me as inconsistent with the finest in judicial temperament. I can't say why this happened. Maybe the judge was showing off for the media, and he disliked sharing the spotlight. Abbe had stopped talking to reporters, but I hadn't, because I wanted to restate my belief to the public that I was innocent and the trial was a politicized hunting expedition. Shortly, I'd conclude that the judge believed I was guilty and wanted me convicted, though it would be a couple days before I came to that conclusion. I felt I had a Damocles sword hanging over me when I went to bed at night and when I woke up in the morning, and if I made one false move, it was going to cut off my head. Whatever Sharpe's reasons, at this juncture he directed his ire at Abbe. Later on, I read that Sharpe had overruled the defense team far more frequently than the prosecution.[3] I haven't gone through the transcript to do a tally, but I remember *The New York Times* reporter Nicholas Confessore describing it as "a rare moment" when Sharpe sustained an objection from the defense.[4] That was how it felt to me, and I was concerned that the jury was being influenced by his hostility.

Regarding the objection, Abbe said, "He felt," emphasizing for the jurors that this was hearsay. Congi wouldn't have the foggiest notion of how Michael Quarcini felt, and Quarcini couldn't speak for himself as he happened to be dead.

Congi continued, "He felt that to make Mr. Bruno happy, that we would invest with this company and he would, in turn, do us favors in return."

That was precisely what Coombe wanted to hear. The honest services law didn't require the prosecution to establish a quid pro. In fact, the government would tell the jury that they weren't out to prove that I did anything in exchange for a payment. The *appearance* of impropriety was enough to sully my choices and condemn me. This was the hideous flaw of the statute, but since the Supreme Court hadn't ruled yet, Coombe was free to use Congi to create the impression of a crime.

Abbe was merciless during his cross-examination. He said, "You started by explaining that you had been convicted of racketeering? What did you do?"

"I ordered people to hurt people."

"Did you lie to people?"

"Not the people that I worked with."

"But to others?" Abbe asked.

"I'm a pretty straightforward guy…. I tell it like it is, so I wouldn't say I'm a liar, no."

"Have you lied to people in the course of getting done what you want to get done?"

"I just didn't always tell them the truth. Or I just didn't tell 'em at all."

"So you ordered people to hurt people and sometimes you didn't lie, but you just didn't tell them the truth. That's different in your head?"

"Sure."

His testimony sounded like the dialogue from a dark comedy, and it grew more comedic when Abbe asked him if he extorted people.

Congi answered that the government claimed he'd extorted jobs from nonunion contractors, but "that's not my definition of extortion…. I call it union activities. That's what I call it."

Abbe led Congi through several meetings the union had regarding the decision to use Wright, and neither he nor Michael Quarcini had attended all of them. An attorney was there along with an independent fund consultant who advised the union, an accountant, and the woman who kept the minutes. None of these people had ever been indicted. They did discuss the disappointing performance of some of the firms handling the union pension funds, and they chose to explore several new firms, Wright among them. Ultimately, the lawyer recommended the firms, and Wright was selected through this process.

And yet, Abbe said to Congi, with all those other people at these meetings, you are the one testifying.

I wished he'd said, "The one that the government brought in to testify," but he didn't, and I hoped that the jurors had understood his argument.

30

THE BATTLE OF
QUID PRO QUO

Despite the prosecutors' claim that they didn't have to prove I was selling favors, for the first eight days of the trial they questioned thirty-five witnesses and tried to suggest that I'd sold my office.[1] It was the government's persistence with this strategy, and Judge Sharpe permitting them to do so while not allowing my legal team to defend me with the appropriate documents, that would lead to my bitter courtroom exchange with the judge.

Here's how it started. The government called Samuel F. Forsina, a business manager from the Eastern New York Laborers District Council, who had held the same position with Laborers Local Union 190 in Albany. Sam testified that he'd known me for twenty years, and during a golf outing I told him that I was working for Wright Investors' Service and asked if he'd be willing to let Wright make a presentation. He told me to have Wright contact Francis X. Lilly. A former White House counsel and solicitor for the Department of Labor with an impeccable reputation, Frank was the chairman and CEO of Independent Fiduciary Services, Inc. When the union decided to invest $37 million of their pension and welfare funds with Wright, it was because Frank recommended it, and later on, when they moved the pension away from Wright, it was Frank who advised them.

Unsatisfied that he'd heard nothing about a quid pro quo, Assistant U.S. Attorney Pericak questioned Sam about my recommending him for the Occupational Safety and Health Hazard Abatement Board. Sam had forty-plus years of experience in the building trades, and Pericak had the gall to intimate that it was a payoff putting Sam together with other experts to assist with organizing training for lead removal. I looked at Pericak, his robot-like gestures, and heard him drone on, and I wondered if he'd ever seen the harm lead could cause laborers—memory loss, high blood pressure, and mood disorders, for instance. No, I decided, he probably hadn't.

Next up was Richard Burdick, my former director of operations who oversaw member items in my district. Assistant U.S. Attorney Coombe showed Rich—and the jury—some paperwork that had passed between us in which I had pushed hard for training funding for unions and low-cost electricity to help a unionized upstate paper mill. Again, the government was insinuating that I did this because of my consultant agreement with Wright. When Bill Dreyer cross-examined Rich, he said, "It would appear that you intervened on a few occasions for members of unions."

Rich replied, "I intervened for almost anybody if it was going to create jobs."

Bill informed Judge Sharpe that he had a matter to take up with him. After Sharpe sent out the jury, Bill said that he wished to introduce into evidence the detailed lists of the member items that I'd submitted from 2000 to 2006.

Sharpe said, "Why do I want to see a thousand records demonstrating all member items other than to try and schmooze the jury about what a wonderful senator your client was?"

Bill replied, "The government has selected a certain number of unions to suggest that there were training initiatives and training programs and member items to unions. Let the jury look through the list and see every single not-for-profit organization that was being given member items, initially by selection by Mr. Burdick, and then by approval by another [state] agency. Let the jury [see] these member items, thousands of them…to youth hockey, YMCAs, school districts, municipalities."

Sharpe appeared unmoved. "What other reasons do you have for the offer?"

Bill replied that it would be "extremely relevant" to demonstrate to the jury that everyonewas treated the same with the member-item program—whether or not I was being paid a consulting fee.

"I decline to admit the items," Judge Sharpe said. "This is not an election campaign.... I understand that it was the government's position articulated in the indictment and...the opening statement that there was no quid pro quo. And yet, they have incessantly opened the door to suggestions that there was.... I think it's time we begin to focus [and] I do not intend to continue the election campaign."

Bill pressed on, saying that "the government has spent a considerable amount of time trying to suggest that Mr. Bruno used his office to try and favor [people] he had business with.... That's the gist of this case, that he did certain things for them—"

Sharpe cut him off. "I don't believe that's the gist of the case.... That would be a quid pro quo, and I don't believe that's what the indictment alleges whatsoever."

Technically, the judge was correct, though that wasn't how the trial was proceeding. Bill said, "But having the Court acknowledge that the government has, in fact, accomplished that."

Sharpe snapped, "I don't know that they have accomplished it at all."

I sat at the defense table, shocked by his comment. Five seconds ago, Sharpe had conceded that the government had been hammering away at this theme, and now he claimed that the tactic had no impact on the jury? That was inconceivable. If I hadn't known that I'd followed the rules and the law, and set up my own wall between my official responsibilities and my business, and knew that I would never, ever trade a payment for a legislative decision, I may well have concluded that I was guilty. Did Sharpe believe himself capable of reading the jury's collective mind?

The prosecutors," Bill said, "have been allowed to use this courtroom to suggest that Joe Bruno has treated certain union members who used Wright Investment in a particular way and we have a right, I think, to counter that."

Sharpe held his ground, asserting that he had given us that right.

My head was pounding. If my lawyers didn't get the record of my member items before the jurors, they'd be more inclined to convict me of something, since if I couldn't fully understand the actual charges, how could they? Nor was this the only time Judge Sharpe refused to admit evidence favorable to me. He wouldn't let in my financial disclosure statements, which proved that I'd adhered to the existing regulations and hadn't violated any provisions of the Public Officers Law. Nor would he allow us to introduce the financials of other legislators, chosen at random, that demonstrated I was more than in line with accepted practices. From the start of the trial, I'd felt that Judge Sharpe was a peculiar hybrid of bully and buffoon, but now, his willful ignorance about what the assistant U.S. attorneys had done confirmed for me that Sharpe was rooting for a guilty verdict. He had no intention of stopping Coombe and Pericak from the constant innuendo. Once the jury came back, the prosecutors called several more union folks and elicited the kind of testimony that Sharpe had contended that he opposed. I put on an optimistic face for my family and friends and the reporters, but from that moment on I thought that Sharpe would do whatever he could to make sure that I died in prison.

For two days, I said nothing, and then, sick of the judge's hypocrisy and a trial that was a perversion of justice, I finally spoke up.

31

CLEARLY

The star prosecution witnesses that day were employees of Wright, Peter M. Donovan, the CEO, and Kenneth H. Singer, a senior vice president who was my primary contact at the company. I think a dozen witnesses had to be granted immunity from the U.S. Attorney before they would testify, and Peter and Ken were among them. This meant that they couldn't be prosecuted for any crimes related to their testimony unless they perjured themselves on the stand.

Elizabeth Coombe called Peter first. She asked him about my not notifying potential Wright clients that I worked for them, but didn't give Peter space to answer. As I've said, the government was painting a villainous portrait of me and the artistry was limiting the testimony the prosecutors wanted the jury to hear. True, the trustees of the union funds hadn't signed the necessary federal form that disclosed my agreement with Wright, but once I became an employee the form wasn't required. Coombe insinuated that my change in status was a dodge, though it was in strict compliance with law.

The issue of notification and conflict of interest was cleared up later that day, when Paul M. Thompson, a former federal prosecutor who now worked with Abbe, cross-examined Peter. I cite some of their exchange here because, rereading some of the newspaper articles from that trial, I noticed that reporters tended to skip testimony that exonerated me.

Paul asked, "You are confident, aren't you, that Mr. Bruno made disclosures about his affiliation with Wright?

"Yes."

"And you know that others at Wright knew that Mr. Bruno was making disclosures about his affiliation, correct?"

"Yes," Peter said.

"Some Wright employees attended presentations where Mr. Bruno was present, right?"

"Yes, in one instance [the paper unions] in particular I can think of."

"And at that presentation, Mr. Bruno, it's your understanding, said he was affiliated with Wright?"

"That's my understanding."

"And there was no agreement to try to conceal his affiliation, was there?"

"No."

Then Paul asked him, "Wasn't there more than one occasion in which Senator Bruno declined to contact a potential client because he felt that entity had significant and specific issues pending [before the Legislature]?

"Yes. I think there are two that I'm aware of."

"And in your experience, Mr. Bruno showed a caution to these kinds of issues and at times would not contact entities, correct?"

"That's right. And I was comfortable that he was very careful."

"Now, Miss Coombe didn't ask you any questions about that on direct examination, did she?"

"No."

I glanced over at Elizabeth Coombe when Paul finished, and to me she looked as though she were about to blow a gasket. Perhaps that accounted for why she beat the next witness, Ken Singer, like a cheap drum.

She covered a range of topics for more than an hour, but let's skip to the end, because that was when the fuse was lit. By then, it was almost time for court to adjourn until the morning, but Coombe kept having Ken read over his grand jury testimony from a transcript. He'd testified that when I contacted a potential client I was upfront about working for Wright and said that if they wanted to meet with Ken Singer that would be fine. If not, "I didn't want [them] to feel any kind of pressure."

Coombe had asked him about my pitch repeatedly before the grand jury, and now she had him read each one. Then, in a spate of questions designed to indicate that Ken wasn't reliable on the subject of my approach to clients, she said, "You told us it was only two or three times you heard Senator Bruno make contact with a union official?"

"Besides [the paper-industry] presentations, yeah, two or three."

"So you have no idea what he said when you weren't there, right?"

"No. I mean, I assume that's what he said."

"But you don't know that, do you?"

"No."

Coombe finished, and she must've figured that we were done for the day, and the jury would file out believing that Ken couldn't genuinely vouch for me. Abbe Lowell had no intention of letting her get away with that, and he asked Judge Sharpe if he could begin his cross-examination of Ken, promising that he'd keep it to five minutes. Sharpe agreed, saying that he wanted to let the jury go, but he didn't "think they'll mind five minutes."

Abbe asked Ken how often he had to testify before the grand jury, and Ken answered that he'd appeared in June and July of 2008 and in January 2009.

"And in addition to the three appearances," Abbe said, "you also met with the members of the prosecution team and the FBI, correct?"

"Yes. Once."

"Miss Coombe just asked you to read from three different portions [of your testimony].... And it was the same question each time. Did they ask you the same question over and over and over again in [your meeting with the prosecution and the FBI]?"

"Yes."

Abbe said, "Did they not like the answer the first time?"

Coombe almost blasted up out of her chair. "Objection, your Honor!"

"Sustained," the judge said.

"I'll withdraw it," Abbe said, but he'd made his point to the jury, and again, he had Ken say that he'd been asked three identical questions by the government, and he'd given the same answer on each occasion, stating that he'd heard me say I worked for Wight and told people that they could take the call from for Ken or not take the call as they saw fit.

Abbe said, "And that was asked to you three different times in the grand jury?"

"Yes."

"And again today?"

"Yes."

Abbe quipped, "See you tomorrow," meaning that he'd pick up his cross-examination then.

Judge Sharpe, his voice rising in anger, answered, "No, you won't," and asked Coombe if she had any follow-up.

"Yes, your Honor," she said.

Even now, seven years on, that moment remains frozen in memory. I thought a judge wasn't supposed to allow a redirect before a cross-examination was completed. Coombe had undermined Ken Singer's credibility, and Abbe had restored it, and by now, given Sharpe's behavior, it was clear to me why he'd want the prosecution to have the last word. But I wasn't a lawyer—maybe I was wrong—so I leaned over to check with Abbe and whispered in his ear, "He can't do that, can he?"

Sharpe said to Coombe, "Hang on a minute." He excused the jury and Ken Singer and, when they were gone, scowled down at me from the bench. "Let me explain somethin' to ya once, Mr. Bruno," he shouted, and I could see the spittle flying out of his mouth. "And I will not explain it again. For once in your life, you don't control something, I do. You ever do what you just did in the presence of that jury again, which is question any of my rulings, I will take measures to make sure you don't repeat that. Do you understand me? Do you?"

He must have seen the consternation on my face, because it was physically impossible for him to have heard me. None of the reporters in the gallery had heard what I'd said.[1] And I was seated near the stenographer, who had the hearing of an owl, and if you don't believe me check the transcript—she documented every mm-hmm.

Standing up, I glared at Sharpe. By that late afternoon in November, I was past eighty and on intimate terms with the frustrations of business and politics, the horrors of poverty and war, and the sorrow of burying lifelong friends and loved ones. But this—this hit me in a way I hadn't experienced—a disorienting blend of despair and fury that our legal system, among the nation's proudest achievements with its noble aspiration to blind justice, could be so corrupted by a prejudiced judge—a judge who seemed to me to be doing his level best to help the prosecutors stick me in a prison. On the surface, Sharpe's response seemed to be his attempt to show the lawyers and me and the media who was boss. But I'd met too many bullies: as a rule, they are scared of their own shadows, which was why they possessed the thinnest of skins, and in the instant before I spoke, it occurred to me that I was witnessing a guilty conscience in action, a man so insecure that a whisper spotlighting his lack of objectivity humiliated him.

With more than a touch of sarcasm, I replied, "I understand very clearly, Judge, what is happening here."

"All right," Sharpe said.

"Very clearly," I added, while Abbe tugged on my suitcoat and told me to sit down.

Sharpe said, "I want you to stop. You have a conversation with Mr. Dreyer and with Mr. Lowell so they can give you the benefit of their professional advice before you say anything further."

Abbe broke in before I could answer and, when he thanked the judge, I sat down and wanted to vomit.

Sharpe launched into a justification for his decision, his language, to my ears, tinged with insecurity. "This is not a strategic contest. I know what's going on in the trial. I was not born last night. Sooner or later, the lawyers are gonna come to grips with the fact that I understand what's going on in courtrooms."

Abbe told Sharpe that he was confused because he wouldn't be allowed to break into the prosecution's cross examination.

"Let's leave it alone," Sharpe said, and scrambled to explain himself. "Nobody will come to grips with the fact that I know what's goin' on…. You asked for five minutes to complete a brief period of cross-examination. That had to do with the impression you wanted to leave in the jury's mind overnight until you resume your cross tomorrow morning."

"And is that improper?" Abbe asked.

"No, not necessarily. I simply, in light of what you did, was going to permit her some additional questions at that point, on that issue and that issue alone."

Why would he do that? Where was it written that the prosecution, not the defense, was entitled to the last word? Nowhere, absolutely nowhere—except in the mind of this particular judge.

Sharpe said, "But it makes no difference. It's irrelevant at this point. That's all superseded by Mr. Bruno's conduct and that's what I'm not gonna tolerate."

There you go—it was my fault, not his. Spoken like a true bully, I thought, and a man who was a disgrace to the bench. It was so emotional for me—it felt like being in the boxing ring with both hands tied, trying to defend yourself with more than one person in the ring pounding on you. I prayed that justice would be served, and that I would be vindicated.

★ ★ ★

The next morning, before the jurors came in, Bill Dreyer asked Judge Sharpe to declare a mistrial, claiming that the displeasure he'd shown before sending out the jury left the impression that he favored the government. Barring the mistrial, Bill asked him to remind the jurors that he was impartial. Sharpe refused to declare a mistrial, but that day he did tell the jurors that when he was "engaged in any exchange with the lawyers or anything else over issues of admissibility, you ignore all of that."

The judge also wanted "to settle the record," so he recited his take on our interchange, quoting me as saying, "See, I told you his rulings are unfair."

Now, not only didn't I believe Sharpe was impartial, I knew that he wasn't above putting words in my mouth.

32

ARGUMENTUM
AD HOMINEM

A s the trial rolled into its third week, the prosecution called my former assistant, Patricia Stackrow, to testify. I felt a little sick watching Pat walk to the witness stand. She had worked as my assistant for twenty-four years, putting in long hours and keeping my life organized. I knew Pat couldn't point to any wrongdoing on my part, so, at first, I wasn't sure why the prosecution had summoned her. Yet as Assistant U.S Attorney William Pericak asked her questions, it was obvious to me that this was an exercise in character assassination.

Pericak asked her, "What does the term 'gatekeeper' signify?"

"The person who pretty much controls who the Senator saw."

"Were you [his] gatekeeper before he was Senate majority leader?"

"Yes. And for a period of time, probably maybe the first ten years that he was majority leader."

"And who succeeded you as the gatekeeper?"

"Amy Leitch."

From the questioning it appeared that Pericak was attempting to establish that Pat knew my business dealings, and that her replacement by Amy was in the natural course of things. Nothing could've been further from the truth, though I was unsure if Pericak was aware of the story

220

behind Pat's replacement. Pat knew it, but I can't say that I blame her for not bringing it up.

Pericak asked Pat about her responsibilities, and she replied, "I wrote checks out of his personal checkbook. I balanced his wife's personal checkbook, I wrote checks out of Capital Business Consultants.... [and] Mountain View Farm. I did a lot of his personal shopping. I did a lot of shopping for his wife or his family periodically over the years. Christmas shopping, gifts for his family, gifts for his wife."

"Did Senator Bruno pay you for the work that you did on his personal business and things you did for him personally?"

"No."

I could imagine what the jury was thinking: Here was this woman in her mid-sixties, prim and proper with short brassy hair and wire-rimmed glasses, a bit schoolmarmish, but perhaps resembling some of the jurors' beloved teachers from grammar school. And there I was, in my dark suit and muted tie, with my thick silver hair, a high-roller, just the sort of unethical guy who would take advantage of kindly, underpaid women like Pat, who, in truth, was earning more than a hundred grand a year when she retired. Pericak was also attempting to mislead the jurors by insinuating that my assigning Pat to handle some personal work for me was illegal, and the next day the newspapers trumpeted this false perception. *Newsday*, in a bold headline, declared: *State Worker: Bruno made me do personal duties.*[1]

It was always controversial when an elected official had a staffer doing personal business. But my theory was that if I skipped the chores that someone else could do, then I could devote more time to my constituents and legislative agenda. But assigning Pat those jobs wasn't against the law, and Pericak knew it. In fact, it wasn't until two months *after* my first trial, that Governor Paterson signed a law closing what was referred to as the "Bruno Gap," and finally made it illegal for public officials to use state resources for these tasks.

What followed were hours of questions about my business dealings, with the paperwork put up on the monitor so the jury could see it, every piece of paper described as a "government exhibit," as though it were evidence of some wrongdoing on my part. The net impact was that it seemed that I'd been running a multinational conglomerate while I was majority leader. Yet a lot of the paperwork was simply the disclosure forms that had to be filled out in order for me to comply with the rules that had been established for legislators.

Pericak asked, "When did you first become involved in typing Senator Bruno's financial disclosure forms?"

Typing? Jesus, Pat didn't just type them—she assembled them from her own records with the help of three different lawyers. This was the main reason the government pursuing this line was nonsense. I did the consulting and made the money, but I had nothing to do with keeping track of the payments or the state-required paperwork. Nor did I ever accept a client without running the potential employment past a lawyer— Frank Gluchowski, the Senate ethics lawyer; Ken Riddett, my counsel; and Tim Collins, a Senate counsel. Interestingly enough, when Pericak put Tim on the stand, and he testified that he'd done everything he could to help me avoid conflicts of interest, Pericak, again hoping to create the impression of impropriety, asked Tim if I'd been helpful securing his appointment by Governor Pataki to a judgeship. Of course, I had, and I was proud of it— Tim was an excellent lawyer and has proved to be a first-rate judge. Tim told him the truth. And it wasn't until Abbe Lowell got a chance to cross-examine Tim that the jury learned that he'd been reappointed to the bench by Governor Spitzer.

Pat went on answering questions, none of which revealed a damn thing except that Pat had handled all the associated banking and paperwork for my outside business, and that I'd been careful and refused to sign forms for the state until I got the OK from lawyers.

Right before Pericak finished with Pat, he said, "Your Honor, at this time, I would

request that the jury be advised of an immunity order issued with respect to this witness."

In a jocular tone, Judge Sharpe replied, "Did we forget, did we?"

Pericak said, "No, no."

"Oh, all right," the judge said with the same inappropriate, jocular tone, "Is this witness aware of the immunity order?"

Give me a break! The feds told us that after looking at my personal accountant that they believed that Pat had stolen somewhere between $50,000 and $100,000, so there was no way she'd have taken the stand without immunity from prosecution.

Pericak told the judge the obvious—Pat knew about her immunity—and Sharpe told the jury, "Ladies and gentlemen, just as the other witnesses who have been immunized, the same limiting instructions I have provided you would apply to the testimony of this witness."

Now Pericak went back to work, attempting to frame Pat's theft as my fault.

"Miss Stackrow," he said. "You mentioned that Senator Bruno did not pay you for all the personal work you did for him on his businesses, et cetera, is that right?"

"That's right."

"OK. Did you take some money yourself?"

"Yes, I did."

"And can you tell us approximately how much money you took?"

"I have no idea."

I didn't believe that. Pat was extremely precise about such things, which was why I had her doing my books. I suspect she was ashamed to admit how large her theft had been.

Pericak asked, "Why did you take the money from Senator Bruno?"

"I don't know."

This may well have been the biggest lie Pat told, but Pericak only had some of the story. The assistant U.S. attorney then read from the testimony that Pat had given to a grand jury:

Question: *"Why did you [Miss Stackrow] take the money from Senator Bruno?"*

Answer: *"Retaliation for the way he treated me at times."*

Question: *"How did he treat you?"*

Answer: *"He was demeaning, very degrading."*

Pericak looked up and asked Pat, "Did you give those answers?"

"Yes, I did."

I had no doubt that Pat found what happened to her "demeaning" and "degrading," but that was not my intention, and she knew it. While Pat worked for me, we'd been very close, and I'd trusted her with everything that I did professionally and politically. Once I became leader her power increased exponentially, because Pat was stationed outside my door and controlled who could talk to me on the phone or in person.

I'd never claim to be the easiest boss, and I could understand Pat feeling resentful at times—employees often do— but apparently the expansion of her power when I became leader went to her head. I began hearing from members, lobbyists, and constituents that you had to sweet talk her to get in touch with me. I discovered that she was going out to dinner with members, and a few times, as people left my office, I heard them say, "Pat, thanks for the help in scheduling the appointment," and Pat would reply, "Well, flowers are always nice," or "Wine is always nice."

Next thing I knew, I saw bouquets and bottles of wine being delivered to her desk, and I was disgusted with her behavior. I'd been abused by staff people in charge of access to leaders, and it had been among the reasons I'd challenged Ralph Marino. So I called Pat into my office and told her to knock it off.

Pat got defensive. "I'm not doing anything wrong. I can't help it if people want to send me flowers or wine. And I have a private life. I can go out if someone asks me to dinner."

On a few more occasions, I tried to convince Pat to stop seeking favors from people who wanted to see me, and when she refused, I replaced her with Amy Leitch. I moved her out of the Capitol to a beautiful, ninth-floor, private corner office in the Legislative Office Building. From my perspective, this was the opposite of demeaning her—technically, it was a step up—but Pat no longer controlled access to me, and I guess she missed the power.

Of course, Pericak would never want the jury to hear that story, and he wrapped up his questioning of Pat, doing his best to keep her victimhood intact.

Now, my lawyer got his chance. Referring to my checking accounts, business contracts, and disclosure forms, Abbe asked Pat: "Do you remember one time, one single time that Mr. Bruno ever went into those files to take any piece of paper out of them?"

"No."

Pat began smiling, and Abbe asked her why. She answered with the truth—that I never went anywhere near those files.

Abbe asked, "And when you were collecting this information and putting it in the files, did there ever come a time when Mr. Bruno said, 'Make sure you don't give this to

Mr. Riddett; make sure you don't give it to Mr. Gluchowski; and make sure you don't give it to Mr. Collins?'"

"Absolutely not."

I listened as my lawyer got Pat to testify that the changes made to my paperwork weren't done at my request, but because the Senate ethics lawyers had requested them. She also admitted that I'd never asked her to hide any aspect of my business affairs or income from anyone.

That was the truth, but, as I looked over at the jury, I had the sense that the damage had been done—that the jurors believed I'd treated this nice lady so badly that I'd turned her into a thief.

Funny thing is, Pat knew that she didn't need immunity as far as I was concerned. Pat knew me well enough to know that I'd never try to prosecute her or reclaim the money she'd stolen. What would have been the point? Revenge? I wasn't angry at her. I was sad, pure and simple, because someone who I'd worked with for so long had repaid me by embezzling from my checking accounts.

33

A FAST ROUND:
THE JAB AND THE CROSS

In boxing, the jab is used as a prelude to one of your power punches, usually a cross. When you're in the ring, during the late rounds, and the man you're boxing is jabbing, there is a terrible instant when you know what's coming yet he hasn't rotated his hips to throw his knockout punch. You envision it while you're defending yourself, exhausted, your arms like lead, sweat stinging your eyes, and though the clock is ticking, time doesn't seem to move, and all you are aware of is that the punch is coming.

That was how I felt when Mary Louise Mallick was called to testify, because I knew the government wanted to get her out of the way before they threw their haymaker—Jared Abbruzzese.

Mary Louise had two master's degrees, one in economics and the other in bioethics, and she is considered by Republicans and Democrats alike to be "one of the state government's top fiscal experts."[1] Prior to joining the administration of Governor Andrew Cuomo as first deputy comptroller, she had been the secretary of the Senate Finance Committee. In that role, Mary Louise represented me and the Republican conference on budget issues, separating the wheat from the chaff, so to speak, and negotiating funding.

Mary Louise told the jury about that the $500,000 in grants that had gone to Evident Technologies in Troy, among the earliest companies in the

Capital Region to utilize nanotechnology for a range of products—from treating cancer to improving decorative lights for Christmas trees.[2] Jerry Abbruzzese had a stake in Evident, but Mary Louise testified that I'd given the company those grants on her recommendation. She also explained the Genesis Program, an initiative of mine to create jobs in New York. Since we have so many research universities, I was hoping that we could use the funding to move their discoveries from the laboratory to the marketplace. To that end, I also directed $2.5 million to Russell Sage College, half the funding they'd need to build a lab that Evident would use. Russell Sage is a women's college, and a side benefit of placing this incubator there would be to encourage young women to pursue careers in math and science.

I had the dispirited feeling that the jury hadn't understood where Mary Louise's testimony fit into the narrative of my case. I became convinced of that once their deliberations were underway, and they requested that her testimony be read back to them. In the jury's defense, the technicalities of state financing are a paper-shuffling bore, and the jurors would've had a better handle on the relevant details had Mary Louise testified right after Jerry Abbruzzese.

Water under the bridge, I thought when she was done, and steeled myself for what I was certain would be the main event of the trial.

34

THE JOKER

The procession of witnesses, the slow-moving hours of testimony, a library of exhibits projected on the monitors, ruling upon ruling from the judge, the lawyers butting heads, the rushed lunches, the icy snap of the wind on the courthouse steps as I spoke to reporters, the millions I was spending to defend myself, the phone calls from well-wishers interrupting dinner, the heart-wrenching evenings of reassuring my children and grandchildren that everything would be fine, the waves of nighttime doubts, tossing and turning in bed, my rage at this railroading by government hacks with lofty titles, all of it part of a gruesome political rite and all of it boiling down to the testimony of Jared Abbruzzese, his words taking up no more than three percent of the monstrous transcript.

I'd met Jerry on the golf course of the Schuyler Meadows Club shortly after becoming leader. He was a turnaround specialist for troubled companies who had made a fortune in the communications field. We became friendly, and so did our families. It was a joy watching him with his wife and four kids—he was so attentive and fun-loving—and yet Jerry was one of those boisterous, rough-cut, wise-cracking guys who underneath his tough exterior was a teddy bear with few friends, a result of his impatience, a tendency to alienate people by yelling at them, and a habit of dominating conversations with an inexhaustible supply of anecdotes, a habit that neither endeared him to the assistant U.S. attorney nor the judge.

In 2004, Jerry hired me as a consultant for two of his two businesses, Communications Technology Advisors and Capital and Technology Advisors, and we negotiated a deal for $20,000 a month. Coombe had already questioned Jerry before the grand jury. His grant of immunity carried over to my trial, so if he told the truth he couldn't be prosecuted based on his testimony. Coombe was intent on implying that the money I'd earned amounted to a bribe but, like any accomplished storyteller, she had to begin by inventing a pair of motives for the jury—one for Jerry and one for me.

Coombe went at her task by questioning Jerry about Evident Technologies. Once Coombe had Jerry say that he'd offered to help Evident position itself to find funding from the public and private sector, she said, "Did you expect to receive some compensation for that?"

Jerry replied that if he were successful, yes.

Coombe asked him if he'd facilitated a meeting with Evident and me regarding state funding. She already knew the complete answer, but she had no intention of allowing Jerry to lay it out for the jury: it would've undermined her fictional motives.

Jerry said, "I did facilitate a meeting with Evident with Senator Bruno so they could collect on the money that was owed them by the state government as part of the $1.5 million commitment made in [the late fall of 2002] by Governor Pataki."

"Move to strike," Coombe said, glancing up Judge Sharpe. "Nonresponsive."

"Granted," Sharpe said.

"Mr. Abbruzzese, my question is: Did you facilitate Evident meeting with Senator Bruno in connection with Evident's request to get a grant from the State of New York?"

"Ma'am, I'm tryin' to answer.... It wasn't a new grant.... I did facilitate a meeting for them to get the payments that were owed them by the State of New York."

Coombe peppered Jerry with questions that suggested his deal with me and the grants for Evident and the money for the Russell Sage lab were connected. When she finished, she moved on to demonstrate that the

$200,000 Jerry had paid me between March and December 2004 was a bribe because I had performed no work for it.

She asked, "What reports did you receive from Senator Bruno for the $200,000 that he was paid?"

"None. I didn't ask for any either, though."

"What correspondence did you receive from Senator Bruno?"

"We spoke by phone."

"What memoranda did you receive from Senator Bruno?"

"No reports, no memorandum," Jerry said. "But neither did I ask for any."

The assistant U.S. attorney read from a letter that terminated my agreement with Jerry and thanked me for my "fine help" with some golf-course opportunities in Florida.

Sarcastically, Coombe asked, "What *fine* help did Senator Bruno provide?"

Jerry answered that the telecommunications restructuring business had slowed, and he wanted to expand into other areas. He had asked me to use my contacts to dig up some parties interested in golf-course development.

Then Coombe made a mistake, bumping her head on the truth and revealing to the jury how a prosecutor manipulates a witness in an effort to caricature a defendant. Coombe asked, "Did you mention anything about starting a new business involving golf courses when you testified in the grand jury?"

"You didn't ask," Jerry said.

Her mistake, I believed, was assuming that because Jerry was bald and paunchy and sometimes flashed a goofy grin, he wasn't too bright. But Jerry was smart as a whip, and he was a careful listener—one of the reasons I liked him.

Coombe inquired about the people Jerry had met through me. He named a couple, and when the prosecutor, apparently unimpressed with his response, said, "Who else?" he launched into one of his anecdotes that would lead the *Times Union* to refer to his testimony as the "comedy hour."[1]

"Donald Trump, which was amazing. I spent some time, a couple meetings with Donald Trump, and I have to tell you, just a brief aside, I went in there to try and work on potential opportunities with Donald Trump, based on an introduction from Joe, and I came out of there having bought a membership at one of his clubs. So, in the art of the deal, he totally walked over me. I mean, it cost me money and I got nothing out of it."

Laughter rolled through the courtroom. Coombe didn't appear amused.

"Jerry said, "But he does comb his hair from the side and swirl it around."

More laughter.

Coombe, again smacking her head on the truth, implied that Jerry was perjuring himself now because at the grand jury he hadn't mentioned his plans to develop golf courses.

"When I testified," Jerry said. "You were very specific on limiting what I got to answer."

"Your Honor, move to strike."

"You kept cutting me off," Jerry was saying.

"Move to strike," repeated Coombe. "Nonresponsive."

"No," Judge Sharpe said. "I deny it."

Coombe's face tightened into a mask of anger. Jerry sometimes had that effect on people, and I suspect the prosecutor was put out that she hadn't gotten her way with the judge. But Sharpe couldn't very well stop Jerry from directly and honestly answering her.

Coombe doubled down, her voice as unpleasant as chalk scraping a blackboard. "Mr. Abbruzzese, you didn't tell the grand jury that you were thinking of having golf course opportunity developments at the time that you testified, did you?"

"No, I did not, ma'am."

"And I repeatedly asked you during various times of your appearance about the golf course opportunities and instead of saying that, you said that those introductions were to help some friends of yours."

"No. I think, ma'am. You asked me on several occasions did I have a golf course business at that time, and I did not."

Coombe gave up and tried to get Jerry to say that I'd done nothing for my payments. "What general telecommunications advice did Senator Bruno give you?"

He told her about our discussions of my early years in telecom and my bringing Coradian out of bankruptcy, and how I'd advised him about being a leader.

"When we would be playing golf and talking about these things, what I would be doing, breaking the rules at the club, always on a cellphone at the golf course, yelling and screaming at people, and [Joe] would say, 'Would you stop…. You gotta lead by making [people] feel enthusiastic about following you and following your beliefs and the standards you want to set as opposed to urging them from behind like a sheep dog herding sheep,' which is the way I was doing it. There are a lot of things I got from my relationship, both direct and indirect, regarding telecom and my business from Joe."

Coombe pointed out, and Jerry agreed, that the technology was vastly different in the early days and irrelevant to him. "At the end of the day," she said. "Senator Bruno didn't give you a tremendous amount of telecommunications advice, isn't that correct?"

Jerry replied. "I didn't need Senator Bruno for telecommunications advice solely. I wanted him for his Rolodex."

Once she had established that Jerry was interested in my connections, Coombe asked him about Friends of New York Racing, a nonprofit group that hoped to recommend approaches to fix or replace the financially troubled New York Racing Association.

Coombe said, "Friends of New York Racing was formed in anticipation of the expiration of the NYRA franchise?"

"Yes, ma'am."

Coombe referenced a meeting I'd had with Jerry and another member of Friends in which I told them that I'd like to privatize NYRA "to improve operations, accountability, results, et cetera."

Of course, this had been my mantra since being elected to the Senate, but the implication in this context was that I would assist Jerry and his group in taking NYRA's place.

And why would I do this, you might wonder?

Not just because Jerry was paying me, but because we both loved the horse business, which Coombe illustrated by circling around to Christy's

Night Out, a horse that Jerry and I had owned in partnership with Dr. Jerry Bilinski, a veterinarian and proprietor of a Thoroughbred farm in Columbia County. The story was convoluted and it didn't become easier to understand with the assistant U.S. attorney interrogating Jerry as if he were a prisoner of war.

Coombe said, "The horse wasn't worth $80,000, was it?"

"Well, you can look back and say the horse isn't worth $80,000 now."

"Mr. Abbruzzese, I am going to direct your attention to page ninety-seven of your grand jury transcript."

"Yes, ma'am."

"Did you give this answer: 'Christy's Night Out wasn't worth $80,000.' Did you give that answer?"

"I did."

"Did you continue on to say, 'But it was not worth zero, but was worth somewhere in between'?"

"Yes, ma'am."

I was nervous listening to this back and forth. Few people understand how a Thoroughbred is valued, and odds were against any of them being on the jury. Pricing Thoroughbreds is about as scientific as predicting the future with a crystal ball. For example, take Sea Biscuit. He could've been claimed for two or three thousand dollars, but nobody was interested, and he turned into one of the greatest horses in racing history. On the flip side of that success story is the disappointment of The Green Monkey, a colt that sold for a record $16 million and never won a race.

"The horse wasn't worth $80,000, was it, Mr. Abbruzzese?"

"No. And I ended up paying forty for it." Jerry was referring to a debt that he owed me of $40,000. I'd forgiven it as part of the horse deal, but Coombe hadn't given him a chance to work that in. I guessed she liked the sound of eighty instead of forty.

"Senator Bruno was owed $80,000 under the terminated TerreStar agreement and you agreed to pay him $80,000 for a horse that was not worth $80,000, isn't that correct?"

From my point of view, Coombe was raising an issue that demonstrated Jerry's essential decency. I'd been working with him on helping TerreStar, a communication company in Texas, when a new CEO took over and told Jerry to get rid of his consultant. Jerry felt obligated to pay me the money left on my contract. Coombe was attempting to portray this payment as a bribe.

"Ma'am, I think if you read on in the grand jury testimony—"

"Excuse me, Mr. Abbruzzese. The question requires a 'yes' or 'no' answer."

"I agreed to purchase a horse for $80,000."

"Your Honor, move to strike, nonresponsive."

"Nonresponsive," Judge Sharpe said. "Answer the question, please, Mr. Abbruzzese."

"I paid him $80,000 for a horse."

"That was not worth—"

"I committed to pay him $80,000 for a horse."

"You committed to paying him $80,000 for a horse that was not worth $80,000, isn't that correct?"

"Looking back on it, that is correct."

Coombe stiffened. She didn't like that answer: it emphasized the fact that neither Jerry nor I knew the real value of Christy's Night Out.

As she forged ahead, Jerry blurted out, "I did not pay 80,000 for the horse; I paid forty."

She said, "You paid $80,000 for a horse that was not worth $80,000 because you paid $40,000 for it at one point and had $40,000 debt forgiven?"

"That would be a $40,000 total, not eighty like everybody talks about it."

"Well, you would have had to pay Senator Bruno another forty."

"Right."

"Mr. Abbruzzese, please let me finish my question."

"I'm sorry. I apologize."

"The bill of sale was for $80,000, isn't that correct?"

"Correct."

"You paid half of it, $40,000?"

"Correct."

"If Senator Bruno had not forgiven the $40,000 debt in connection with the termination agreement, then you would have owed him another $40,000, isn't that correct?"

"Correct. But he did forgive it and so...I made good on the TerreStar contract, I made good on getting out of all the horse dealings with Jerry Bilinski, I made good on severing all my economic ties for $40,000. It was never an $80,000 transaction; it was a $40,000 transaction. Forgiveness of debt—and people in the newspaper misprint this all the time because they don't bother to think about it. Forgiveness of debt is him forgiving my debt. If I forgave him $40,000 in debt, that would be $40,000 to Joe Bruno. This was $40,000 to Jerry Abbruzzese, so it was a $40,000 transaction."

I felt as though I was listening to Abbott and Costello performing their "Who's on First?" routine. It had the same absurd feeling of going round and round, except it wasn't funny to me, because I could see the jury losing track of the discussion and responding only to Coombe acting as if she had Al Capone himself on the stand and Jerry, understandably worn out, becoming defensive.

Abbe Lowell questioned Jerry, and he was able to explain that he'd bought the horse for his wife, who had named it for her best friend, and Jerry had paid out another $10,000 or $12,000 to board and train the horse before deciding that he had no future as a racehorse and gave him away to a little girl.

Abbe also asked Jerry about our business relationship, and Jerry made the jurors laugh again by saying that my advice about leading companies had been valuable, making him "a little bit of a people person [and] much less of a jerk."

Coombe got her chance to take a final run at Jerry, and it struck me that she was less interested in information than she was in pushing him around, setting him off, and making him less sympathetic to the jury.

With phony good cheer, she said, "Good morning again, Mr. Abbruzzese."

"You have fifteen minutes left of morning, but yes, good morning."

"I usually check before I say that."

"Good for you."

35

THE LONGEST WAIT
OF MY LIFE

The closing arguments sounded like white noise, a tedious, befuddled rehash of the testimony, with the government referring to me as a bully and my lawyer as a benefactor, and I marveled at the jurors' ability to remain awake.

I listened far more intently to Judge Sharpe charging the jury. My impression was that he spent far more time telling the jurors how they could come back with a guilty verdict than how they could acquit me.

On top of that was the ridiculousness of the honest services law. The judge told that jury that my "state of mind is a fact you are being called upon to decide," and instructed them that "rarely is direct proof available to establish a person's state of mind [so it] may be inferred from what he says or does at the time of the occurrence or nonoccurrence of certain events."

Therefore, my fate hinged on the subjective perceptions of five men and seven women who had become acquainted with me through the jaundiced lens of this trial.[1] That was intimidating, but worse, as the jury retired to begin deliberating, was my chewing on an observation that Abbe Lowell had made in his closing. Abbe had compared the prosecutors' thirty-five pages of allegations to "throwing a bowl of spaghetti on the wall with hopes that one strand or another might stick." Abbe had intended to demean the government's strategy, to characterize it as unfair, as a miscarriage of justice,

236

but while this was true I realized that logically it didn't follow that such a strategy, however unconscionable, would be ineffective.

During the first day of deliberations, Tuesday, November 24, the jury asked the judge for some guidance about payments I received from a wireless company and for the testimony of a Senate ethics lawyer and my Senate counsel to be read to them. The jurors reached no verdict, and Judge Sharpe excused them until the Monday after Thanksgiving.[2]

Over the long holiday weekend, my mood bounced between elation and despair, but on Monday, after lunch, when the jury came into court to have the testimony of Mary Louise Mallick read to them, I felt a surge of optimism.[3] The next day, the jury sent a series of notes to the judge. One requested "clarification about 'beyond a reasonable doubt' versus 'beyond a shadow of a doubt,'" and another, the note that made me believe I'd be exonerated, was delivered in the late afternoon and stated that they had "come to a consensus on two counts," but were deadlocked on the other six and requested "some guidance as to how to proceed."[4]

Sharpe gave them an *Allen* Charge, which urges a jury, in the strongest terms, to keep at it until arriving at a verdict on all counts. I sat with a few reporters in the courtroom and told them that "the magic words in my mind are 'reasonable doubt.' There certainly is a reasonable doubt that has to be in people's minds as to whether we've done anything that we shouldn't have been doing."[5]

My spirits soared, and I was delighted the next morning when I opened up the *Times Union* and read a quote from Daniel J. French, a former U.S. Attorney from the Northern District. "If the jury has acquitted on two counts and ultimately can't reach a verdict on six, I do not think the government should feel compelled to bring this to trial again. Obviously, a jury has struggled with whether the conduct is illegal. Resources would be better spent demanding that the Legislature eliminate outside income, which of course is the source of the problem."[6]

I couldn't have agreed more.

My optimism lasted up until 4:20 in the afternoon on Monday, December 7, when the jury filed into Courtroom 6, and Judge Sharpe read out their verdicts.[7] They found me not guilty on five counts, couldn't reach consensus on another, but convicted me for two acts—my consulting payments from Jerry Abbruzzese and the sale of Christy's Night Out, which the jurors deemed gifts.[8]

I felt as I'd been gut-punched, but that gave way to a merciful numbness that not even the cold air outside could dispel while I made a statement to the media on the courthouse steps.

"I am very, very disappointed in the verdict. The legal process is going to continue. In my mind and in my heart, it is not over until it's over. And I think it's far from over. Thank you all, have a good night and merry Christmas."[9]

I believed what I'd said. This wasn't over. Not by a long shot.

36

SENTENCED

In April 2010, Bill Dreyer wrote Judge Sharpe requesting that he postpone my sentencing "in the interests of judicial economy and fundamental fairness." The honest services law was being reviewed by the U.S. Supreme Court; a decision was expected soon; and all signs from legal scholars and the Court itself indicated that the section I was tried on would be declared unconstitutional and my conviction would be vacated.

If what I'd done wasn't illegal, then I didn't want to walk around as a convicted felon, and I'm sure Sharpe understood this. Yet even though judges across the country had done what Bill had proposed, Sharpe rejected the postponement with a one-line decision. Bill told me that the terse rejection had shocked him and a number of lawyers. It didn't shock me. In court, when my lawyers had raised the issue, Sharpe snapped, "I am the Supreme Court in this courtroom,"[1] and because I'd spent decades among people addicted to power and public attention, I never thought that Sharpe would miss his chance to throw his weight around and sentence a big fish, with the media for an audience.

My sentencing took place on May 6. According to Jeremy Peters of the *New York Times*, I "bounded" into Courtroom 6 and greeted my family and friends in the gallery as though I were working "a rope line at a campaign rally."[2] Indeed, I did say hello to everyone and shook hands, but I knew that some of these people felt worse than I did, and I was banking on my customary display of confidence to cheer them up.

Then I stood before the judge, and I remember looking up at Sharpe's dull, angry eyes, as if no light burned behind them. I remembered the stories I'd read about the show trials in the Soviet Union, and I understood, in a way I wish I hadn't, the helplessness of those defendants in those grim kangaroo courts, facing the unbridled power of the state, a power indifferent to rational argument and the rule of law, the power of bullies, small gray men with bloated egos whose greatest joy in life was their government-sanctioned ability to flatten others on a whim.

Before Judge Sharpe sentenced me, I had a chance to speak. I remember talking about my background and telling Sharpe that I'd "been up at night, thinking about this moment. I can say this to you as honestly as I can say anything in my heart and mind: I did nothing wrong.... Maybe I used bad judgment. Maybe I was a little cavalier in the way I handled my business judgments," but I earned my pay as a consultant and "did a lot to change people's lives."[3]

I shifted my focus to the prosecutors, saying that I was still waiting for somebody to "prove I didn't do my job as a senator," adding that I had no idea how the jury could have understood their arguments. "I didn't understand the eight counts—and I was the one on trial!"[4]

I pointed out that I'd earned a good deal of money before entering the Senate, and I was worth a lot more before getting into politics.[5]

Friends in the courtroom later told me that they thought Sharpe had listened carefully while I spoke and his expression had softened. I can't say whether I reached him, but when I finished he began coughing and excused himself and disappeared into his chambers. However, when he returned, he had a strange look on his face, as if God had visited him in chambers and whispered in his ear that he wasn't on the bench because of a political assembly line that rewarded slavish devotion over talent and judiciousness, but because he was the prophet Jeremiah reborn.

"You committed a crime," he said. "The jury told you that. You can't accept it. You have blinders on. You simply can't see it."[6]

The hypocrisy of this statement made me gag. Sharpe and I both knew that if the Supreme Court had issued its ruling, then I wouldn't have been guilty of anything, and I wondered about the motivation for his statement.

Was it possible that a judge could suffer from such prejudice that he couldn't do his job? I could accept that my thirty-two years in the Senate were spent navigating, as best I could, through a putrid, ethically challenged system, which I'd attempted—and failed—to change. Even so, Sharpe had been birthed by that same system. The difference was that if I put on a dog-and-pony show at the expense of the taxpayers, all the while knowing that shortly my efforts would be rebuked, then I risked being removed in a primary or a general election. Sharpe didn't run that risk. No mechanism existed to check his power beyond the limited scope of the courts. He was a menace to society hiding under his robes, and he couldn't be thrown out on his ass for hubris or exercising bad judgment or trying to show the defendants that came before him that they were wrong and he was right. So there he sat, puffed up with moral indignation, as though he'd been doused in sacramental rose water instead of giving off the stink of an unmucked stable.

Sharpe began to speak again, and he sounded as though he'd appointed himself the savior of New Yorkers everywhere: "I firmly believe Mr. Bruno has engaged in charitable and good works in his life. But the conduct alleged to be part of your charitable and good works was also conduct that feathered your own nest.... I wonder how important the citizens of Buffalo, of Rochester, of Syracuse, of Binghamton, think Joe Bruno Stadium is.... People think you're the greatest thing since ice cream because of what you got them. And you got that because you took money from other taxpayers."[7]

Ah, Judge Gary L. Sharpe, the blowhard political theorist: if you ask me, he was a mile or two shy of Aristotle and the conception of the common good. To Sharpe, public works would appear to be stealing from taxpayers if they don't directly benefit from a specific public investment. Therefore, when the Senate majority leader, Warren Anderson, funded an extension of Interstate 88 that connected Albany to Binghamton, where Sharpe had worked as an assistant district attorney, Anderson was cheating the residents of Rochester? Because the University at Buffalo, where Sharpe had attended college, boasted the largest state-run medical school, dental school, education school, business school, and engineering school, the students attending the University at Albany got screwed?

How ignorant, but not surprising. With his tunnel vision, Sharpe would tend to see every exchange as a zero-sum game, the type of I-Win, You-Lose man who has become so prevalent—and done such harm—to our public life.

I knew I was wasting my breath, but I explained that my interest was in creating jobs wherever I could, and for that reason I used my staff to free me up for those responsibilities. In response, Sharpe accused the Senate lawyers of being prostitutes.[8]

"Those are not your lawyers," he said. "They belonged to me, to everyone in this courtroom, to the citizens of the state of New York. They should not have been negotiating your private contracts."[9]

This may have been the most perverted statement I've ever heard from a judge. Sharpe knew from the evidence that no lawyer had negotiated my contracts. I sought their input so I wouldn't make a mistake, and neither I, nor the other legislators who took on employment outside their elective duties, had a choice. The legislative lawyers were the experts in this murky, arcane field of rules and laws, so where the heck should legislators go for guidance?

Don't misunderstand me. It's a lousy arrangement, which was why I suggested to Spitzer that we raise salaries and forbid outside income. But no one seemed to want to fix that problem. After all, if journalists, prosecutors, judges, and good-government think tankers couldn't excoriate New York legislators for being crooks, what would they do for a blood sport?

Assistant U.S. attorneys Elizabeth Coombe and William Pericak had requested that Judge Sharpe sentence me to more than eight years in prison.[10] It seemed that they believed justice demanded that an eighty-one-year-old convicted of committing what, in reality, had never been a crime, should die behind bars. I wondered if Coombe and Pericak would've preferred the guillotine, which would've been a real boost to their careers. Think about it: how many prosecutors could brag that they had the head of a Senate majority leader chopped off?

Bill Dreyer argued that their request, given my age and accomplishments and that I was no longer in office, was ludicrous. Judge Sharpe commented that he didn't view these as mitigating factors and stated that my refusal to admit any wrongdoing rankled him—despite the fact that the Supreme Court was about to agree with me, a turn-of-events that the judge obviously thought shouldn't impact his decision.

Sharpe sentenced me to two years in prison, said that I had to pony up $280,000 in restitution and, upon my release, had to remain on probation for three years.[11] I suspect he would've given me a reporting date to begin serving my sentence, except that would've made him appear to be what he was—a judge out to punish me regardless of the law. Bail would be continued until after *Skilling v. United States* was decided and, depending on the result, my lawyers would either submit a bail application to the Court of Appeals or I'd no longer be a convicted felon.

I squared my shoulders, held my head high, and walked out to the courthouse steps. I told the reporters waiting there that I was "proud of my public service, and I don't believe I have anything to apologize for because I listened to our [Senate] attorneys.... and I am confident and praying, as others are praying, that the Supreme Court comes out soon and strikes down this law, as most people believe it will be struck down, and when that law disappears, we're going to be appealing to this judge to have this all go away."[12]

Richard Hartunian, the U.S. Attorney for the Northern District of New York, held his own news conference and crowed that the sentence was "a landmark step."[13]

I speculated that by gloating before reporters, Hartunian would be reluctant to eat his words after the Supreme Court weighed in.

This was how it played out, and his refusal to do so would cost me another four years of my life, leaving me to wonder what sort of hideous legal system allowed an out-of-control prosecutor to wield such power and why nothing could be done to stop him.

37

THE CRIME
THAT WASN'T

On June 24, 2010, the Supreme Court ruled unanimously in *Skilling* that the law making it a crime to deprive another of the intangible right of honest services was unconstitutional and could "cover only bribery and kickback schemes."[1] Writing for the majority, liberal Justice Ruth Bader Ginsburg highlighted why I considered my trial a travesty and refused to admit that I'd committed a crime. Justice Ginsburg wrote that a penal statute had to be defined so "ordinary people [could] understand what conduct is prohibited" and added that a law should not "encourage arbitrary and discriminatory enforcement,"[2] which was what I believed had happened to me and which accounted for my disgust with the U.S. Attorney, his eager-beaver prosecutors, and the power-drunk judge who had assisted them.

One could have reasonably concluded that once the Supreme Court issued its ruling that my troubles would be over, but I wasn't dealing with reasonable people. Hartunian said he was going off to consider the decision and promptly disappeared for a while, leaving me to twist in the wind. Elizabeth Coombe and William Pericak, in all probability urged on by Hartunian, informed my attorneys that they were going to require us to file a notice of appeal from the judgment of conviction. The *Skilling* decision had made it clear that I was guilty of nothing. However, because no independent, meaning de-politicized, inspector general's office was tasked with reining in the behavior of prosecutors—a remedy to prosecutorial misconduct that ought to be considered in the future—we were forced to file. (Republican Senator Chuck Grassley of Iowa has introduced legislation *to oversee the federal judiciary and "to ensure that taxpayer dollars are not lost to waste, fraud, or abuse," and that the system "remains free of corruption, bias, and hypocrisy."*[3]) In addition, we applied to Judge Sharpe for a continuation of bail. In a move that revealed how unhinged the prosecutors had become, Elizabeth Coombe recommended that my application be opposed and that I should start serving my sentence.

I can only speculate why she—again, most likely ordered to do so by the U.S. Attorney—made this recommendation: a bid for headlines or frustrated careerism. Whatever the explanation, the Justice Department wasn't willing to go that far and consented to bail. The entire process chewed up a few weeks—along with $50,000 in legal fees—when the matter should've been disposed of within a few minutes.

In late October, U.S. Attorney Hartunian wrote a letter to Bill Dreyer saying that because Judge Sharpe's instructions to the jury had included a statute struck down by the Supreme Court, tossing the conviction was proper. Then he offered me a deal, and it was a real doozy, demonstrating that the U.S. Attorney knew he was on shaky legal ground if he sought to retry me. Hartunian said that he'd dismiss the charges if I agreed to waive my protection from double jeopardy.

I didn't require a conference with my lawyers to decide against it. All I had to do was read the *New York Post*. Stephen Coffey, an enormously talented trial attorney, spoke to Fred Dicker, and his response was quoted in Fred's column: "There's not a chance that any defense attorney in the world would ever agree to such a stupid request. I think the federal prosecutors are making fools of themselves with this."[4]

I refused to waive my protection and, behaving like a guy with a wicked case of diaper rash, Hartunian let my conviction stand, forcing me to spend more time and money on an appeal. This is a standard tactic that, in a fairer world, would be outlawed by the legislature. Sadly, legislatures are dominated by lawyers, who profit handsomely from the petulance of prosecutors.

Bill wrote Hartunian that his tactic would be seen as vindictive and petty. It was both of those, yet I guessed that the U.S. Attorney had another problem beyond being a sore loser. His office was burning through a fortune pursuing me, another dreadful aspect of a government prosecutor's power. Thanks to the taxpayers, he had unlimited resources to chase a target and the ability to extract a plea by exhausting the target's resources. Subsequently, I'd hear that the feds wasted $30 million coming after me, and though unlike an elected official, Hartunian wouldn't be dropkicked to the curb for diverting public resources from the pursuit of gun-and-drug traffickers, organized crime kingpins, and terrorists, it would be a black eye for Hartunian and could embolden future innocent targets to stand up to him.

With regard to money, I was fortunate. I poured my life savings into my defense; exhausted the remains of my campaign account; and I had friends who raised funds to help with my legal bills. Still, it was a burden, because I had to resign my position at CMA, and being a convicted felon doesn't make you the hottest prospect on the job market. I never knew what the end of my story was going to be in my life.

Joe with daughters Natali and StefaniOne year after the Supreme Court ruling, I appealed my conviction to the United States Court of Appeals for the Second Circuit, and five months later, the three-judge panel ruled that my conviction had to be thrown out, but I could be retried for accepting bribes and kickbacks. I was chagrined by the ruling, but I shouldn't have been. The Court of Appeals is famous for its rubber-stamping tendency.

On May 3, 2012, Hartunian indicted me again in the Federal District Court in Albany. According to the U.S. Attorney, I took $440,000 in bribes and kickbacks from Jerry Abbruzzese. My alleged payoff to Jerry was to send a $250,000 grant to Evident Technologies and a $2.5 million grant to Russell Sage.

This was ridiculous. To begin, I'd done no such thing, but still, in the first trial, the jurors convicted me for taking money from Jerry *without* performing any services for him. Now the government, in a nauseating exhibition of prosecutorial zeal and unfettered discretion, was alleging a quid pro quo between Jerry and me, a peculiar claim given that during my first trial, the government had repeatedly told the jurors that no quid pro quo existed.

If you are finding this confusing, join the club.

Abbe Lowell was an out-of-towner, and for my second trial I decided to use someone closer to home and retained E. Stewart Jones Jr., to work with Bill. Stew, whose grandfather had founded the family firm in Troy in 1898, was not only local, he was one of the finest lawyers in the country, and after my indictment he didn't waste any time before lashing out at Hartunian.

"The government won't let this go," he said. "They can't tolerate someone standing up to them. With all their resources and might and money, Joe…refuses to collapse. They have spent seven years investigating, harassing, and intimidating [him]. And for what? To harm a man who has done more for this community…than anyone who has walked the face of this region in the last fifty years? Joe Bruno does not deserve this."[5]

I agreed, but life is frequently unfair in the What-We-Do-Or-Don't-Deserve Department. Legal experts supported the idea that the re-indictment violated my double-jeopardy protection. Vincent Bonventre, an Albany Law School professor, erstwhile Army prosecutor, and constitutional scholar, commented that "one of the fundamental [legal protections] is that the government…doesn't keep getting another try until they get it right."[6] Judge Andrew Napolitano, the senior judicial analyst for Fox News, opined that Hartunian's course of action was "a trick England played on their political opponents, including many Colonists. A trick so abominable that the Framers expressly prohibited it in the Constitution." The trick was to rename the crime and retry the defendant.[7] I even heard that my old nemesis, Eliot Spitzer, upon learning of the indictment, commented, "They can't do that. It's double jeopardy."

Judge Sharpe could've thrown out the case, but then he would've been wrong calling me a criminal at my first trial, and who in the world could imagine Gary L. Sharpe ever being wrong? Certainly not the man himself.

So I had to file again at the Court of Appeals for the Second Circuit, asking them to dismiss the charges. Once again, the judges wielded their infamous rubber stamp.

Before my second trial could begin, the doctors discovered a malignant tumor on my right kidney, and I had surgery to remove it and a third of my kidney at Memorial Sloan-Kettering Cancer Center in New York City. Somewhere in the midst of the pain and the fog of recovery, I remember thinking that I wasn't going to give these people the satisfaction of dying so they could go around telling themselves and anyone dumb enough to listen that they would've gotten Joe Bruno if only he hadn't croaked.

Righteous indignation may not be a balm for the soul, but it can do wonders for your will to live.

38

NIGHTMARE ON BROADWAY: PART 2

Opening statements for my second trial began on May 5, 2014. Elizabeth Coombe served up her tired leftovers to the jury about my no-shows jobs and the sale of a worthless horse, and Bill Dreyer referred to them as "hogwash," which in my opinion was an overly polite term.

William Pericak called Mary Louise Mallick to the stand. As in the first trial, the government tried to plant the false idea in the minds of the jurors that my consulting agreement with Jerry Abbruzzese was why Evident Technologies had received their appropriation, and Pericak tried to shape Mary Louise's answer to leave that impression.

Nevertheless, because this trial was focused on an alleged bribery, the jury paid strict attention to Mary Louise's testimony, and Pericak's ploy didn't pay off. The jury was able to hear that Mary Louise was impressed by Evident and, after her usual thorough due diligence, had recommended the appropriation in no uncertain terms; that in all the years she'd worked at the Senate, I'd only rejected her recommendations twice; that Clint Ballinger, the president of Evident, was anxious to get his hands on the already-approved funding; and my contribution was to free the check from the state bureaucracy.

As far as I could tell, the prosecution's whole case rested on the testimony of Jerry Abbruzzese. Pericak put Jerry on the stand again, and Judge

Sharpe, losing patience with Jerry's rambling, cut him off, and when Jerry kept trying to answer, Sharpe said, "Are you going to debate me?"

"No," Jerry replied.

"I didn't think so," Sharpe said, his voice filled with a smugness you'd expect to hear from a dictator, not a judge.

Once again, the prosecution attempted to get Jerry to say that the money appropriated to Evident was a result of our consulting agreement. Jerry stuck to the truth, saying that he had made that deal with then-Governor George Pataki well before I did any consulting for him.[1] Coombe would go on to suggest that Jerry was paying me so I'd provide a $2.5 million grant for the lab at Russell Sage, which could be utilized by Evident, and because Jerry was involved with some investors who wanted to take over the New York Racing Authority.

I was proud that the state had provided half the funding for that lab—the first of its kind to be located on the campus of a women's college—and to counter the prosecution's charge, Jeanne Neff testified. She had taken the stand in 2009 after Jerry Abbruzzese. To this day, I believe that Jerry, with his wisecracks and humorous tales and his jousting with Coombe, had become such a large and lingering presence in that trial that the jury quit listening to anyone who followed him. The prosecution, I thought, must have agreed with me, because they didn't even bother to cross-examine Neff.

My second trial was a different story. With the jurors considering a narrow set of circumstances, they listened carefully to each witness, and Jeanne Neff had a solid-gold reputation as an educator and administrator. She'd been president of The Sage Colleges for thirteen years, and seeing this tidy, well-spoken, middle-aged woman on the stand made one think of the word "rectitude." Neff said that the Incubator for New Ventures in Emerging Sciences and Technologies (known by its acronym, INVEST) had been the brainchild and result of the persistence of Sage Professor Thomas C. Keane.[2] She hadn't heard of any involvement by Jerry Abbruzzese, and she added that INVEST was already paying dividends, pairing students with companies that had hired them after graduation.[3]

My alleged effort to pave the way for Jerry to take over the New York Racing Association was laughable. NYRA had been a cesspool of corruption and mismanagement and had been indicted for fraud by the U.S. Attorney of the Southern District of New York. In 2006, NYRA had filed for bankruptcy, and as a fan of horse racing and the Senate majority leader concerned about the business climate of my state, I wanted to fix this problem and weighed the pros and cons of privatizing it. I did try to replace NYRA's incompetent leadership, but the notion that I was doing this to benefit Jerry was preposterous. I told Jerry that if his group—first the Friends of New York Racing and later Empire Racing—was going to bid on the franchise, I had to conclude my business arrangements with him, which was why we ended our joint investment in Christy's Night Out.

I had appointed John Nigro to an ad hoc committee to review the applicants for the franchise. Nigro testified that I never attempted to influence his decision. The proof was that the committee voted for a group that had nothing to do with Jerry, and in the end, NYRA wasn't privatized. Governor Eliot Spitzer cut a deal with the association to continue in its role.[4]

And finally, my second trial wouldn't have been complete unless the tale of Christy's Night Out was revived, the horse that Jerry had bought from me, and Stew Jones cleared that up in his final remarks to the jury.

Despite the effective rebuttals to the prosecution's charges, in my opinion the outcome of the trial can be boiled down to Stew's cross-examination of Jerry and the plain-spoken logic of his closing in which he berated the U.S Attorney for indicting me and attacked his motives and the shoddiness of his office's behavior. As with my first trial, Jerry was a government witness and testified under immunity, which meant that his only worry was that he'd get caught in a lie and the government would go after him hammer and tong. Otherwise, Jerry could've testified that we robbed banks once a week and twice on Thursday, and nothing would've happened to him.

Seeing Stew work was a pleasure, like watching DiMaggio patrolling center field, and at the beginning of his questioning, his baritone voice was as muted as his blue, pinstriped suit.

"Good afternoon, Mr. Abbruzzese," he said, then cut right to the heart of the matter. "Did you ever bribe Senator Bruno?"

"Absolutely not."

Stew waited, giving the jury a chance to let that answer sink in. Then, like an avenging angel dropped down to protect the innocent, he thundered, "Did you ever intend to bribe Senator Bruno?"

"Absolutely not."

Again, Stew gave the jurors the chance to digest that information. "Did you—" he began, his voice rising so it seemed to echo. "Did you enter into the consulting agreement with Senator Bruno in the expectation that it would influence his official acts to the benefit of Evident or any other entity with which you were involved?"

"No," Jerry said.

Still blasting away with his deep baritone, Stew asked, "Did Senator Bruno ever ask you to enter into a consulting agreement with him for the purpose of influencing his actions or conduct officially?"

"No."

Stew paused. I noticed that the jury was staring at him, as if unable to avert their eyes. Suddenly, it seemed as if the air had quit moving. The courtroom was so silent that had the proverbial pin dropped, it would've sounded like the ceiling caving in.

Lowering his voice, Stew asked, "Was any of the money that you paid in consideration for any present or future or official act on the part of Senator Bruno to the benefit of any company that you had an affiliation with or interest in?"

"No."

Louder now, Stew said, "Did you have any understanding of any kind with Senator Bruno in 2004, 2005, 2006, that any money that Senator Bruno received was for the purpose of influencing him and his acts and conduct as a New York State Senator and as the majority leader of the State Senate?"

"No. Not ever."

"Until I asked these questions of you just now, have you ever been asked those questions by the government?"

"Absolutely not."

Stew took a deep breath, allowing the jurors to contemplate Jerry's response. Then, with a tone of accusation and disgust, Stew shouted, "So in the six years the government questioned you, they never asked if you bribed Senator Bruno?"

"No."

Stew began to reword the question and ask it repeatedly, like a boxer hitting the speedbag—jab jab jab jab jab jab. He waited only long enough for Jerry to say no before asking it again. The hair was standing up on the back of my neck, and I was bowled over by my lawyer's performance and the meaning of Jerry's answer.

Between 2006 and 2014, FBI agents and the U.S. Attorney's office had been prodding and poking Jerry Abbruzzese and granted him immunity so he would have every reason to spill the beans, and now it was clear that they never even bothered to ask him about a bribe or kickback or quid pro quo. The explanation for the government avoiding that question was common sense. Had one of the FBI agents or assistant U.S. attorneys asked Jerry that question, and he answered no, it would've become part of the record, and that record had to be turned over to my legal team during discovery. My lawyers would've seen Jerry's reply, and it would've made it harder for the U.S. Attorney to indict me the first time, and nearly impossible for him to do it the second. How could you convince a judge, even one like Sharpe, that you were charging me with bribery while the guy I supposedly bribed, who was protected from prosecution if he didn't lie, swore under oath that I hadn't bribed him?

And if there had been no bribe, then the government had no case.

I watched Jerry get off the stand and concluded that the legal system that had permitted the U.S. Attorney to hound me had been decayed by prosecutors and judges enthralled by their own uncurbed power and suffering from what Stew Jones would refer to as their "bloodlust" for convictions. You'd get no argument from me that the New York State Senate and Assembly were in dire need of ethics reform. Yet if the citizens of our state ever got around to demanding those changes, it would behoove the people to pay special attention to the behavior of prosecutors and judges who cared more about making a splash in the media than they did about justice.

Both assistant U.S. attorneys spoke during the prosecution's closing arguments, speaking before and after Stew. If I hadn't been listening as intently as any person facing a two-year stay in prison, I wouldn't have believed what I heard. William Pericak attacked Stew for making "vicious and slanderous allegations about the position and the conduct of the government." Apparently, not asking your own witness if he'd ever bribed the defendant you've put on trial for accepting bribes shouldn't be standard operating procedure, and Stew was deplorable for underscoring this absurdity.

Pericak also accused Jerry, his own witness with immunity, of telling "falsehood after falsehood after falsehood" and claimed that the government couldn't trust him. Strange as it seemed and as unfair as it was to a defendant, the government didn't have to vouch for its own cooperating witness, which allowed them to try to persuade the jury that it was OK to infer guilt because the witness was a liar. What appalled me was that Pericak was attempting to substitute himself for Jerry. He was suggesting to the jurors that they ignore Jerry's sworn testimony and accept that the sole reliable witness in the courtroom on this subject was an assistant U.S. attorney.

This tactic defied logic, because it would be only natural for the jurors to ask themselves why, in God's name, would Jerry Abbruzzese risk being prosecuted for perjury and going to jail to help me?

The answer was plain as day. He wouldn't.

During Stew's summation, he took to pacing the courtroom, and wherever he went the jurors followed him with their eyes.

"What you have just heard," he said in that thunderous voice, "is a continuation of an elaborate, deceitful, and misleading shell game that this prosecution has pictured for you since the beginning of this case. That shell game takes half-truths, innocent events, benign timelines, and completely ignores the testimony…because the testimony does not support, in any way, manner, shape or form, the central allegation in this case: A bribery in order to obtain an official act from the Senator. It never happened. The testimony tells you it never happened."

Stew was, as I recall, standing behind the prosecutors' table when he made that claim, and they were glancing nervously over their shoulders, as if wondering what he was going to do next.

"The government never, ever asked Jerry Abbruzzese any questions about bribery, about kickback, about quid pro quo…. When you don't ask a question, it means you don't want to know the answer." Stew walked over behind me and put his hands on my shoulders. "They didn't want to know the answer because the answer was the truth and…the truth [derailed] their obsession to prosecute this good and decent man, Senator Bruno."

Stepping out from behind the defense table, Stew kept hammering away at the government, saying that they wanted my scalp. I had been subjected to years of investigations "by the most extraordinary investigative agency in the entire world…the FBI, and not a single person comes forward and says I never, ever heard anybody talk in any way, manner, shape or form, in any language, that suggested a bribe or a kickback or a quid pro quo."

Stew went through each of the government's claims, underscoring that none of them were supported by testimony. Then he warned the jury that "the criminal justice system is haunted by the ghost of an innocent person wrongfully convicted."

The explanation for these miscarriages of justice, he said, was often because a steamrolling government "ignores the truth, does not present facts, skips over what is inconvenient to their theory," and because "jurors don't recognize that truth is from the witnesses' lips, not from the government's mouths."

As Stew began to review the years that the government had wished

Perciak interrupted him. "I object, your Honor," he said, a whiny note in his voice, as if Stew were picking on him. "That is not the government's fault."

This had to be one of the nuttiest statements I heard in either of my trials. *Not the government's fault?* Pericak, for my money, was nothing more than the U.S. Attorney's arrogant water boy, but still—who did he figure had been after me? King Solomon? The Pope?

Not even Judge Sharpe could take his objection seriously, and he replied, "Overruled. Finish, please, Mr. Jones."

And finish Stew did, saying that the time had come "for the government to let go," and exhorting the jurors, "as representatives of justice, to do justice," and not to "condemn an innocent man by a wrongful conviction." I imagined myself going to prison and the thought terrified me—but I always had a lot of faith. I made my peace with whatever outcome it would be, and knew in my heart that justice would prevail and prayers would be answered and we would be totally vindicated of wrongdoing.

Much of the prosecutors' summation had the tenor of schoolchildren making up answers because they hadn't done their homework. I do remember Coombe starting out as if she were narrating an episode of *Lifestyles of the Rich and Famous*—her effort, I guessed, to stir up a storm of class resentment among the jurors. In ominous tones, she told them that the government had "taken them behind the scenes…into country clubs, restaurants, meetings at NYRA, the Jockey Club and even Jerry Abbruzzese's home," all so they could understand how I, "one of the most powerful three men in New York State," had sought financial gain by targeting Jerry, "a businessman who had a private plane and lots of money."

Coombe rambled on for close to an hour. Most of the particulars escape me, though I do remember her defending the government's not asking Jerry about bribing me by saying that wasn't how "the FBI does or should investigate bribery." I recall thinking that it damn sure would've been an appropriate place for the agents to start. After that, she proceeded to twist facts into such torturous spirals of innuendo that I—and in all likelihood the jury—couldn't follow her speech. One thing I haven't forgotten was that she referred to me as "disgusting."

I always thought that was a description that Coombe and Pericak must've come up with one morning when they were looking in the mirror.

Sharpe instructed the jury that to find me guilty they had to believe that I'd accepted a bribe or received a kickback, though evidence of a payment didn't have to be paired with an act. In what I considered an atypical burst of fairness from Sharpe—maybe in an effort to avoid an appeal if I were declared guilty— he told the jurors that if they concluded I'd been operating in good faith then that would be a "valid defense."[5]

At my first trial, the jury had struggled for a week to reach a verdict, so now, once the jurors had received their instructions, I settled in for a long, excruciating wait. Around noon on Friday, the opening day of the jury's deliberations, I was standing in the hall outside the courtroom talking to Stew when we were summoned back to court. I didn't know it then, but the judge had been given a note by one of the jurors asking she had to be excused because she'd told her boss that she'd been selected to serve at my trial.[6]

When we walked in and took our seats at the defense table, Sharpe was staring into his lap, his chin on his chest. He didn't glance up. A minute passed, then another, and to me, anxious about the verdict, it felt like an hour. Stew was looking at the judge in disbelief.

I whispered, "Have you ever seen anything like this?"

Stew shook his head.

"Is it possible he's fallen asleep?"

"I don't know," Stew replied.

More time went by, then the jury filed in. It had only been four hours. I didn't think they'd had adequate time to complete their deliberations. I was confused and trying to figure out what was going on, when Sharpe quietly said, "The jury has reached a verdict. On the first count, not guilty. On the second count, not guilty."

For one frozen instant, I couldn't comprehend what Sharpe was saying, then it hit me, and I shouted out something but can't remember the words, and I heard Kay scream, and my daughters, Katie and Susan, and my son, Ken, were surging toward me along with some friends, all of them cheering and hugging me and clapping me on the back while relief, warm as the sun on a bright summer afternoon, enveloped me, and I could feel tears gathering behind my eyes. I thought at that moment of a quote I had kept in mind during the trial that helped me to keep going. It was from a ballad about Sir Andrew Barton, and said something that I will always remember; "Fight on, my men, I am hurt but I am not slain; I'll lay me down and bleed awhile, and then I'll rise and fight again." That thought sustained me. I had been wounded, and I had bled- but I rose and fought, and for that reason, I was not slain.

Judge Sharpe called for order and dismissed the jury, leaving me to ponder if, while he was staring at his lap, he was attempting to conjure up another way to keep the government on my tail, perhaps by declaring a mistrial, so I'd have to face another round of legal wrangling, a round I doubted that I could endure given my health and anemic financial condition.

Out on the courthouse steps, reporters surrounded me and aimed microphones and TV cameras in my direction.

"I can't describe to you what it feels like to have the government, the federal government, day and night on your mind [and] their mission is to put you in prison.... I really thank the good Lord for answering our prayers."[7]

And it was truly one of those "let go and let God prayers". Let go knowing that God is going to look after you, protect you, and help you. I knew that justice would be served. I truly believe that it is not our faith to avoid crisis, but as long as you have faith, nothing can harm you, nothing can hurt you, and will be delivered.

U.S Attorney Hartunian would give a statement denying that his office ever sought anyone's scalp or that he had any "personal animus" toward me. Then he made himself scarce, understandable given that the *New York Times* would describe the verdict as "a jarring rebuke for prosecutors who had pursued Mr. Bruno despite his age, failing health and reputation as a local hero."[8]

What no newspaper ever reported was something that I learned later when I spoke to one of the jurors. I was told that after a brief discussion the jury concluded that it was obvious I wasn't guilty, but they thought that if they came back in ten minutes, it would look bad, so they sat around talking about their children and grandchildren, their vacation plans, sports, and where they liked to go to dinner—anything they could think of to pass the time. Finally, they decided that four hours was long enough to pass muster with the judge, so they informed him that they had reached a verdict.

News of my acquittal must've spread quickly. As we walked to Jack's Oyster House for lunch, people stopped me on the street to shake my hand and wish me well, and after a bus driver waved to me and I waved back to him, I had to stop and wipe the tears out of my eyes. Everywhere I went people shook my hand and congratulated me on my courage and my willingness to fight a big battle and to overcome. I was so touched by the support I received from others, and their unwavering belief in me is what kept me going and gave me strength.

Lunch was splendid, as it always is at Jack's, and the celebration was terrific, though with the passing of time it has melted into a magical, colorful blur.

Of one thing I'm certain: as I drank a glass of wine, it never occurred to me that these trials would follow me for the rest of my life.

39

LADIES AND GENTLEMEN, IN CLOSING

I've long thought that the poet Rudyard Kipling had it right—you're better off if you can "keep your head when all about you are losing theirs." That was what I tried to do during my trials, and I highly recommend Kipling to anyone who might be unlucky enough to have the government spend tens of millions of dollars and nine years trying to lock you up.

Beyond the advice of a poet—and keeping in mind that Hemingway defined courage as demonstrating "grace under pressure"—what sustained me was knowing in my own heart that I wasn't guilty and that I'd always, regardless of the cost, stuck to my guns when I believed that I was right. I turned to my faith, and to me, the power of prayer is that you have the ability to overcome and persevere. Judge Sharpe would say that I had blinders on. He wasn't even close: I simply knew that I was innocent and ultimately the Supreme Court and a jury agreed with me.

It was also helpful that I was blessed with wonderful friends—though noticeably less than I had before I was indicted—a loving family, and Kay Stafford, my miracle woman, who was at my side every day in court. Every morning Kay and I would read a couple of prayers together—and that's what held me together. I would read those prayers many times in the morning, and knew that with God I would overcome any obstacle.

During these tough times people would stop me on the street and write me letters- reminding me about how I saved their businesses or had helped their lives. This kept me going and gave me strength. I think it was right during my trial going into a bistro when a little old lady with a walker motioned for me to walk over to her. I'm not kidding you when I say little old lady! I lean over and she says, "Keep fighting those bastards". I almost fell down. I couldn't repeat that to anybody—and her daughter that was with her didn't even know what she had whispered in my ear. Moments like these pushed me forward.

Finally, it was the memory of my parents that kept me from caving into the U.S. Attorney's onslaught. My mother and father would've been horrified if I ever gave up and permitted the government to designate their son a criminal. I could imagine them reading the headlines and feeling as though they had failed at the job I knew they had considered one of their primary tasks—teaching their children right from wrong.

I wish I could report that once the second trial ended, the clock rolled back to my pre-indictment days, but the clock stayed right where it was, and I found myself appreciating a remark made by Raymond J. Donovan, a secretary of labor under President Reagan. Before he joined the Cabinet, Donovan and some others had allegedly plotted to defraud the New York City Transit Authority. Donovan claimed that the charges were false and politically motivated. He had been butting heads with organized labor since joining the administration, and indeed as soon as the trouble started union leaders began demanding his resignation.

When a judge ordered him to stand trial, Donovan resigned, and two and a half years later, following a nine-month trial, he was judged not guilty by the jury on the first ballot. After the verdict was read, jurors gave the accused a standing ovation.

Speaking to reporters, Donovan asked a question that I'd been asking myself ever since my acquittal: "Which office do I go to to get my reputation back?"[1]

Regrettably, no such place existed, and as journalists and commentators continued to lay bare the ethical lapses in Albany, most kept mentioning my "conviction," which made it appear as if I'd broken a law—an opinion that was contradicted by the Supreme Court. This mix-up was fed by U.S. Attorney Hartunian, who referred to the *Skilling* case as a change in the law. Bill Dreyer publicly refuted Hartunian, pointing out that the Supreme Court had never referred to a change, but had ruled that the honest services statute as used by the government was unconstitutional. I can't say whether Hartunian was attempting to save face or if his unchecked power had led him to dismiss a Supreme Court ruling, but dismiss it he did and responded to Bill that they had a disagreement on the issue.

I noticed the same disregard for facts from journalists after I applied for $2.4 million in reimbursement for my legal fees under the New York Public Officers Law. According to this law, the state is on the hook for litigation expenses for any of its employees acquitted of criminal charges while "acting within the scope of his public employment or duties." Yet one reporter—and his attitude wasn't uncommon—wrote that I "should check [my Christmas] stocking for a generous $2.4 million gift from the state."[2]

Gift? I applied for $2.4 million, spent well over $4 million, and lost a fortune in earnings when I resigned from CMA. Comptroller Thomas DiNapoli reduced my request to $1.8 million, and it took nearly a year for me to receive the check. If journalists want to blame someone for this expenditure, I suggest they pay a visit to the U.S. Attorney.

I settled my outstanding legal bills and, as permitted by law, transferred $1.4 million to the State Senate Republican Campaign Committee. This wasn't purely a partisan gesture, but in keeping with my view that it's unhealthy for the state to be dominated by one party. When I was in the Senate, I'd pushed hard to create Tech Valley High School, and I was thrilled to give them $100,000 to set up a scholarship fund for students and teacher training. The remainder of the money went to local not-for-profits, much of it in health-related fields.

Once that was done, I had the opportunity to focus on what was most important to me now— spending time with my family and loved ones, traveling and enjoying all that life has to offer. I also, after leaving the frenetic pace of the political arena, had a chance to reflect.

The life I've led was a long shot from the start. No one stopping by 25 Walnut Street in Glens Falls during the 1930s would've predicted that one of those hungry children in that cold-water duplex would become the majority leader of the New York State Senate. On the other hand, no one would have prophesied that this same child would grow up to lock horns with federal prosecutors for years. Throughout my struggles growing up through the tribulations of the trial, I learned to be strong, and to have faith. If you have the courage of your convictions, you will overcome. You will be delivered and you will be victorious, no matter what the obstacles are. That's where "keep swinging" in my life comes from —and it's what I kept doing, no matter what I faced.

Keeps swinging to me means to keep moving forward and to keep fighting. If you don't swing, you'll never get a homerun, if you don't throw towards the basket you'll never get a point, and if you don't throw punches in the ring, you'll get knocked down—so just keep swinging. No matter how many times you're beaten down, you get up, and you keep swinging.

If I've learned anything it is that if you got a rough deal early in life, forget it, put your head down, and move forward. You're going to get hit and you may go down, but you're not out, so get up, shake it off, and continue toward your goals. Life is often filled with one challenge after another. Savor them, learn from them, and remember this above all else: No matter how eager someone is to take your integrity from you, don't let them. Fight. Fight with everything you have. No matter what the odds are against you, always keep swinging. If you keep swinging, you have a chance to score and a chance for victory. Any way you want to put it, but you have to take action in order to come adversity because you will not accept defeat. That's why Winston Churchill said, "Never, never, never give up."

One question I get a lot is whether I'm bitter about that battle. I'll admit: I have bad days thinking about it. I resent that my retirement from the Senate, which I wanted to spend pursuing my interests in business and working for causes I believed in—chiefly in the fields of medicine and high-tech education—was devoured by a needless prosecution. But throughout all of that, and what I hope people would take away from this is that in a difficult time, remember that you're wounded but you're not dead. Whether it's depression, a broken marriage, a dying loved one, it may wound you—you may be hurt—but you're not dead, so you rise up and fight again. You keep smiling, and you keep swinging.

As for the resentment I still feel from time to time, there is a remedy for that. I get in my car and drive past the updated train station and airport, the nanotech megaplex in Albany, GlobalFoundries in Luther Forest, the East Greenbush Technology Park, the Rensselaer Technology Park, and occasionally, a memory strikes me—throwing out the first pitch every year to open the season at the Joseph L. Bruno Stadium on the Hudson Valley Community College Campus, or the day in the fall of 2007 when I stood next to President Shirley Ann Jackson of Rensselaer Polytechnic Institute, and we both had a shovel in our hands for the groundbreaking of General Electric's new digital mammography production facility. I laugh to myself, thinking about the $10 million appropriation I'd secured for GE because they made noise about relocating to a plant they owned in Minnesota, where it was less expensive to operate, and how I'd taken a hailstorm of flak for that appropriation, for being strong-armed, and maybe that was true but here was this state-of-the-art facility in the Capital Region with a total investment of more than $165 million and an employee payroll of some $10 million.

I think about how privileged I was to be a public servant and keep on driving, taking my time now and passing all the brick-and-mortar proof of what I'd helped to accomplish during my thirty-two years in the Senate, and I recall the old Gershwin song about the things that can't be taken away from you.

There's your reward, I tell myself, and it's the only one that you'll ever get. And on most days, it is more than enough.

I am still alive, still here, and still blessed to have my incredible family, supportive friends, my partner Kay, and God watching over me. In life, we never know what good things are about to happen. For this reason, I always end my speeches with "stay tuned"…for whatever comes next. Stay tuned, and keep swinging.

Acknowledgments

I never imagined myself writing and publishing a memoir. I've done the best that I can to recall my past and to bring it to life for the reader. Of course, memory is an imperfect instrument, so I have used other sources, and I believe the result is as close as I can come to telling my story.

Now that the book is done I find myself in debt to a number of people who deserve my heartfelt thanks.

First, to my children—Joe, Sue, Ken, and Katie—and to my grandchildren, whose love has motivated and sustained me ever since they arrived, and to my brothers and sisters, your love and support all these decades has meant more to me than words can say.

I'm grateful to Peter Golden, the writer who helped me construct this memoir, and to Lacy Lynch for her counsel.

At Post Hill Press I'd like to thank Anthony Ziccardi, my publisher, for his care with the manuscript; Michael Wilson, Hannah Yancey, and Rachel Shuster.

To the staff members who worked with me in the Senate and my legal team who defended me at both trials, thank you one and all.

I owe much that I have accomplished to the voters in my Senate district and my colleagues in the Senate and Legislature; and to Governor George Pataki, whose friendship remains a bright spot in my life; and to countless others who have helped me along the way.

Finally, I'd like to thank my very best friend and companion, Kay Stafford, whose love and support makes every day of my life an adventure.

ABOUT THE AUTHOR

Joseph L. Bruno served on the campaign staff of governor Nelson Rockefeller (1966), special assistant to speaker of the assembly Perry B. Duryea (1969–1975), president of the New York State Association of Young Republicans (1968–1969), Chairman of the Rensselaer County Republican Committee (1974–1977), member of the New York State Senate (1977–2008), and majority leader of the New York State Senate (1994–2008). The minor league baseball stadium in Troy, NY, the Joseph L. Bruno Stadium, is named after the senator, and he holds honorary degrees and doctorates from seven universities.

He splits his time with his beloved partner, Kay, in Troy, New York, and Palm Beach, Florida.

ENDNOTES

CHAPTER 1

1 Nicholas J. Wagoner, "Honest-Services Fraud: The Supreme Court Defuses the Government's Weapon of Mass Discretion in Skilling v. United States," *South Texas Law Review*, Vol. 51, No. 4, p. 1087, 2010.
2 Editorial, "Albany's 'Ethics' on Trial," *New York Times*, 11/23/2009.
3 Mike Robinson, "Honest-Services Fraud: Law Used To Indict Blagojevich Challenged As Vague," AP, 11/12/2009.

CHAPTER 7

1 Bill Fagan, "Bruno Takes Close Senate Race," *Troy Record*, 11/3/1976.
2 Ibid.
3 Ibid.

1 Joe Picchi, " 'Ahead of his Time,' Ned Pattison, Politician, Lawyer, Succumbs to Liver Cancer at 58," *Times Union*, 8/24/1990.

CHAPTER 9

1 Sewell Chan, "Warren Anderson, Albany G.O.P. Leader, Dies at 91," *New York Times*, 6/2/2007.
2 Ibid.
3 Emma Green, "A Lot Has Changed in Congress Since 1992, the 'Year of the Woman'," *The Atlantic*, 9/26/2013.
4 James McKinley, "G.O.P. Leader In New York Steps Down After Decade," *New York Times*, 2/27/2001.
5 Kevin Sack, "Republicans Open Convention Today," *New York Times*, 6/23/1994.

6 Kevin Sack, "G.O.P. Backs a Legislator to Oppose Cuomo," *New York Times*, 5/24/1994.

7 Ibid.

8 Alison Mitchell, "Giuliani, Defying His Party, Backs Cuomo for 4th Term; Sees Pataki as Bad for City," *New York Times*, 10/25/1994.

9 Kevin Sack, "Poll Finds Cuomo Has Edged Ahead of Pataki in Race," *New York Times*, 10/31/1994.

CHAPTER 10

1 James Dao, "Dissident G.O.P. Senators Bid To Topple Marino as Leader," *New York Times*, 11/24/1994.

CHAPTER 12

1 Jane Gottlieb, "The Ax Hangs Over 11,400 Workers," *Times Union*, 2/2/1995.

2 Michael McKeon, "The High Cost of State Thrift," *Times Union*, 3/5/1995.

3 Editorial, "Mr. Bruno Ends His Jobs Program," *New York Times*, 5/7/1995.

4 Ibid.

5 Adam Sichko, "Joe Bruno calls it quits," *The Business Review*, 6/26/2008.

6 Ian Fisher, "Political Memo; Budget Brawlers Bloody, but Smiling," *New York Times*, 6/13/1995.

CHAPTER 13

1 Robert A. Caro, *The Years of Lyndon Johnson: The Passage of Power* (New York: Alfred A. Knopf, 2012) p. 459.

CHAPTER 14

1 Michael Finnegan with Bob Liff, "Big Win for Police and Fire Union," *New York Daily News*, 2/13/1996.

CHAPTER 15

1 Keri P. Mattox, "New Flights Ready for Takeoff," *Times Union*, 9/15/2000.

CHAPTER 16

1 Deborah Sontag, "Up With Their Rents! Albany Aims at the Rich," *New York Times*, 5/2/1997.

2 Dennis Hevesi, "As Battle Looms On Rent Law, Skirmishing Has Begun," *New York Times*, 6/16/1996

3 Don Fedorisko, "Will Rent Reform Hurt or Help Middle Class?" *New York Times*, December 14, 1996.

4 James Dao, "The Rent Battle," *New York Times*, 6/12/1997.

CHAPTER 20

1 Andrea Bernstein, "Power Guy Joe Bruno Risks Pataki's Wrath by Embracing Giuliani," *New York Observer*, 04/19/1999.

2 Ibid.

3 Associated Press, "In Surprise Move, Union Endorses Pataki," *Los Angeles Times*, 3/20/2002.

4 Al Baker, "State Legislature Overrides Pataki on Budget Vetoes," *New York Times*, 5/16/2003.

5 Danny Hakim, "Legislature Overrides Most Budget Vetoes, but Pataki Says He Will Block Some Items," *New York Times*, 4/27/2006.

6 Claire Hughes, "Bruno Promises to Fight for Chip Plant," *Times Union*, 12/9/1999.

7 Jean DerGurahian, "$100M Boosts Tech Center," *Times Union*, 4/24/2001.

8 Roger Parloff, "Suit: Intel paid Dell up to $1 billion a year not to use AMD chips," http://money.cnn.com/blogs/legalpad/2007/02/suit-intel-paid-dell-up-to-1-billion _15.html, 4/7/2007, Retrieved 9/12/2015.

9 Larry Rulison, "$3.2B AMD plant big lift to region," *Times Union*, 6/24/2006.

CHAPTER 21

1 Alan Finder, "Spitzer Concedes That His Father Has Helped to Pay for Campaigns," *New York Times*, 10/28/98.

2 Michael Cooper, "Hevesi Pleads Guilty to a Felony and Resigns," *New York Times*, 12/23/2006.

CHAPTER 22

1 Associated Press, "Poll: Gov. Eliot Spitzer reclaiming some popularity," *New York Daily News*, 1/21/2008.

2 Danny Hakim, "Spitzer Is Sworn and Begins Push on Ethics Rules," *New York Times*, 1/2/2007.

3 Gov. Eliot Spitzer's Inaugural Address, *New York Times*, 1/1/2007.

4 Joel Siegel, "Spitzer Enters Race," *New York Daily News*, May 5, 1998.

CHAPTER 23

1 Fredric U. Dicker, "Eliot Spitz Fire," *New York Post*, 1/31/2007.

2 Peter Elkind, *Client 9: The Rise and Fall of Eliot Spitzer* (New York: Portfolio/Penguin, 2010), pg. 142.

3 Lisa Foderaro, "Homeless Sex Offender Held in Stabbing Death Near Mall, *New York Times*, 7/1/2005.

4 Danny Hakim, "Dysfunction Junction No More?" *New York Times*, March 1, 2007.

CHAPTER 24

1 Bruce Lambert, "Democrat Wins Senate Seat on Long Island," *New York Times*, February 7, 2007.

2 Bruce Lambert, "Democrat Wins Senate Seat on Long Island," *New York Times*, February 7, 2007.

3 Geoffrey Gray, "The Un-Reformed," *New York*, March 1, 2008.

4 Danny Hakim, "The 'Wimp' Factor in Albany," *New York Times*, 12/3/2007.

5 Observer Staff, "1199's 'Remember Me' Ad," *New York Observer*, 03/19/2007.

6 Danny Hakim and Raymond Hernandez, "Rangel Tells State's Delegation That Spitzer Is Too Combative," *New York Times*, 3/9/2007.

7 Danny Hakim, "Spitzer: Senate Outdoes Enron," *New York Times*, March 13, 2007.

8 Ibid.

CHAPTER 25

1 Danny Hakim and Michael Cooper, "Spitzer Visits Bruno Turf to Push Campaign Reform," *New York Times*, 4/25/2007.

2 Danny Hakim, "Spitzer's Campaign Reforms Stall as G.O.P. Senators Resist," *New York Times*, April 24, 2007.

3 These quotes are taken from the transcript of "Investigation D" from the Office of the Albany County District Attorney, March 28, 2008. The expletives were deleted but I took my best guess at what had been edited out.

4 Fredric U. Dicker, "Police State: Gov sicced cops on Joe," *New York Post*, 7/5/2007.

5 James M. Odato, "Key Republican official flew with Bruno," *Times Union*, July 11, 2007.

6 Jimmy Velkind, "Judge tosses Dopp challenge," *Times Union*, July 9, 2010.

7 Sewell Chan, "Latest Poll: Can It Get Any Worse for Spitzer?" *New York Times*, December 10, 2007.

8 Danny Hakim, "Senator Bruno's Wife Is Eulogized," *New York Times*, January 14, 2008.

CHAPTER 26

1 Michael Cooper and Danny Hakim, "Bruno Is Subject of Inquiry by F.B.I.", *New York Times*, 12/20/2006.

2 Michael Cooper and Danny Hakim, "Bruno Is Subject of Inquiry by F.B.I.", *New York Times*, 12/20/2006.

3 Danny Hakim, "Bruno Quits Job at Financial Firm Where Unions Were Investors," *New York Times*, 12/22/2007.

4 Ibid.

5 Fredric U. Dicker, "Bruno Files Seized," *New York Post*, 6/25/2008.

6 Glenn Blain, "Former state Senate Majority Leader Joe Bruno indicted on corruption charges spanning 13 years," *New York Daily News*, 1/23/2009.

CHAPTER 27

1 Mike McIntire and Jeremy W. Peters, "Ex-Senate Leader Bruno Is Indicted for Corruption," *New York Times*, 1/23/2009.

2 Tom Caprood, "Feds indict Bruno on corruption matter," *The Saratogian*, 01/24/09.

3 Ibid.

4 Lyle Denniston, "Analysis: 'Honest services' law in jeopardy?" www.scotusblog.com /2009/10/analysis-honest-services-law-in-jeopardy, 10/13/2009, Retrieved June 9, 2015.

5 Roger Parloff, "The catchall fraud law that catches too much," *Fortune*, 1/26/2010.

6 John Schwartz, "Justices to Weigh Honest-Services Law," *New York Times*, 12/06/2009.

7 Alan Dershowtiz, Foreword to *Three Felonies a Day* by Harvey A. Silvergate (New York: Encounter Books), 2009, p. xxxi.

8 Conrad M. Black, John A. Boultbee, and Mark S. Kipnis, Petitioners v. United States of America, Respondent, Brief of the Chamber of Commerce of the United States of America as Amicus Curiae in Support of Petitioners, www.americanbar.org/content /dam/aba/publishing/preview/publiced_preview_briefs_pdfs_07_08_08_876 _PetitionerAmCuUSCoC.authcheckdam.pdf, Retrieved 10/9/15.

9 Adam Liptak, "Justices Appear Skeptical of Anticorruption Law," *New York Times*, 12/8/2009.

CHAPTER 28

1 Unless otherwise noted, quotes from both trials are drawn from the court transcripts.

2 Edward Walsh, "Counsel Lowell: A Defender Of Democrats in Trouble," *Washington Post*, 10/6/1998.

3 Phil Kuntz, "Rep. McDade Wins Acquittal After Lengthy Legal Fight," *Wall Street Journal*, 8/2/1996.

4 Nicholas Confessore, "Mistrial Request Rejected in Ex-State Senator's Trial," *New York Times*, 11/13/2009.

5 Brendan J. Lyons, "Trial judge warns Bruno's attorney," *Times Union*, 10/29/2009.

6 Ibid.

CHAPTER 29

1 Nick Powell, "Prosecution or Persecution: The Saga of Joe Bruno," http://archives .cityandstateny.com/prosecution-or-persecution-the-saga-of-joe-bruno, 10/22/2012, Retrieved 12/08/15.

2 Danny Hakim, "Bruno Quits Job at Financial Firm Where Unions Were Investors," *New York Times*, 12/22/2007.

3 Roger Stone, "Sharpe Shenanigans: Federal Judge Prods for Bruno Conviction," www.breitbart.com/big-government/2009/12/06/sharpe-shenanigans-federal-judge -prods-for-bruno-conviction, 12/6/2009, Retrieved 9/30/15.

4 Nicholas Confessore, "Secretary Describes a Scolding From Bruno," *New York Times*, 11/17/2009.

CHAPTER 30

1 Adam Sichko, "Bruno trial: Judge chides lawyers for getting off track," *Buffalo Business First*, 11/10/2009.

CHAPTER 31

1 Stephen Williams, "Sparks fly in fraud trial of former political heavyweight," *The Daily Gazette*, 11/13/2009.

CHAPTER 32

1 Bloomberg News, "State worker: Bruno made me do personal duties," *Newsday*, 11/16/2009.

CHAPTER 33

1 Press Release Office of the New York State Comptroller, "DiNapoli Taps Former Top Senate Fiscal Expert to Review State Budgets," www.osc.state.ny.us/press/releases/apr07/041707a.htm, 4/17/2007, Retrieved 9/16/2015.
2 Chelsea Diana, "Nanotech company shifts focus to meet industry demands," *Albany Business Review*, 4/10/2015.

CHAPTER 34

1 Robert Gavin, "The Jared E. Abbruzzese comedy show and testimony," *Times Union*, 11/20/2009.

CHAPTER 35

1 Nicholas Confessore and Danny Hakim, "Bruno, Former State Leader, Guilty of Corruption," *New York Times*, 12/7/2009.
2 Nicholas Confessore, "After Some Requests, Bruno Jury Chooses to Reconvene Monday," *New York Times*, 11/24/2009.
3 Jilly Bryce, "No verdicts just read-backs," *The Record*, 12/1/2009.
4 Danny Hakim, "Jury Said to Reach Partial Verdict in Bruno Corruption Case," *New York Times*, 12/1/2009.
5 Ibid.
6 Brendan J. Lyons, "Jury struggles with 6 counts," *Times Union*, 12/2/2009.
7 Nicholas Confessore and Danny Hakim, "Bruno, Former State Leader, Guilty of Corruption," *New York Times*, 12/7/2009.
8 Press Release U.S. Attorney's Office, Northern District of New York, "Former New York State Senate Majority Leader Joseph L. Bruno Convicted," www.fbi.gov/albany/press-releases/2009/alfo120709a.htm, 12/7/2009, Retrieved August 28, 2015.
9 Nicholas Confessore and Danny Hakim, "Bruno, Former State Leader, Guilty of Corruption," *New York Times*, 12/7/2009.

CHAPTER 36

1 Michael Caputo, "Prosecutor Abuse: The Crucifixion of Joe Bruno," www.breitbart. com/big-government/2013/01/27/prosecutor-abuse-the-crucifixion-of-joe-bruno, 1/27/2013, Retrieved 4/4/2015.

2 Jeremy W. Peters, "Swagger and a Speech Before an Ex-Lawmaker's Sentencing," *New York Times*, 5/6/2010.

3 Adam Sichko, "Lawyer: Bruno 'refuses to collapse and cave' to prosecutors," *Albany Business Review*, 5/4/2012.

4 Ibid.

5 Ibid..

6 Nicholas Confessore, "Bruno Gets 2-Year Prison Term, but Stays Free," *New York Times*, 5/6/ 2010.

7 Adam Sichko, "Bruno: 'I did nothing wrong,'" *Albany Business Review*, 5/7/2012.

8 Ibid.

9 Ibid.

10 Nicholas Confessore, "Prosecutors Seek an 8-Year Term for Bruno," *New York Times*, 4/25/2010.

11 Nicholas Confessore, "Bruno Gets 2-Year Prison Term, but Stays Free," *New York Times*, 5/6/2010.

12 Jon Campbell, "Ex-Senate chief Bruno gets 2 years for fraud," *The Journal News*, 5/7/010.

13 Nicholas Confessore, "Bruno Gets 2-Year Prison Term, but Stays Free," *New York Times*, May 6, 2010.

CHAPTER 37

1 Supreme Court of the United States, *Skilling v. United States*, Certiorari to the United States Court of Appeals for the Fifth Circuit No. 08–1394, www.law.cornell.edu/supct /html/08-1394.ZS.html, Retrieved 12/8/ 2015.

2 Supreme Court of the United States, *Skilling v. United States*, Certiorari to the United States Court of Appeals for the Fifth Circuit No. 08–1394, www.law.cornell.edu/ supct/html/08-1394.ZS.html, Retrieved 12/8/ 2015.

3 Senator Chuck Grassley, Text of Grassley's floor statement regarding the bill, www.grassley.senate.gov/news/news-releases/grassley-bill-would-improve-oversight -federal-judiciary, 5/22/2015, Retrieved 9/9/2015.

4 Fredric U. Dicker, "Bruno conviction to be nixed," *New York Post*, 11/16/2010.

5 Adam Sichko, "Lawyer: Bruno 'refuses to collapse and cave' to prosecutors," *Albany Business Review*, 5/4/2012.

6 Nick Powell, "Prosecution or Persecution," http://archives.cityandstateny.com /prosecution-or-persecution-the-saga-of-joe-bruno/, 10/22/12, Retrieved 12/1/2015.

7 Andrew P. Napolitano, "Double Jeopardy," Release, 7/18/2013.

CHAPTER 38

1 Stephen Williams, "Abbruzzese: No bribes," *The Daily Gazette*, 5/9/2014.

2 Invest, http://www.sage.edu/invest/, Retrieved 12/12/15.

3 Molly Eadie, "Jury: Bruno not guilty of honest services mail fraud," *The Record*, 5/16/2014. |

4 Stephen Williams, "Jury hears witnesses from both sides," *The Daily Gazette*, 5/14/14.

5 Associated Press, "Joe Bruno found not guilty—again—in Albany corruption trial," 5/16/14.

6 Molly Eadie, "Two ex-NYRA officials testify at Bruno retrial," *The Record*, 5/12/2014.

7 CBS6, "Bruno Found Not Guilty," www.youtube.com/watch?v=bNl9euqsArc; WGY, "Bruno Acquitted of Fraud," www.youtube.com/watch?v=QaeWtAF6A24, Retrieved 10/29/2015.

8 Jesse McKinley, "Bruno, Ex-State Senate Chief, Is Acquitted of Fraud in Retrial," *New York Times*, 5/16/2014.

CHAPTER 39

1 Selwyn Raab, "Donovan Cleared of Fraud Charges in Bronx," *New York Times*, 5/26/87.

2 Aaron Short, "State taxpayers to cover $2.4M in Bruno criminal defense costs," *New York Post*, 12/25/14.

DEDICATION

Bobbie and I celebrating our fiftieth wedding anniversary with our children and grandchildren.

My brothers and sisters in my Senate office. From left to right: Tony, Peter, Rose, Bob, Florence, Art, and Vito.

Ken's girls